D1532293

Parent-Infant Intervention

Communication Disorders

Grune & Stratton Rapid Manuscript Reproduction

Based on the International Conference on Parents and Young Children held at Washington University, Saint Louis, Missouri, June 20–22, 1978

Parent-Infant Intervention

Communication Disorders

Edited by
Audrey Simmons-Martin, Ed.D.
Donald R. Calvert, Ph.D.

Central Institute for the Deaf
Department of Speech and Hearing
Washington University
Saint Louis, Missouri

Sponsored by
The Central Institute for the Deaf

GRUNE & STRATTON
A Subsidiary of Harcourt Brace Jovanovich, Publishers
New York ☐ San Francisco ☐ London

Grune & Stratton, Inc.
111 Fifth Avenue
New York, New York 10003

Distributed in the United Kingdom by
Academic Press, Inc. (London) Ltd.
24/28 Oval Road, London NW1

Library of Congress Catalog Number 79-83870
International Standard Book Number 0-8089-1185-6
Printed in the United States of America

Dedication

This book is dedicated to the memory of Ira J. Gordon, Kenan Professor and Dean of the School of Education, the University of North Carolina at Chapel Hill. As a distinguished investigator, teacher, author, and administrator, he set an eminent example of applying theory to practice for the benefit of teachers, parents, and especially young children. His chapter in this book, "Parents as Teachers—What Can They Do?", one of his last contributions, exemplified this rare and creative blend. His work will long serve as a model for all those concerned with parent-infant intervention.

Contents

Preface

This book is a product of the International Conference on Parents and Young Children held at Washington University, St. Louis, Missouri, on June 20–22, 1978. The Conference was a timely expression of contemporary activity and interest in young children and their interaction with parents. Its deliberations document several prominent features of the current scene in this field. Among these is the growing and encouraging influence of scientific investigation on the management of parent-child relations whether in the home, the clinic, the pre-school, or in variously organized "centers." Also reflected is the promising convergence of the study and experience on normal child development with that for children having handicaps that impair development. The theories, practices, and research findings of the psychology of learning, of child development, of sociology, of neurophysiology, of speech pathology, of audiology, and of education of the hearing-impaired all find expression in the Conference contributions. Common to all is recognition of the importance of "parenting" in the early years, in what has come to be called the "optimum" period for total beneficial development of the child. The essence of parenting is communication, and when it is disordered, for whatever reason, indifference to the condition of its mismanagement courts disaster for the child and his family. It is their needs and the improvement of our competence to meet them that motivated us to stage the Conference and to organize it as we did.

It is appropriate that the Conference, sponsored by the Central Institute for the Deaf, be held in St. Louis. This was the city which established the first free public kindergarten in the United States, and where education of hearing-impaired children at three years of age was put into practice as early as 1914. St. Louis is also the site of Central Institute's Home Demonstration Center, a model for parents and their infants with hearing and language disorders. The Conference was planned at a time when early education as a field of endeavor is emerging from its own infancy, when the nature of parent-infant interaction is just beginning to be understood, and when intervention to stimulate effective parent-child interaction that facilitates development or remediation for communicatively handicapped children seems to be attainable.

We are reminded that the basic themes of the Conference are not new. As far back as 1680, in his book, *The Deaf and Dumb Man's Tutor*, published at Oxford, George Dalgarno advocated that we address the deaf child ''unto the cradle.'' Juan Pablo Bonet, in the first recorded book on educating deaf children, published in Madrid in 1620, advised that *all* members of the family be involved in the education of deaf children. Three and a half centuries should be adequate gestation for such ideas.

The Conference purposely brought together people who represented different points of view on intervention. Over 300 people from 44 states and 7 countries participated. Included were audiologists, speech/-language pathologists, classroom teachers of hearing children, research scientists, psychologists, teacher educators, students learning to teach or test, teachers of hearing-impaired and other handicapped children, teacher/counselors of parents, parents themselves, government representatives, and administrators of public and private programs. The contributors represent both theory and practice. They come from different states, nations, and cultures. They hold differences of opinions and espouse different approaches to accomplishing a goal. Even different generations participated, representing, on the one hand, the empirical, experience-oriented pioneers who by trial and error rough-furrowed the unplowed soil, and, on the other hand, the young disciplined observer, data-oriented and skeptical of all things that cannot be measured. From such diversity may eventually come a new kind of ''knowing'' about the subject.

Preparation of the Conference was assisted by a grant (PR# 451AH60117) from the Bureau of Education for the Handicapped, Office of Education, of the United States Department of Health, Education and Welfare. We are indebted to the speakers whose papers appear as chapters in the text, and to the many participants whose questions and discussion helped illuminate an idea or represent a point of view. We especially thank all those whose encouragement, advice, planning, implementation, and moment-to-moment handling of the logistics required for convening 300 people at such a Conference made the undertaking possible.

Contributors

Nicholas J. Anastasiow, Ph.D.
Director, Institute for Child Study
Indiana University
Bloomington, Indiana

Barbara J. Anderson, Ph.D.
Department of Psychiatry and Pediatrics
Washington University Medical Center
St. Louis, Missouri

Lovenger H. Bowden, Ed.D.
Research in Communications
Department of Communication Arts and Sciences
Howard University
Washington, D.C.

Norman P. Erber, Ph.D.
Research Associate in Audiology
Central Institute for the Deaf
St. Louis, Missouri

Bernard Z. Friedlander, Ph.D.
Professor of Psychology
Director, Infant/Child Language Research Laboratory
University of Hartford
West Hartford, Connecticut

Ann E. Geers, Ph.D.
Research Associate
Central Institute for the Deaf
St. Louis, Missouri

Joan Godshalk, M.A.
Supervisor, Infant Center and Preschool
Lexington School for the Deaf
Jackson Heights, New York

Ira J. Gordon, Ed.D.
Kenan Professor and Dean, School of Education
University of North Carolina
Chapel Hill, North Carolina

June M. Grant, Ph.D.
Director, Special Education
Trinity University
San Antonio, Texas

Michael Hanes, Ph.D.
Director, Preschool Education Department
High/Scope Educational Research Foundation
Ypsilanti, Michigan

Ralph L. Hoag, Ed. D.
Superintendent, Arizona State School for the Deaf and the Blind
Tucson, Arizona

Barry A. Kaufman, Ed.D.
Assistant Professor of Education
Graduate Institute of Education
Washington University
St. Louis, Missouri

Joan Kiser, M.S.
Director, Center for Hearing-Impaired Children
Tucson, Arizona

Phyllis Levenstein, Ed.D.
Director, Verbal Interaction Project
Freeport, New York

Gerry McCarthy
Visiting Teacher of the Deaf
Department of Education
Dublin, Ireland

Jean S. Moog, M.S.
Supervising Teacher
Central Institute for the Deaf
St. Louis, Missouri

Winifred H. Northcott, Ph.D.
Associate Professor, Special Education
Mankato State University
Mankato, Minnesota

Luisa E. Pachano, M.S.
Director
Center for Early Language Development
Caracas, Venezuela

Sylvia O. Richardson, M.D.
Associate Director, University Affiliated Programs for Learning Disabilities
Associate Clinical Professor of Pediatrics
University of Cincinnati College of Medicine
Cincinnati, Ohio

Virginia Shipman, Ph.D.
Senior Research Psychologist and Chair
Early Learning and Socialization Research Group
Princeton, New Jersey

A. M. J. van Uden, pr., Ph.D.
Principal of Research
Institute for the Deaf
St. Michielsgestel, Netherlands

Burton L. White, Ph.D.
Senior Research Associate
Harvard Graduate School of Education
Cambridge, Massachusetts

Introduction

This text has been prepared for the following readership: 1.) those who directly influence the lives of young children with communication disorders—teachers, speech/language pathologists, audiologists, counselors, and parents; 2.) those who study human communication or the development of infants — sociologists, linguists, psychologists, and pediatricians; 3.) those who are preparing as students to enter one of the above fields; and 4.) those who as administrators have the important responsibility to fund, support, and shape programs of service and study.

The book is designed accordingly both as an introduction and reference. It is also, in a sense, a state-of-the-art presentation, time-bound and linking the events and understanding of the past with some directions for the future. As we have pointed out in the Preface, this publication and the Conference from which it was developed are very timely. This is particularly true when one considers the important, immediate, and long-range ramifications of Public Law 94-142, the Education of All Handicapped Children Act, which mandates both early education of handicapped children, and the direct and ongoing involvement of parents in the process. It is as though, while we were casually reflecting on theories, sifting through data, and speculating on techniques pertinent to parent-infant intervention, a new momentum, a saltation of ideas, studies, and procedures bursts upon us, forcing us to identify where we are now, and describe where we most likely will be going. The Conference and this publication are a product of that moment.

As editors we have puzzled over the best among many ways to present this broad body of knowledge. Certainly the variety of issues that emerged, the spectrum of viewpoints, and the heterogeneous backgrounds of an international group suggest a number of possible formats. Our decision was to group chapters into three sections which reflect the primary ways we (both contributors and readers) organize ourselves to learn and to serve: (1) Theory and Rationale, (2) Practice and Procedures, and (3) Research and Analysis.

In "Theory and Rationale," we begin with Nicholas Anastasiow's fine delineation of the current issues in child development, since it raises a number of important questions dealt with in later chapters. Then, with

Ira Gordon, we shift focus from the child to the parents and what they can do as teachers in the light of the concepts of transaction, systems, and instructional theory. From her considerable experience with hearing-impaired children, June Grant ably presents the thesis that appropriate experience is the foundation of language acquisition interrelated with cognitive development. Burton White next introduces a theme of the Conference, now also emerging prominently in child development, that is, the special importance of hearing ability for the development of infants and toddlers, not only for their language but for their social and emotional adjustment as well. Lovenger Bowden poignantly reminds us of how self-concept importantly influences language development, especially when negative conditions set off the dynamics of self-fulfilling prophecy. Sylvia Richardson, selected as the Conference banquet speaker, poses Bowden's theme in the context of handicap, warning of the promiscuous application of labels of abnormality when we really don't know the range of "normal." To conclude the section, Michael Hanes calls upon his study and experience with deprived children to bridge theory and practice, describing how the choice of curriculum directly affects many aspects of child management.

"Practice and Procedures" is initiated by the Netherlands' Father Anthony van Uden who starts at point Alpha, instructing on how to converse with infants and toddlers using his "seizing techniques." Jean Moog further develops the van Uden theme, pointing out the forgotten art of carefully listening to the child's spontaneous ideas in order to select the best strategy for language development. We again change focus from children to parents, as in Chapter 10 Joan Godshalk responds to the questions posed by Ira Gordon in Chapter 2 with her practical approach to putting parents on the team. Winifred Northcott elaborates the Minneapolis model of a local education agency coordinating educational services in partnership with parents and the health care system. Other models reported include Gerry McCarthy's individual-oriented visiting teacher service for the sparse population of Ireland, and Luisa Pachano's group-oriented program for Venezuela with over eight million people. Father van Uden returns to describe the comprehensive home-training service for prelingually profoundly deaf children in the Netherlands. The role of American state schools for deaf children in early childhood and infant education, as exemplified by Arizona with its multilingual population, is presented by Ralph Hoag and Joan Kiser.

Bernard Friedlander leads off the section on "Research and Analysis" with his thoughtful chapter on finding facts of value and value in facts. Then Barbara Anderson presents a study which exemplifies use of the scientific method to analyze what really takes place when parent and child interact. Phyllis Levenstein focuses directly on the verbal interaction component of the mother-child dyad. Is it possible to evaluate the effectiveness of an educational program at the pre-school level? Ann Geers presents data from Central Institute's validated program, suggesting a positive answer to that question. Next, in Chapter 20, Virginia Shipman examines the persistence of early education gains at a later age, finding they can be maintained, with the important variables being the quality of parenting and excellence of teachers. Norman Erber further emphasizes the importance of the classroom teacher in early childhood through his model of optimizing oral communication.

Finally, to give his impressions as a general educator, Barry Kaufman notes the importance of interaction among theory, practice, and research which emanates from the exchange of views and ideas by the professionals whose chapters appear above. He urges care in considering single aspects of a child, rather than regarding each child as a whole.

Part I

Theory and Rationale

The rationale underlying the role of the parent in early childhood development is reflected in the papers of this section. While each paper focuses on a distinct aspect of child development, the central theme is to understand the direct and indirect effects of parents on the child. In past years the field of early education has focused on the child's development, the child's needs, the child's behavior. With emphasis on the ecological perspective, viewing the interaction of an organism with his environment, there is a growing need to understand parent's development, parent's needs and the parent's behavior as educators, caretakers and as language developers.

NICHOLAS J. ANASTASIOW, Ph. D.

Director
Institute for Child Study
Indiana University
Bloomington

1

Current Issues in Child Development

In this chapter, the current status of our knowledge about young children and programs designed to facilitate their growth will be examined. It should be clear that any one chapter cannot do justice to the vast amount of new knowledge that has been generated in the past fifteen years. The reader is referred to two excellent volumes produced by the Society for Research in Child Development for a more comprehensive coverage of recent research (Horowitz, 1975; Hetherington, 1976). The following sections will focus on the importance of the child's first year of life, the competencies that the infants possess in their innate capacity to actively pursue information about the environment from birth on, the discontinuities in development, the effectiveness of intervention programs and the major shift from basic behavioral theories to cognitive theories in order to explain thinking and learning.

THE EFFECTS OF INTERVENTION

There are now sufficient data to indicate that intervention programs are effective in facilitating the growth of young children. These data are impressive and can be found in numerous publications, research reports, newspaper articles and Sunday supplements. (See Stedman et al., 1972 and Wynne et al., 1975, for summaries). What these reports indicate is that children who live in poverty and participate in early childhood programs do better in school on a number of dimensions than those children of a different socio-economic background who do not have such experience. Many of the effects of the preschool programs are found to last well into the upper elementary grades with fewer of the children who had early childhood education experiences being placed in remedial or special education programs, or being classified as mentally retarded.

Similarly, programs which intervene early in the life of the handicapped or impaired child can offset the negative effects of impairment as Northcott, Pachano, McCarthy and van Uden describe elsewhere in this volume. These programs have shown that severely hearing-impaired children can function in regular classrooms if intervention is begun before the third year of life and in some cases success has been achieved with program initiation even after the third year. Others have demonstrated similar effects for children with other impairments (Wynne et al., 1975). Blind children have learned to ski in Raynor's Michigan project. Deaf children who are integrated with normal-hearing youngsters early in life do not develop the grimaces and excessive physical contacts that severely hearing-impaired children develop when raised without normal-hearing peers. Fraiberg (1977) has demonstrated that many of the autistic-like behaviors typically associated as a condition of blindness may be due to a lack of social and physical stimulation rather than a physiological state. These have been "miracles, miracles, miracles," as one mother stated to the author as she recounted how her physically impaired child moved from a condition of little body control to a state of walking in a two year period while enrolled in an early childhood intervention program. Similar stories can be found in other HCEEP projects (DeWeerd, 1974). Early intervention does have a major impact on the life of the child and on his parents. Peters (1977), in an impressive summary of early childhood programs, reports that intervention programs have enhanced children's cognitive and socioemotional growth, IQ scores, achievement test scores, and overall adjustment to school. Further, the parents of these children show positive changes in attitudes, skill development, communicative ability and openness to new experiences and are more secure in their overall environmental mastery.

The studies reported above are, in the main, concerned

with remediating genetic or environmental deficits. Other studies (Werner et al., 1972, Broman et al., 1976, and Neligan et al., 1974) have also shown that conditions which have been associated with stress factors just before birth or which occur during the birth process can also be overcome by positive childrearing attitudes. In the Werner study, it was found that the best criterion for differentiating children who had school-related problems (achievement, language, perception) and those who did not was the educational stimulation received in the home. Ten times more children had problems associated with less facilitative childrearing attitudes than with sensorimotor or perinatal stress. As Broman et al. (1975) states, breech birth and anoxia are trivial compared to what a mother does in the home. The child who overcomes perinatal stress is one whose caregiver is generous in the use of warmth and verbal interaction and encourages development by setting appropriate but firm achievement standards.

Thus, intervention programs which also train parents tend to maximize the probability of offsetting or remediating a child's impairments. Some broad characteristics of successful programs for parents and children have been described and the reader is referred to Gordon et al., 1975 and Anastasiow, 1976 (in Hanes et al., 1976) for a detailed description of those characteristics. In the main, the findings indicate that intervention programs which emphasize the training of parents to deal with their children and which stress the parents' cognitive development appear to have children who make greater gains. These data suggest that what a caregiver does during the early portion of a child's life does much to facilitate or hamper his development. Babies are born with reflexes to deal with the environment; however, they need the stimulation of the environment to develop their skills.

"A BABY IS VERY INTELLIGENT FOR HIS AGE"

The quote above is attributed by McKeachie (1976) to Harlow. It summarizes nicely the multiple competencies with which the normal infant is born. The infant, at birth, can see, hear, locate sounds, move his body in rhythmic response to spoken speech, make perceptual discriminations and so on. The reader is referred to the chapter on infancy in Horowitz (1975) for an excellent overview of these multiple talents.

It is generally conceded that the infant, born with innate mechanisms (usually called schema or schemata), utilizes these schemata to take in information about the environment much as Piaget has observed (Piaget and Inhelder, 1969). Let's take one example of an infant's amazing learning capacity. An infant can be observed lying in a crib apparently looking at a mobile suspended from the ceiling above the crib. The infant thrashes and makes cooing sounds. To the adult, he appears to look at and "talk to" the mobile. In an experiment, a string is tied to one of the infant's arms so that movement of that arm produces movement of the mobile. In a series of "trials," the infant reduces his overall thrashing and yet moves the arm to which the string is attached, yielding continued movement. Most infants can learn to do this between the ages of two and four months. In addition, if the mobile will move faster when the arm (or in some experiments the string is tied to the leg) is moved faster, then the infant will "learn" to move his arm (or leg) more rapidly.

These data, and others like it, have caused developmental psychologists to reexamine their notions about infants and infancy. For one, there is a great push towards the completion of development. Infants grow in size, and develop more complex skills given a healthy physiological state and an adequate environment. (Scarr-Salapatek, 1976). This fact has caused one developmental psychologist to comment mistakenly that it does not appear to be important what happens in the first year to 18 months of life (Kagan, 1976). This is to miss the point of the interaction between even the youngest child and his surroundings. Innate dispositions, which mature in most environments, will, if the child is impaired or possesses deficits due to stress, mature most readily in those environments which enhance development. The critical factor underlying the enhancement of development by the caregiver (usually the mother) is in the affective relationship established with the child during the first year of life (Lewis and Rosenblum, 1977, Scarr-Salapatek, 1976). Basic trust (in Erikson's (1950) sense) established during infancy does much to encourage the development of the genetically programmed innate dispositions into more complex schemata through the child's own actions upon the environment. For the impaired child, it would appear that the caregiver must learn how to encourage the utilization of other schemata when basic physiological processes are not fully operational. For example, Fraiberg (1977) has demonstrated that mothers of blind infants need to learn how to give touch and voice feedback when the child cannot observe the reassuring smile. The broad general outlines of what facilitates growth and development that leads to school success are known. It is many of the details which are still unclear. However, some new light is being shed on the regularity of development itself.

CONTINUITY VERSUS DISCONTINUITY IN DEVELOPMENT

The regularity of development of the infant moving from simple to complex skills is in serious question today. It has been known for some time that there are massive bio-behavioral shifts that occur, such as in the five-to seven-year-old period (White, 1965). However, infancy itself seemed smooth and regular. Emde et al. (1977) in their study of the Emotional Expression In Infancy, conclude that there are major periods of discontinuity in development in infancy as well. They demonstrate that major bio-behavioral changes occur between the two-to three-month-old and the seven-to nine-month-old periods. They found that the infant smile in early infancy was related to both sleep and wakeful states and occurred during periods of rapid eye movements (REM). This smile did not appear to be related to stomach conditions. They observed that the smile at two months, occurring with increasing periods of wakefulness, changes and resembles the social smile save for the fact the infant smiles at everything and everybody. At the end of the three month period the smile is a full social smile, under the control of the infant who smiles at objects he appears to enjoy. The authors report that parents of the infants they studied described their three-month-olds as more human, curious and engaging than they were at two months of age.

Following the seven-to nine-month-old-shift, Emde et al. (1977), report that infants are more discriminating and are able to communicate their wants more specifically. Similarly, Zelazo (1972) has observed that, by measuring heartbeat acceleration rates, infants can be shown to comprehend the meaning of a message following the age shift. Infants, when asked to "show me a big smile" before the shift, show no change in heartbeat, while they do so following the shift.

These spurts or shifts are probably due to mutations selected during our long evolutionary history (Fishbein, 1976). Recent data tend to place more emphasis on innate dispositions which appear to be better understood utilizing cognitive theories than behavioral ones.

COGNITIVE VERSUS BEHAVIORAL THEORIES

Recent summaries of research have emphasized that reinforcement (or the law of effect) doesn't quite operate in the way it has been proposed by such theorists as Thorndike, (1926), McKeachie, (1976), and Bandura, (1977). Whereas reinforcement does seem to operate to maintain a behavior, it does not seem to be as powerful as a tool in learning a new behavior. Learning is predominately under control of the learner and is a complex interaction of the learner's current state (level of development, absence or presence of impairment), the environment and the nature of the facilitator (mother, parent, teacher) in the environment. As Luria (1976) and Gibson (1975) both posit, babies have genetic neural schemata to control their sense organs. The infant also uses these schemata to aid in seeking information about the environment. The infant "knows" how to find out about the world into which he is born and how to organize new information in order to be able to use it and to be able to "seek" more information.

These cognitive views are currently in ascendance in several fields of psychology such as in social psychology, psychology of reading and personality theory, as well as child development. The cognitive view is also present in current language theory (Bates, 1976; Moerk, 1977). These language theories suggest that each child creates language out of attempting to communicate needs and wants in the environment. The first attempts at communication are non-verbal in gestures and oral in terms of cries (Wolff, 1969). As the child learns about things in the environment he attaches words to them. These words are provided to infants by the caregiver in the environment. Thus, the "real language acquisition device" is a whole child, learning by acting on and perceiving things and events in an environment in which an agent provides the appropriately agreed-upon "social" word for the object or event (Bates, 1976). Thus, English children are provided with English words, Russian infants with Russian. However, each infant, whether Russian or English, appears to learn language in the same manner, that is, by making hypotheses and testing them out through their observations and utterances; by being provided with feedback and correction in a setting where they are given opportunity to correct their utterances in an environment of support and love.

Behaviorism as a theory has shown great utility in analyzing skills and preparing sequences of lessons in which skills can be obtained. For the impaired child these efforts have greatly facilitated the acquisition of skills which so many children acquire normally and which, due to a sensory lack or deficit, the impaired child does not. Bricker et al. have done much to combine behaviorism and cognitive theory into viable theories for impaired children (Anastasiow, 1977, in Guralnick).

SUMMARY

The current research data in child development leave implications for how programs are designed for children and their parents, whether it be for normal or impaired children. This is not to say that every child and every parent need to attend preschool education classes. As Moerk (1977) suggests, most middle-class mothers are superb teachers of language. It does suggest that if a child suffers an impairment or if a parent is in doubt of the effects of praise, warmth, and verbal interaction, intervention must begin as early as possible, for infants are born learning. In the opinion of this author, if the parent-to-be is not aware of knowledge of child growth and development currently available to facilitate growth, that information might best be obtained before becoming a parent (Anastasiow et al., in press).

A few years ago Gallagher (1967) commented on the role of the special education teachers and their impossible task. He wrote:

> We may ask of composers that they be very good at writing music, we ask of musicians that they master their instruments, we only require of conductors that they coordinate the instrumentation and weld it into an expressively pleasing whole, and we expect that critics will bring their unique skills to the examination of musical efforts. But in special education, we expect the teacher to write the music, play all the instruments with one hand while conducting with the other, and having done all this, write a scintillating critique of the whole effort.

Today the field is much further advanced. Well developed programs such as those described in this volume are available for implementation, refinement and modification. The field recognizes the need for the cooperative and joint effort of the teacher, parent, therapist and research evaluator. As new knowledge is gained and new light is shed on the complexities of development, the role of the parent assumes new stature and importance which will lead to the fulfillment of an old but constantly renewable goal: maximizing the potential of each human being born into this world.

REFERENCES

Anastasiow, N. J. An overview of parent-oriented early intervention programs. In M. L. Hanes, I. J. Gordon, and W. F. Breviogel (eds.), Update: The first ten years of life. Gainsville, FL: Division of Continuing Education, University of Florida, 1976, 245-258.

Anastasiow, N. J. Strategies and models for early childhood intervention programs in integrated settings. In M. Guralnick (ed.), Early intervention and the integration of handicapped and nonhandicapped children. Baltimore, MD: University Park Press, 1977.

Anastasiow, N. J., Everett, M., O'Shaughnessy, T. E., Eggleston, P. J. and Eklund S.J. Using a child development curriculum to change young teenagers' attitudes toward children, handicapping conditions and hospital settings. American Journal of Orthopsychiatry. (in press).

Bandura, A. The self system in reciprocal determinism. American Psychologist. 1978, 33, 344-358.

Bates, E. Language and context: The acquisition of pragmatics. New York, NY: Academic Press, 1976.

Broman, S. H., Nichold, P. L. and Kennedy, W. A. Preschool IQ. Hillsdale, NJ: Erlbaum Associates, 1975.

DeWeerd, J. Federal Programs for the Handicapped. Exceptional Children. 1974, 40, 441.

Emde, R. N., Gaensbauer, T. J., and Harmon, R. J. Emotional expression in infancy: A biobehavioral study. New York, NY: International Universities Press, Inc., 1976.

Erikson, E.H. Childhood and society. New York, NY: W. W. Norton, 1950.

Fishbein, H. D. Evolution, development, and children's learning. CA: Good Year Publishing Company, 1976.

Fraiberg, S. Insights from the blind. New York, NY: Basic Books, Inc., 1977.

Gallagher, J. J. Presidential address. Annual Convention, Council for Exceptional Children, Dallas, Texas, 1964.

Gibson, E. J. How perception really develops: A view from outside the network. In D. LaBerge and S. J. Samuels (eds.), Basic processes in reading: Perception and comprehension. NJ: Lawrence Erlbaum Associates, 1977, 155-173.

Gordon, I. J., Hanes, M., Lamme, L. and Schlenker, P. with the assistance of Barnett, H. Parent oriented home-based early childhood education programs: A decision oriented review. Gainesville, FL: Institute for Development of Human Resources, College of Education, University of Florida, 1975.

Hetherington, E. M. Review of child development research. Chicago, IL: University of Chicago Press, 1975.

Horowitz, F. D. Review of child development research. Chicago, IL: University of Chicago Press, 1975.

Kagan, J. Resilience and continuity in psychological development. In A. M. Clarke and A. D. B. Clarke (eds.), Early experience: Myth and evidence. New York, NY: The Free Press, 1976, 97-121.

Lewis, M. and Rosenblum, L.A. Interaction, conversation, and the development of language. New York, NY: John Wiley and Sons, 1977.

Luria, A. R. Cognitive development, its cultural and social foundation. Cambridge, MA: Harvard University Press, 1976.

McKeachie, W. J. Psychology in America's bicentennial year. American Psychologist. 1976, 31, 819-833.

Moerk, E. L. Pragmatic and semantic aspects of early language development. Baltimore, MD: University Park Press, 1977.

Neligan, G., Prudham, D. and Steiner, H. Formative years: Birth, family and development in Newcastle upon Tyne. London, WI: Oxford University Press, 1974.

Peters, D. L. Early childhood education: An overview and evaluation. In H. L. Horn, Jr. and P. A. Robinson (eds.), Psychological processes in early education. New York, NY: Academic Press, 1977, 1-21.

Piaget, J. and Inhelder, B. The psychology of the child. New York, NY: Basic Books, 1969.

Scarr-Salapatek, S. An evolutionaly perspective on infant intelligence: Species patterns and individual variations. In M. Lewis (ed.), Origins of intelligence. New York, NY: Plenum Press, 1976, 165-197.

Stedmam, D. J., Anastasiow, N.J., Dokecki, P.R., Gordon, I. J. and Parker, R. K. How can effective early intervention programs be delivered to potentially retarded children? Report No. OS-72-305-DHEW for the Office of the Secretary of the Department of Health, Education, and Welfare, 1972.

Thorndike, E. L. et al. The measurement of intelligence. New York, NY: Bureau of Publications, Teachers College, Columbia University, 1926.

Werner, E. E., Bierman, J. M. and French, F. E. The children of Kauai. Honolulu, HI: University Press of Hawaii, 1971.

White, S. H. Evidence for a hierarchial arrangement of learning processes. In L. P. Lipsitt and C. C. Spiker (eds.), Advances in child development and behavior. New York, NY: Academic Press, 1965, Vol. 2.

Wolff, P. H. The natural history of crying and other vocalizations in early infancy. In B. Foss (ed.), Determinants of infant behavior. London: Methuen, 1969, Vol. IV.

Wynne, S., Ulfelder, L. S. and Dakof, G. Mainstreaming and early childhood education for handicapped children: Review and implications of research. Washington, DC: Division of Innovation and Development, Bureau of Education for the Handicapped, U. S. Office of Education, U. S. Department of Health, Education and Welfare, Final Report Contract No. OEC-74-9056, 1975.

Zelazo, P. R. Smiling and vocalizing: A cognitive emphasis. Merrill-Palmer Quarterly. 1972, 18, 349-367.

IRA J. GORDON, Ed.D. (deceased)

Dean, School of Education
University of North Carolina
Chapel Hill

2

Parents as Teachers—What Can They Do?

The title of this chapter suggests that you will be presented with a cookbook list of activities parents should engage in with their children, or a long list of behaviors presented in a column of "oughts" and "shoulds." Rather, this chapter is based upon my surveys of the field of parent education and parenting, particularly in the early years of the child's life, conducted in both an informal fashion as well as through the usual scholarly pursuits of literature review. It seems important that we attempt to develop some conceptual scheme from which we can infer those lists that people seek. Further, that conceptual scheme, while by no means a theory, should be data-based and subject to continual empirical check. This paper is designed to present some major conceptualizations, and present their implications for practice and research.

There are three major conceptualizations: transaction, systems (ecology), and an instructional theory model. These are not independent: that is, the boundaries that separate a conceptualization of transaction from a systems theory are highly permeable. It is possible to talk about transaction inside of a systems theory. Indeed, transactions occur within and across systems. But nevertheless, separating them may make the issue clearer for our purposes.

TRANSACTION

> Behavior and development is a continuous process of transaction between the child's biological organism and his sociophysical environment. . .The child creates a world of meanings for himself from his experience with his own body and his social milieu. Our basic assumption is that the human being is a meaning-seeking animal. He finds clues in his environment and develops an assigned meaning on the basis of the feedback he gets when he responds to both bodily and external sensations. (Gordon, 1975, pp. 2-3)

This means that the individual always functions as a whole, and behavior has to be understood in the social context. "If we have learned anything from ecology and the history of science, it is that at any moment in time the behavior of an individual is a function of the total of what he brings to it, both from nature and nurture, and of the demands of the situation" (Gordon, 1969, p. 155). There is, then, no dichotomy between heredity and environment. At any given moment, behavior is a total expression of both.

Kessen (1965), in examining the way we have looked at children over the years, states:

> Three variations of a basic melody appear regularly over the entire story of the child in history... Is the child a creature of nature or a creature of nurture? Is the child an active explorer or a passive receiver? Is the behavior of the child best conceived as a bundle of elements or as a set of integrated structures? (Kessen, 1965, p.4)

A transactional orientation answers these questions by saying the child is the creature of both nature and nurture. The child is an active element in the process, and behavior can best be conceived of in an integrated fashion.

What has this to do with the parent as teacher? It means that the child is contributing to the family relationship and influencing the behavior not only of the parent towards him or her, but also of the parents and other adults and other siblings towards each other. If behavior is to be understood in context, and if it is truly transactional, then any list of how one is to behave toward the child runs the risk of being unilateral. That is, it may fail to take into account what the child himself or herself is contributing to the situation.

A second aspect in this transaction is summed up in the word uniqueness. It comes as no shock to you to be told that each child, each person, is unique, but each family setting is also unique. Murphy perhaps said it best: "Every individual is an almost infinitely complex pattern of biochemical tendencies. . .Biochemical individuality is recognizable even in the embryo and clearly in the newborn; and upon this early individuality are impressed still further individualities due to the vicissitudes of the individual life process." (Murphy, G., 1947, p. 31) A 1978 example of this is provided by Williams (1978), who demonstrates that even anatomical structures such as the stomach or the heart do not resemble in vivo the marvelous textbook pictures studied in anatomy textbooks. There is tremendous individuality of organ structure within the human being.

This uniqueness is reflected at birth and shortly thereafter in a variety of ways. These have been called temperaments, and Thomas et al., (1964) has presented us with a list of eight or nine of these, such as activity, mood, responsivity, rhythm, and the like. In the transactional relationship between child and family, these temperamental variables of the child influence caretaker behavior and are in turn influenced by that behavior. Not only does the child have an individual set of characteristics, but also so do each of the parents and other adults with whom he relates. The excellent longitudinal studies conducted by Lois Murphy and her colleagues at the Menninger Foundation in the 1950's (Murphy, 1962) dealt with such questions as "Are the active babies now active preschool children? What is the relation between other persistent aspects of equipment or temperament and the techniques used by each child as he confronts the demands made upon him?" (Murphy, L., 1962, p. 13)

Children in the Murphy and collaborator's study were rated on various temperamental characteristics. For example, low sensory thresholds and drive were among these. They state:

> Perceptual sensitivity determines to a considerable degree both the scope of the stimulus pressures upon the young child and his awareness of resources he can draw upon in meeting his needs and implementing his interests . . . Children with

> markedly low sensory thresholds (or high sensitivity, since sensitivity is high where threshold is low) were evenly divided between those whose mothers were anxious, tense, unstable, or in other ways might have contributed in obvious ways to the sensitizing of the baby, and those mothers who were unusually relaxed, permissive, and giving ..., or who were actively aware of the baby's needs and responsive to them, as well as apparently well adjusted . . . Children who reach clinics are often both sensitive themselves and have anxious, tense mothers; this has tended to lead to the assumption that the mothers cause the child's sensitivity. But there is a flat contradiction here to the hypothesis that low thresholds in the baby are necessarily a resultant of anxious interaction with the mother. It might be suggested, however, that unusually gentle mothers give the baby minimal occasion for development of defenses against stimulation, and this may tend to stabilize thresholds at a low level when the infants are initially sensitive. (Murphy, L., 1962, pp. 334-335)

Thus the parent's own uniqueness is matched or mismatched with the child's own uniqueness, not only in the area of sensitivity, but also in all other aspects of temperament. Children, in their striving to cope and master, thus learn to adapt to this and to develop those patterns of thought and behavior which permit the integration of their own biology with the demands of the world. As Murphy and her collaborators summarize: "We can say that the child creates his identity through his efforts in coming to terms with the environment in his own personal way." (Murphy, L., 1962, p. 374). Lists of advice to parents rarely take such a position, and instead assume the _tabula rasa_ child or the unilateral relationship in which children will become what parents demand of them. Transaction implies that all those involved are constantly influencing each other, and that each individual's uniqueness is being modified by environmental press.

A SYSTEMS APPROACH

The first system is the development of the self. We are meaning-seeking animals actively searching our environments to make order out of it, or, as Piaget and Inhelder say, "The formation of personality is dominated by the search for coherence." (Piaget and Inhelder, 1969, p. 158) Even though the surrounding world may be chaotic, each of us takes in information and organizes it to make sense out of it. One way of making sense of the environment is to develop concepts of ourselves--to place order inside even if order may not exist outside. We develop views of ourselves which allow us to organize our world, perhaps even to consciously influence it, and also to understand and assign reasons to our own successes and failures. The self begins to develop early in life, but it, too, is permeable and therefore modifiable throughout life. Its origins lie in the transaction. Thus the role of significant others in the early years is of great importance in determining or influencing the original views one holds of one's self, which in turn shape the future meaning of the world. Murphy stated:

> Not only is uniqueness rooted in the biochemical composition of the individual, but also it is fostered by the nature of his (or her) cultural experience. When the child is born, he (or she) comes into contact with an already ongoing social environment that immediately begins to shape his (or her) development...Cultural role expectations --although these may be rapidly changing--present images and create situations, so that each child experiences something somewhat different from the other...(Murphy, G., 1947, p. 31)

As a modern social learning theorist presents it:

> In the social learning view of interaction, which is analyzed as a process of reciprocal determinism, ...behavior, internal personal factors, and environmental influences all operate as interlocking determinants of each other...Contrary to common misconception, social learning theory does not disregard personal determinants of behavior. Within this perspective, such determinants are treated as integral, dynamic factors in causal processes rather than as static trait dimensions. (Bandura, 1978, pp. 346, 348)

The self begins in the first moments of life, and we tend to see family as the first major cultural agency with continuing impact on the child. But, even in the hospital, the larger culture makes itself felt in the way the baby's birth is handled, and the procedures which either allow or bar family participation in the delivery and immediate after-care of baby and mother. So that, from birth on, "in addition to family experiences, the child participates in the life of the neighborhood, the school, and the community at large." (Gordon, 1975, p. 14) These cultural forces can be understood as a series of systems embedded in each other. Brim (1975) and Bronfenbrenner (1976) have described these, and Figure 2-1 is adapted from their description. At the center of Figure 2-1 is the family as a micro-system.

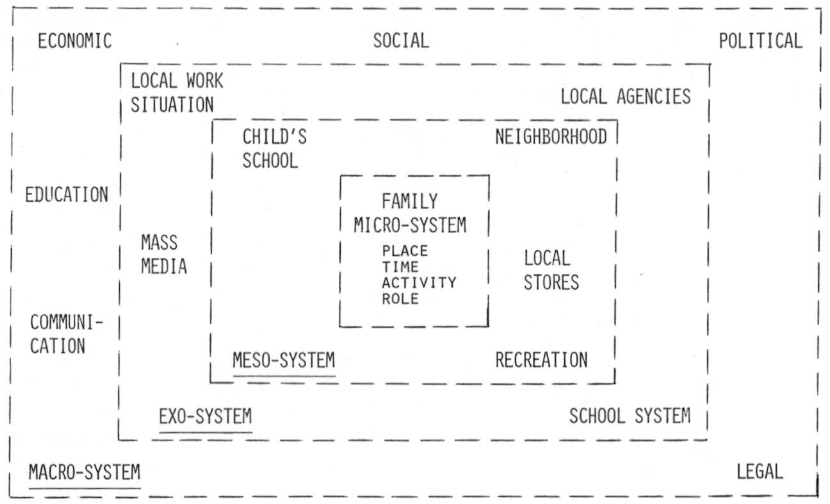

FIG. 2-1

The System Network Influencing a Child's Development. Adapted from Orville Brim, Macro-structural influences on child development and the need for childhood social indicators. American Journal of Orthopsychiatry. 1975, 45, 516-524, and Urie Bronfenbrenner, The experimental ecology of education. Educational Researcher. 1976, 5, 5-15.

The family can be examined from a multiplicity of theoretical positions, but generally we might agree that regardless of how it is defined, it assembles in some place. Its members spend some portions of time with each other. They engage in certain activities as a group, and they perform certain roles which enable the family to function in an organized way. All of those factors are the family's part (including the baby) of the transactional process. But the family in turn is surrounded by three additional systems. The first of these is the meso-system, consisting of the neighborhood, the local stores, recreation facilities, local T.V., the nearby school. The meso-system includes both formal and informal forces which shape and are shaped by the family. One can then move to the exo-system: to agencies, the world of work, mass media. Finally, the economic, political and social systems which compose the macro-system all play fundamental roles in shaping the place, time, activity, and roles which occur within the family. The baby and young child and all children are influenced directly not only by that family, but also by these other systems. Television, for example, although the set is in the home, brings in a variety of images and experiences. The neighborhood and life conditions are experienced directly very early by the child. The child is also influenced indirectly by the ways the family screens and interprets the world, as well as by the parents' position in the world of work, their income level, and by the attitudes and values which surround the family. So in order to understand the parent as teacher, we need to examine not only the family micro-system but also the ways in which the family copes with and interprets for the child those systems with which the family must come to terms. Just as the teacher in the classroom is influenced by the principal, his or her professional organizations, the action of the school board, legislative behavior, newspaper editorials, so also is the parent as teacher influenced by all of the other agencies and systems which make up our total society. It is interesting to note that the Brim and Bronfenbrenner models do not single out religion as a significant system, or show the church as a major agency. Further, the system which might be labeled the science system is also omitted, although both religion and science perhaps are part of the social, educational and communication networks. For many people, however, answers for child rearing are sought from these two sources, and they influence strongly the attitudes and values of many families. We need only to mention the word abortion to make this case.

Current sociological and anthropological perspectives tend to shift the responsibilities for origins of children's difficulties in school, for example, from the micro-system of the family or the exo-system of the school, to the macro-system. Indeed, the recent book by Ogbu (1978) states that the basic cause for lower school performance of blacks is caste.

> The elimination of caste barriers is the only lasting solution to the problem of academic retardation. Programs that seek to change school policies and practices and to help blacks develop new attitudes and skills are necessary but auxiliary components of this strategy, and cannot, by themselves, prove effective in solving the problem of school failure among caste-like minorities in the United States and elsewhere. (Ogbu, 1978, p. 357)

If one takes this position, what are the implications for parents as teachers? One might infer that what parents do in the micro-system makes little difference, or is so governed by the external caste system that there is no point in spending much time helping individual families learn new modes of parent-child relations which have been found to relate to child achievement. But Ogbu has concluded, as have some others, that the early intervention studies, which he calls the compensatory education strategy, have failed. (Ogbu, 1978, pp. 93-94). The more current data of the longitudinal studies, including several he cites, such as the Perry Preschool Project, the Early Childhood Project in New York, the Early Training Project in Nashville, Karnes's preschool projects, Levenstein's Verbal Interaction Project and our work in Florida, now show that the programs did indeed have a lasting impact into the middle school, and in some cases--where time has permitted--into the high school years (Lazar et al., 1977). Nevertheless, Ogbu's point of the significance of the macro-system cannot be overlooked in any discussion of parents as teachers--what can they do?

AN INSTRUCTIONAL THEORY MODEL

We can now examine the transactions which occur in the family micro-system and between that system and other systems from the perspective of a model of instructional theory. We are getting closer to answering the question, What can parents do? Figure 2-2 was developed by the Commission on Instructional Theory of the Association for Supervision and Curriculum Development. The Commission struggled to deal with the fact that a learning theory and an instructional theory are not the same thing. Rather than constructing an instructional theory, we ended up describing what ought to go into one. If we look at the first circle on Figure 2-2, called Pupil Characteristics, we can define that as the baby's characteristics. We can define goal characteristics as the goals the parents hold for that baby. The instructional situation characteristics would then consist of the variables within the family that influence and are influenced by the other two circles. (Gordon, 1968)

Let us first define teaching in the family context. What is teaching? It is the manipulation of the instructional situation characteristics which are under the control of the parent to move the child in his or her own uniqueness toward the parental goals. For most parents, this is not a conscious, organized, rational act. It is only that type of act to us external parent watchers and interveners who study the transaction to find its rules, or it may be that

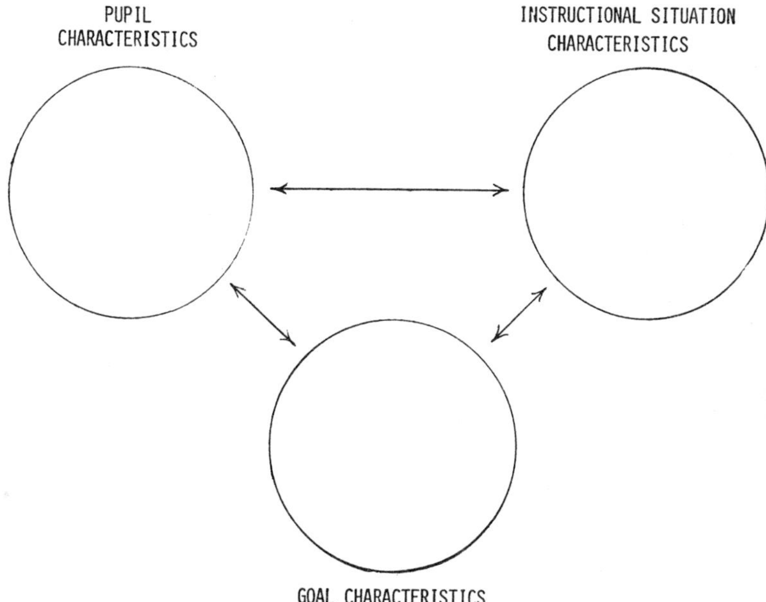

FIG. 2-2
The transactional network between pupil, goal, and instructional situation characteristics. From I.J. Gordon, (ed.), Criteria for Theories of Instruction. (Association for Supervision and Curriculum Development, 1968), p. 17.

overt in authoritarian societies such as China and Russia which organize and systematize the situation. Using this conceptualization, we can now turn to the question, "Parents as teachers--what can they do?"

GOAL SETTING

First, the parents can set the goals. These goals influence instructional setting characteristics and also their responses to the systems which surround the family. But it must also be understood that the family is in a transactional relationship with these other systems, so that the goals they set and the efforts they make are influenced by the other systems up to and including the macro-system. Also, the parents are in a transactional relationship with the child so that the child's own individuality, behavior and responses continually influence and modify the goals which are set.

What are goals that parents set? First, they set expectations for sex role behavior. Depending upon their view of women's liberation, their own cultural background, their relationships with each other, they convey to the child very early on how one of a particular sex is to behave. If they have adopted a tabula rasa view or a heavy environmentalist position, they may feel that one's sex role behavior is completely governed by their own goals and by the instructional situation characteristics. If, however, they adopt what Rossi calls a biosocial perspective on parenting (Rossi, 1977), they ascribe certain elements of sex role to the basic biology and physiology of the child, and realize that it is only within certain limits that one can influence or should influence sex role behavior. As Rossi states, "A biosocial perspective does not argue that there is a genetic determination of what men can do compared to women; rather, it suggests that the biological contributions shape what is learned, and that there are differences in the ease with which the sexes can learn certain things." (Rossi, 1977, p.4)

Parents set expectations for intellectual and academic achievement. We have long known that these expectations actually influence the achievement of children. The variety of research summarized by Hess (1969) and Gordon (1970), as well as the British longitudinal studies (Davie et al., 1972; Douglas et al., 1971; Miller, 1971; Wedge and Prosser, 1973; Kellmer Pringle et al., 1966), and the international educational studies (Coleman, 1975; Comber and Keeves, 1973; Purves, 1973), all indicate, in the vernacular: if you don't ask, you don't get.

A third goal area is general life satisfaction for their child. Parents wish the child to be happy, to have a good self-concept, to be able to get and hold a satisfactory job, to make a reasonable income, and the like. But all of these goals are influenced by the parents' assumptions about the nature of children and the nature of learning. If we turn back to Kessen's original three items, that is nature/nurture, active/passive, organize/discrete, then we see that the ways parents try to establish the instructional situation characteristics and even the goals they set depend upon whether they view learning as distinct from maturation, the child as a passive recipient and a tabula rasa, whether they believe that what a child can become is completely dominated by the genes or by the environment, or whether they hold a transactional perspective.

INSTRUCTIONAL SITUATION CHARACTERISTICS

Parents can and do set these characteristics. Every home has them, whether they are so labeled or understood.

The micro-system, as we indicated, consists of activities and roles and time. These are part of instructional setting characteristics. First, parents organize the home. It can be an orderly and predictable place or chaotic. It can function on an industrial time clock or a more primitive sun clock. It can be organized around the needs of the parents or their perception of the child's needs. Included also in the organization of the home are the number of people and the roles that they play, the organization and assignment of space, the type of furniture and its accessibility to the baby, and the like.

Parents determine the type and availability of materials. It has also been clear for a long time, and found again in current research, that the existence of books and other learning materials in the home plays a major role in the intellectual and academic development of the child. Those references cited above for expectations also contain these data. In addition, the more recent work by Bradley and Caldwell (1976), by my colleague Barry Guinagh and myself (Gordon and Guinagh, 1974; Guinagh and Gordon, 1976), and by Ramey and his colleagues (Ramey et al., 1975), all of whom used versions of a home environment scale, demonstrate the importance of the organization of the home and the materials available in the achievement of low-income children.

The parents play two kinds of major roles in the home. They play management roles and instructional roles. These instructional roles include academic guidance, planning of cultural activities, the direct instruction of the child, the modeling of intellectuality, and language interaction. All of these have been found to relate to child development, particularly in the intellectual domain (Hess, 1969; Gordon, 1970). But they also play management roles, and here two factors seem important: 1. the consistency of management by the individual parent and 2. the disciplinary pattern when several adults are involved. Pavenstedt (1967) stressed the importance of order and predictability, and the summaries by Hess and Gordon also indicate that the child needs a consistent environment. The studies by Burlingham and Freud of orphanages in World War II led them to conclude that young children need consistency of care in a loving environment along with stimulation (Burlingham and Freud, 1944). These are all to some degree under the control of the parent. As indicated above, they reflect the perceptions that the parents hold of the infant and child as a learner as well as their concepts of themselves as teachers. Schaefer (1977) collected data from parents of kindergarten children on a parent-as-educator interview scale and found that the Kessen historical view is still current. He found a factor of parental belief that "children learn passively, children should be treated uniformly, the aim of education is to instill information, children are born bad and will misbehave if uncontrolled...," and belief in the absolute authority of the parent (Schaefer, 1977, p. 8). A second factor "includes a belief that children learn actively, parental attitudes of support for encouraging the child's own ideas, encouraging the child's verbalization of those ideas, encouraging imagination and playfulness...(Schaefer, 1977, p. 8). Obviously these parental attitudes influence the instructional setting characteristics and influence what parents will do in performing the role of teacher.

Third, the parents can and do attempt to influence the systems which surround the child, which also possess instructional setting characteristics. Particularly parents of children with handicaps, such as parents of deaf children, face this task. The professionals and agencies with whom they deal also have a set of attitudes and beliefs in which they place the parent, and then develop a set of instructional setting characteristics to move that parent toward the goals that the professionals take. Parents Speak Out (Turnbull and Turnbull, 1978) reveals the anger and frustration experienced in trying to convince professionals that parents know many things about their children and are not to be treated either as automatically sick or as overanxious or indeed as incapable of facing reality.

PARENT EDUCATION

If the above conceptualizations are somewhat accurate, that is from a transactional perspective, 1. the child is an active learner and meaning seeker, 2. the child's behavior is a function of the complete intermix of biology and experience, 3. the child's uniqueness influences the family, 4. the family can be understood from a systems approach, and 5. parents as teachers can be described in terms of the instructional theory model, where does this leave us? How do we finally answer the question, What can they do?

Let me pose one more question. What do parents need to know in order to make the goals they set and the instructional setting characteristics of the home consistent with the current state of the science--or should I say art--of child development? First, parents (as well as professionals) need to understand the transactional approach, that is that the child is not a *tabula rasa* upon which they can write whatever behavioral prescription they desire, that the child will influence them, that transactions are two-way streets that the child's own biology is an important element in their lives, and that truly each child is unique. Therefore, prescriptions which worked for one child in the family may not necessarily and probably will not work for any other child.

In keeping with this, they need to learn how to see their child. What is this uniqueness? How do they look at those temperamental variables of rhythm, intensity, activity, mood, persistence, adaptability, responsiveness, openness, distractibility? How do they appreciate and understand their child's own maturation rate? These are not mysterious acts which can only be studied by clinical psychologists or highly trained pediatricians. Indeed, most parents are aware to some degree, just as each of us are aware, of differences in activity rate, energy, mood, responsiveness, of the people with whom we come in daily contact. As the book cited above (Turnbull and Turnbull, 1978) indicates, very often parents are more aware than the professionals with whom they deal. They pick up the clues but they may not understand the ranges of normality nor how one should respond to these clues. Indeed, Thomas and Chess indicate that "as a general rule, the nature of the parents' response to the child's temperament was determined not so much by the degree of congruence with their own personality characteristics as by consonance with their goals, standards and values" (Thomas and Chess, 1977, p. 77).

Parents need information on how to provide what seem to be common elements, across studies and cultures, of the positive instructional setting characteristics in the home, if one's goals are for intellectual and emotional achievement. Parents can attempt to organize the home so it provides for order and predictability, some sense of stability, language interaction, reading and other intellectual materials, other opportunities to play with parents as well as with toys, to explore, to interpret. The research cited above as well as the work of White and Watts (1973) indicates the importance of a reciprocal relationship. I have used the term "ping-pong" to describe it (Gordon and Jester, 1972). It is a playful interchange between parent and child in which each person's behavior grows out of the behavior of the other. The studies of home environment also show the importance of planning for cultural activities, of the father as an interactor with the baby, and for parents to play the roles which Carew lists as: participator in the child's intellectual experiences (most important up to age 2.5), teacher, entertainer, playmate, converser, and blender (Carew, 1976).

Finally, parents need information and support on how to cope with and influence the agencies with which they have to deal. This means that parents as teachers need to look beyond the home to change the systems which impact, and often impact detrimentally, upon them. One major pathway, of course, is organization. The second is individual political action. A third is, either through organizations or individually, economic action. We are witnessing the latter with respect to the content of television--the power of a group to have Sears Roebuck give up sponsorship of "Charlie's Angels." We also see it in the Action for Children's Television (ACT) group. This needs to be done not only, however, at the macro-system level but also at those immediate levels that surround the family. The health delivery system is another one which all of us realize imposes great difficulties, not only on low-income families, but also on families with exceptional children, and on middle-class families now attempting to cope.

CONCLUSION

I have not offered a shopping list or cookbook of acts that parents must do. These abound in the literature, and I have contributed my share in the past. Rather, I have attempted to present you with a conceptual scheme for analyzing the role of the parent as teacher, which I hope will indicate what further research is necessary in child development, in family life, and in instruction. I hope the scheme also offers you practical ways of working with individual families to assess where they are, what they need, and how you can enable them to set their goals, understand their child, and define for themselves, with your help, the appropriate family setting to enable them to accomplish their goals.

REFERENCES

Bandura, A. The self system in reciprocal determinism. American Psychologist. 1978, 33, 344-358.

Bradley, R. H. and Caldwell, B. M. The relation of infants' home environments to mental test performance at fifty-four months: A follow-up study. Child Development. 1976, 47, 1172-1174.

Brim, O. Macro-structural influences on child development and the need for childhood social indicators. American Journal of Orthopsychiatry. 1975, 45, 516-524.

Bronfenbrenner, U. The experimental ecology of education. Educational Researcher. 1976, 5, 5-15.

Burlingham, D. and Freud, A. Infants without Families. London: George Allen and Unwin, 1944.

Carew, J.V. Effective home learning environments in the preschool years. In M. L. Hanes, I. J. Gordon, and W. F. Breivogel (eds.), Update: The First Ten Years of Life. Gainesville: University of Florida, Division of Continuing Education, 1976.

Coleman, J. S. Methods and results in the IEA studies of effects of school on learning. Review of Educational Research. 1975, 45, 335-386.

Comber, L. C. and Keeves, J. P. Science education in nineteen countries. International Studies in Evaluation. Stockholm: Almqvist and Wiksell, 1973, Vol. 1.

Davie, R., Butler, N. and Goldstein, H. From Birth to Seven. London: Longman, 1972.

Douglas, J.W., Ross, J.M. and Simpson, H.R. All our Future. London: Panther Books Ltd., 1971.

Gordon, I. J. (ed.), Criteria for Theories of Instruction. Washington, D.C.: Association for Supervision and Curriculum Development, National Education Association, 1968. (ERIC Document Reproduction Service No. ED 030 607).

Gordon, I. J. Our view of the child: 1970. Theory Into Practice. 1969, 8, 152-157.

Gordon, I. J. Parent Involvement in Compensatory Education. Urbana: University of Illinois Press, 1970.

Gordon, I.J. Human Development: A Transactional Perspective. New York: Harper and Row, 1975.

Gordon, I. J. and Guinagh, B. J. A home learning center approach to early stimulation [Final report to the National Institute of Mental Health, Project No. 5 R01 MH16037-01]. Gainesville: University of Florida, Institute for Development of Human Resources, 1974. Published: JSAS Catalog of Selected Documents in Psychology. 1978, 8, 6. (Ms. No. 1634).

Gordon, I. J. and Jester, R. E. Instructional strategies in infant stimulation [Final report to the National Institute of Mental Health, Project No. 5 R01 MH17347-02]. Gainesville: University of Florida, Institute for Development of Human Resources, 1972. Published: JSAS Catalog of Selected Documents in Psychology. 1972, 2, 122. (Ms. No. 237).

Guinagh, B. J. and Gordon, I. J. School performance as a function of early stimulation [Final report to the Office of Child Development, Grant No. N1H-HEW-OCD-09-C-638]. Gainesville: University of Florida, Institute for Development of Human Resources, 1976. Published: JSAS Catalog of Selected Documents in Psychology. 1978, 8, 6. (Ms. No. 1637).

Hess, R. Parental behavior and children's school achievement implications for Head Start. In E. Grotberg (ed.), Critical Issues in Rresearch Related to Disadvantaged Children. Princeton, N.J.: Educational Testing Service, September 1969, Seminar No. 5.

Kellmer Pringle, M. L., Butler, N. R. and Davie, R. 11,000 Seven-year Olds. London: Longman, 1966.

Kessen, W. The Child. New York: John Wiley and Sons, 1965.

Lazar, I., Hubbell, V. R., Murray, H., Rosche, M. and Royce, J. The Persistence of Preschool Effects: A Long-Term Follow-up of Fourteen Infant and Preschool Experiments. A National Collaborative Study by Twelve Research Groups for the Education Commission of the States. Ithaca, N.Y.: Cornell University, New York State College of Human Ecology, Community Service Laboratory, 1977.

Miller, G. W. Educational Opportunity and the Home. London: Longman, 1971.

Murphy, G. Personality: A Biosocial Approach to Origins and Structure. New York: Harper, 1947.

Murphy, L. The Widening World of Childhood. New York: Basic Books, 1962.

Ogbu, J. Minority Education and Caste: The American System in Cross-Cultural Perspective. New York: Academic Press, 1978.

Pavenstedt, E. (ed.), The Drifters: Children of Disorganized Lower-Class Families. Boston: Little, Brown and Co., 1967.

Piaget, J. and Inhelder, B. The Psychology of the Child. New York: Basic Books, 1969.

Purves, A. C. Literature education in ten countries. International Studies in Evaluation. Stockholm: Almqvist and Wiksell, 1973, Vol. 2.

Ramey, C. T., Mills, P., Campbell, F. A. and O'Brien, C. Infants' home environments: A comparison of high-risk families and families from the general population. American Journal of Mental Deficiency. 1975, 80, 40-42.

Rossi, A.S. A biosocial perspective on parenting. Daedalus, 1977, 106, 1-31.

Schaefer, E. S. Parent Interview Predictors of Teacher Ratings of School Adaptation: Concepts, Methods, and Findings. Paper presented at 2nd International meeting on Developmental Screening, Santa Fe, N.M.,September 1977.

Thomas, A. and Chess, S. Temperament and Development. New York: Brunner/Mazel, 1977.

Thomas, A., Chess, S., Birch, H.G., Hertzig, M.E. and Korn, S. Behavioral Individuality in Early Childhood. London: University of London, 1964.

Turnbull, A. P. and Turnbull, H. R. Parents Speak Out. Columbus, Ohio: Charles E. Merrill, 1978.

Wedge, P. and Prosser, H. Born to Fail? London: Arrow Books, 1973.

White, B. and Watts, J. Experience and Environment. Englewood Cliffs, N. J.: Prentice Hall, 1973.

Williams, R. J. Nutritional individuality. Human Nature. 1978, 1, 46-53.

JUNE M. GRANT, Ph.D.

Director, Special Education
Trinity University
San Antonio, Texas

3

Experience: The Foundation of Language Acquisition

One of the most confounding phenomena of human development is the child's acquisition of language. This amazing feat occurs typically at a very early age, and is virtually completed in a very short period of time. McNeill (1966) states that grammatical speech begins early in the second year of life and within twenty-four to thirty-six additional months, the child has inferred the rudimentary rules of the grammar of his culture. Lenneberg (1966) anchors the process to biological development, pointing out, for example, that babbling coincides with the emergence of unilateral reaching and sitting alone. Bloom's (1973) stance is that language acquisition is dependent upon cognitive development and that the reason the child does not talk earlier than he does is that he has not yet acquired the cognitive prerequisites. Interest in language acquisition has produced a large body of literature, especially during the past two decades. It is apparent that the various aspects of language cannot be effectively divorced one from the other (phonology from syntax, syntax from semantics, semantics from pragmatics), yet the focus of attention appears to have shifted over the years. Jakobson's (1941) monograph deals with phonological universals, the most visible aspect of language. He contrasts dissolution of language, aphasia, with the child's acquisition of phonology. It is interesting to note that at that time, a great deal of information concerning the pathologies of language had been documented and yet there was little in the literature concerning "normal" language acquisition. However, the advent of Chomsky's Syntactic Structures (1957) stimulated, by implication, great interest in theories of language acquisition (Edmonds, 1976). Many early studies concentrated on the child's acquisition of syntax (Brown, 1963, 1964; McNeill, 1970; Cazden, 1968, 1970); later investigators included the semantic aspects of language in their studies (Bloom, 1970; Clark, 1973, 1975; Fillmore, 1971; Antinucci, 1975); and more recently, research reports concerning the pragmatics of language have been appearing (Rees, 1978; Bates, 1976; Moerk, 1977). It would seem that as each level of language was intensely investigated, linguists and psycholinguists continue their search in other components in hopes of unraveling more of the mystery of how and what exactly the child has acquired when he has mastered the language of his culture. It is the purpose of this paper to examine the role of language in the development of the young child and to discuss strategies for fostering its development in hearing-impaired children. It will be demonstrated that experience is the vital prerequisite for language acquisition.

FUNCTIONS OF LANGUAGE

The debate concerning the functions of language (Feldman, 1977) cannot be dealt with in this paper, but likewise the subject of language cannot be discussed without some clarification of the role of language in the growth and development of the child. Among the various possible and debatable functions of language, three appear to be particularly salient: 1. language as a means of communication, 2. language as a cognitive tool, 3. language as an avenue for creativity. Clearly, no matter what the philosophical issues might be, the objectives of a language acquisition program for hearing-impaired children should include the fostering of language growth in these three areas.

LANGUAGE AS COMMUNICATION

Communication, itself, both inter- and intra-species, is not specific to homo sapiens. Anyone who has a pet dog or cat can testify to high degrees of communication between man and animal. The highly developed intra-species communication systems of bees (von Frisch, 1950), birds (Marler and Hamilton, 1966), dolphins (Lilly, 1961), and apes (Premacks, 1971, 1972; Gardners, 1971), are well documented, but none of these systems is what can be considered human language (Brown, 1973; Chomsky, 1968; Lenneberg, 1975). While many animals exchange information very effectively and human beings use animal-like cries of alarm and pain, human communication is a more complicated system than that of animals (Cherry, 1966). According to some investigators animal communication lacks novelty in that new ideas cannot be expressed and received; and it lacks the ability to structure morphemes built upon phonemes (Critchley, 1975; Hockett, 1960). In this respect, communication, as one facet of language, serves human beings in a unique fashion.

In order to investigate the role of communication as a function of language it is necessary to limit the term. In its most rudimentary connotation, communication is the transmission of meaning with the intent to do so (Boyle, 1971). The word meaning, itself, is fraught with ambiguity and controversy, and no attempt will be put forth here to clarify or elucidate the issue. Instead, a common interpretation of the word, the message one intends to convey, is the sense in which the term is used here. First of all, before an infant can communicate, he must have attained a prerequisite level of cognition (Leonard, 1978). Sometime toward the end of the sensorimotor period, eighteen months to two years of age (Piaget, 1952), the child begins to see himself as an entity separate from the rest of the world, and the realization of this separation makes possible the distinction between objects and actions (McNeill, 1970). This differentiation signals the need for communication (Beilin, 1975).

According to Bloom (1973), the very young child has a limited number of ideas to communicate; during the sensorimotor period he communicates with words such as there, gone, and more in order to state that objects and events exist, they disappear, they recur. Later, when the child has developed object constancy, more substantive words appear attesting to his knowledge of objects and the ability to act upon them. As the child accrues more sophisticated cognitive structures, this development is reflected in his linguistic performance. The emergence of two-word utterances, the beginning expression of grammatical relations or syntax, signifies the attainment of the preoperational period of intelligence. The child can now communicate concerning objects and entities that are not in his immediate presence (Ginsburg and Opper, 1969). Such communication would appear to require that the child be capable of manipulating two aspects of an event such as agent and object (Bloom, 1973). Another observation is that the child communicates about actions and states associated with objects and persons which he perceives or remembers (Beilin, 1975).

As the child progresses from two-word utterances to three-word utterances, and on to sentences, he is communicating more complex ideas and notions. As his cognitive and linguistic capabilities develop, so do the expressions of semantic functions. Even very early speech demonstrates the highly communicative nature of language; the child intends to communicate and have an effect on the listener (Greenfield, 1976). Hence, there is evidence of need, early in the child's life, to communicate. A language program for hearing-impaired children will need strong objectives to provide the children with linguistic skills for communication.

LANGUAGE AS A COGNITIVE TOOL

Many researchers conclude that the early stages of language acquisition are highly dependent upon and under the control of the cognitive development (Bloom; 1973; Brown, 1973; Leonard, 1978; Beilin, 1975). Bloom (1973) goes as far as to state that during the first two years of life, the child is preoccupied with organizing his perceptions within the environment, and that this is accomplished through cognitive, not linguistic functioning. The child discovers that various linguistic items can be used to symbolize certain of his concepts, and he utilizes syntax as a means of structuring his cognitive representations rather than as a linguistic device. This dominance of cognition over language probably persists well into the operational stages, although it is not complete. For there comes a time when linguistic structures demonstrate relations that seem best explained only by a generative transformational grammar (Beilin, 1975). Such incidents point to the possibility of a transition of the relative positions of cognition and language. The one-way mapping becomes a two-way mapping with language controlling cognition as much as the reverse by the time the child is capable of formal, logical thinking at about ten to twelve years of age (Beilin, 1975).

Bruner states that "cognitive growth, whether divergent or uniform across cultures, is inconceivable without participation in a culture and its linguistic community" (Bruner et al., 1966, p. 2).

The role of language as an aid to cognitive growth is discussed by Vygotsky (1962) who believes that at a certain point in the child's life, thought becomes verbal. Heretofore, thought and language have had different roots with a prelinguistic period of thought, and a preintellectual period of language. He states further that inner speech which is intimately tied up with ordering the child's behavior is a refinement of external speech which has evolved to egocentric speech and then to inner speech. While Vygotsky is careful to point out that even though thought and speech coincide to produce verbal thought, and that verbal thought does not include all forms of thought, he states "an indisputable fact of great importance: Thought development is determined by language, i.e., by the linguistic tools of thought and by the sociocultural experience of the child." (p. 51).

The above-stated position, that language is the precursor of cognition at some point in the intellectual development of the child, has been challenged in recent years (Sinclair-de Zwart, 1969, 1971, 1973; Schlesinger, 1971; Bloom, 1973; Slobin, 1973; Clark, 1973, 1974; Nelson, 1973, 1974). The more recent position that children acquire a great many concepts completely independently of linguistic forms is supported by observed strategies children use to express linguistically cognitive concepts they have already acquired. One such strategy is described by Slobin (1973) as children's use of old forms to express new functions. For example, a child who has not yet acquired the present perfect tense used the word <u>yet</u> with a verb in the past tense to express the correct time frame (<u>I didn't make the bed yet</u> for <u>haven't made</u>) (Cromer, 1974, 1976). Also the fact that children overextend and underextend already-learned linguistic forms is taken as evidence that the cognitive structures already exist, and the linguistic forms are being attached in not completely appropriate ways (Clark, 1973; Bowerman, 1976; Brown, 1973). More evidence for this point of view comes from the fact that children interpret the meanings of utterances in accordance with their view of the nature of the world. They systematically rely on "non-linguistic expectations about the nature of things in processing linguistic input" (Bowerman, 1978, p. 105).

In spite of the current tendency to refute the "language dominace over cognition" position, there are strong reasons to support it; conceptual development alone cannot explain all aspects of language acquisition. Conceptual development does not explain how the child advances to the stage of finding the proper linguistic devices for his concepts (Brown, 1973; Slobin, 1973); it does not explain why a child will learn a more complex means of expression after he has acquired an appropriate one (Cromer, 1976); it does not explain how a child acquires the purely formal, arbitrary distinctions in language that are not governed by semantics. For example, one can say He tried it out or I gave it to Harry, but one cannot say He tried out it or I gave Harry it (McCawley, 1974); it does not explain why some children with certain pathological conditions encounter extreme difficulty in acquiring language although their conceptual development appears to be normal (Cromer, 1976); and finally, it does not explain some strictly linguistic devices not based on conceptual relations, used by children to help them deal with a particular linguistic structure. For example, children have been observed to use strictly linguistic forms, such as repeated or meaningless syllables to serve as "placeholders" for lexical or structural patterns not yet acquired (Leonard, 1975). It would appear, then, that there is ample evidence in both directions: cognition influences language acquisition and growth, and language influences cognitive growth. Clearly, a language acquisition program for hearing-impaired children must provide abundant opportunities for the development of concepts with appropriate linguistic structures provided so that the child may manipulate, store, and retrieve information at will.

LANGUAGE AS AN AVENUE FOR CREATIVITY

A third aspect of language, that of an avenue for creativity, requires the attention of those who would strive for complete language curricula for hearing-impaired children. This use of language differs from the others discussed above in that it can be non-communicative and possibly non-cognitive in that its source may be even a different cortical center from that of other types of language. It is known that spoken words are analyzed in the auditory region of the left cerebral hemisphere for most human beings whereas music is analyzed in the auditory region of the right hemisphere (Rosenzweig et al., 1972). It is not unreasonable to speculate that creative language and other art forms are likewise stimulated and analyzed in the so-called "non-cognitive" hemisphere. The use of language as a creative medium is not far-fetched, for language, itself, is highly creative. One of the important qualities of human language is that very quality of creativity: a person (even a very young child) constructs each utterance anew and is capable of understanding utterances he has never heard before (Cazden, 1972). Chomsky (1968) alludes "to some efforts to found a theory of artistic creativity on the creative aspect of normal language use" (p. 102). He cites Schlegel's argument that poetry is unique among the arts in that poetry, or language, used in a creative fashion, is an expression of the human mind as opposed to a product of nature, and that language's recursive principle "permits each creation to serve as the basis for a new creative act" (p. 102). Language can be thought of as a medium for creativity just as clay is the medium for the potter. A well-rounded language curriculum provides ample opportunities for the development of creative attitudes and the expression of creative ideas.

EXPERIENCE, THE FACILITATOR OF LANGUAGE ACQUISITION

The utilization of language for the purposes of communication, cognitive activity, and creative expression is by no means an exhaustive listing. As pointed out above, there is not unanimous agreement of the functions of language among the linguistic researchers, much less among teachers. Chomsky (Feldman, 1977) believes on the one hand, that language has many non-communicative functions: contemplation, inquiry, self-guidance, clarification of thought, thinking in words, among others. Feldman, on the other hand argues that the functions at issue are, in reality, communicative since the individual is communicating with himself. It seems unimportant whether a teacher aligns herself with one or the other of these views; the important issue is that hearing-impaired children should acquire the ability to use language for all these functions and the essential element of each area is experience.

The consequences of experience in the growth and development of children have been the subject of a great deal of research. Hunt (1961) concludes from his extensive work with animals that it might be profitable to structure the experiences of children, especially very young ones, in an effort to increase the rate and level of adult intellectual capacity. He states that the evidence is clear that impoverishment of experience during the early months can retard the development of intelligence. Later experiments with animals have demonstrated both chemical and weight changes in the brain as a response to environmental experiences (Rosenzweig et al., 1972). However, the changes brought about by operant-conditioning devices or learning mazes are small and of a different pattern from those induced by environmental experience. It is interesting to note that post-mortem examination of the brain of Laura Bridgman, one of the first deaf-blind pupils to be taught at the Perkins School for the Blind in Watertown, Massachusetts, revealed that the parts of her cortex that were involved with vision and hearing were thin and lacked the characteristics of the normal brain whereas the cortical region for touch had a normal appearance. Bruner (1966) states that experience and mental operations must be prepared for before language can be used, and that for the child to transform a perception into a verbal or symbolic formula, he must organize his experience into a form which will allow more complex language to be used as the tool for this transformation.

It is the child's experiences and his way of coping, categorizing, and storing these experiences that form his concept of the world. Bruner's (1966) hierarchy is tri-leveled. He defines three levels of representation: first, enactive, next the ikonic, and finally the symbolic. In the first stage Bruner states that the child establishes a link between action (his own) and perception. The fusion is such that the child cannot separate the two and perceives action as a property of the objects he perceives. This enactive level is the exclusive means of representation for the child during the Piagetian sensorimotor period, "a stage in which action and external experience are fused" (p. 16). It is not until the child can free himself from the necessity of action that he can progress to action-free imagery, or the ikonic level. At this stage a child is able to represent the world to himself by an image. However, the type of imagery the child is capable of at early stages is in many respects unstable and rather primitive in that he is still not completely independent of action and sensory input which dominate the enactive level. When he matches an image in his mind to an object or situation, he is relying on a sensory correspondence between the two. The emergence of the symbolic, or highest level which involves language, is dependent upon the establishment of the prerequisite levels (Bruner et al., 1966). It is important to point out that the levels are not mutually exclusive, that images are often involved with symbolic activity as are motor activities involved with imagery and symbolic activity. It seems obvious that action involving sensory input, in other words, experience, is a necessary ingredient at all three levels of representation.

EXPERIENCE AS RELATED TO COMMUNICATION

To return to the functions of language, attention is now directed to the role of experience in the use of language as a means of communication. It is necessary to examine what forms children's communication take at various stages in their lives. At the earliest stages, the child's babbling appears to be for self-gratification (Spire, 1949) although it serves the important function of establishing the auditory feedback loop, the important link between kinesthetic and auditory sensations (Whetnall and Fry, 1971). But early on, the child expresses ideas of existence, disappearance, and recurrence as mentioned above (Bloom, 1973). The human need to communicate is so urgent that very young children manage to do just this by means of their holophrastic utterances. Slobin (1971) feels that children communicate in order to describe their world and to manipulate people. However, the environment must be rich enough for the child to have hopes, imagination, and anxieties to communicate thoughts, ideas, needs, desires, and this richness must be derived from the child's experiences. Two decades ago, Groht (1958) wrote that the child talks because he is motivated to tell something, or find out something, to express an idea or desire, to promote companionship, or sometimes just to hear himself talk.

The importance of first-hand experiences to provide the raw materials from which communication is derived cannot be overemphasized. For the child to reach the symbolic level of representation, he must have accumulated a great many experiences at the enactive and the ikonic levels before he can progress to the highest symbolic level. The younger or more naive the child, the more essential is the sensorimotor activity as a basis for subsequent ikonic and symbolic representation. Adults, in general, are constantly functioning at the symbolic representational level; therefore, it is hard for them to realize that young children have not made the transition to that state. Sigel (1971) very effectively demonstrated that "children's ability to deal with representations of their environment is indeed a function of life experiences and will vary accordingly" (p. 16). His research revealed among other findings that lower-class children could not classify two-dimensional materials (pictures) as well as they could the actual objects, whereas middle-class children could classify either group equally well; that the story-telling and play activities of lower-class children involved mostly motoric-action level whereas middle-class children's play demonstrated symbolism. It would appear that the experiences of the lower-class children have not provided the breadth and depth to elevate these children from the enactive stage to the higher levels. These inadequacies and inabilities existed in spite of the fact that the children could label the pictures of the objects. An important analogy can be drawn here between these lower-class hearing children and hearing-impaired children: simply teaching hearing-impaired children the labels of objects and actions will not necessarily provide them with requisite ability to manipulate the labels meaningfully at the symbolic level; they will have to have sufficient motoric experience for this transition to occur. Before children can communicate, they must be motivated to communicate and have something to say, and first-hand experience is the main contributor to both motivation and means.

EXPERIENCE AS RELATED TO COGNITION

Having examined the significance of varied and abundant experiences in providing hearing-impaired (or hearing) children the wherewith to communicate, it is appropriate to scrutinize the need for experience as a vehicle for using language as a cognitive tool. It is apparent that so long as a child is functioning primarily at the enactive stage his communication will be very primitive. One can expect more sophistication when the child is able to maintain images, but there are limitations to ikonic representation, also. Images are static, and it is not possible to rearrange or combine the elements of an image. For example, children who function no higher than this level have not achieved Piaget's conservation stages since they are making judgments on one property only: usually, in the case of conservation of liquids, the height of the water level (Dale, 1976). In contrast, when the child can function at the symbolic level of representation, that is with language, he has an added flexibility which permits him not only to represent experience, but to transform it (Bruner et al., 1966). It has been reported that children use language in solving problems (Olson, 1966), and often language becomes an instrument for ordering perceptions and thought. If one is to assume Bruner's point of view, that language becomes an instrument for ordering perception and thoughts, it becomes essential for the child to have a broad base of experiences upon which to operate.

EXPERIENCE AS RELATED TO CREATIVITY

The third aspect of language, that of an avenue for creativity, presents rather a different picture, but yet it too is highly dependent upon experiences for its fruition. The term creativity has many different connotations and definitions and therefore requires some discussion. There are as many different definitions for the word as there are writers, but certain descriptors persist. The words new and novel appear frequently, and often creativity is associated with problem-solving. Definitions range from creating ideas or products which are new to the world, to the type of activity that produces new and original thoughts for the thinker (English and English, 1958; Good, 1959; Warren, 1934; Torrance, 1967). Bruner (1962) in his definition involves the element of surprise in addition to novelty. The surprise can take different forms, such as predictive effectiveness, as in the formula for falling bodies, or formal surprise as is common in mathematics and possibly music, or as metaphoric effectiveness where facts are synthesized within the arts. But in all cases, the effective surprise is brought about by the mediation of symbol, metaphor, and image. Such surprise transcends common ways of experiencing the world and provides man with new instruments for manipulating it, e.g., the creation of the wheel or the creation of formula $e = mc^2$. In addition to such lofty acts of creativity, Bruner (1961) discusses a more common form of creativity: discovery. He describes discovery as containing surprise and requiring rearranging or transforming facts so that one is able to acquire new insights. It would seem apparent then that creative experiences are available to anyone at any level of development. However, creativity cannot occur in a vacuum, and abundant and varied experiences are an essential ingredient in any curriculum which aspires to provide opportunities for creative activity.

THE QUALITY OF EXPERIENCES

The type of experiences at every level of development, of course, will vary; nevertheless, the spectrum is broad, and at each stage the experiences can bring about and/or enhance language in the three roles outlined above. White (White and Watts, 1973) distinguishes between the characteristics of mothers of A children and C children in his study. A children were those who were highly socially competent at ages three to six, and C children were those less competent who were likely to encounter problems upon entry into elementary school programs. Observations were made of the mothers and children during the age span of one to three years. Some of the observed behaviors of the mothers of superior children were that the mothers provided access to many objects and diverse situations, and that the mothers, perhaps unwittingly, served as consultants and designers of a physical world which was very conducive to curiosity and investigation. The physical environments included materials to nurture motor interests and development as well as cognitive and imaginative stimulation.

Teachers of all young children, but especially of hearing-impaired children, would do well to emulate the practices of these mothers of competent children. In developing curricula for young children, the teacher must design experiences which will provide opportunities for children to acquire perceptions through their actions on objects (Simmons-Martin, 1978), and through these perceptions, the child can develop appropriate concepts to which the appropriate verbal symbols should be attached (Simmons, 1971). The child cannot achieve conservation of liquids until he has had water-play experience pouring liquid from one-sized container to another; he needs to form the same amount of clay into balls, snakes, and pancakes before he can achieve conservation of solids. The young child must have first-hand experiences (Read, 1960), and these experiences must be of the enactive type before he can progress to vicarious experiences and ikonic and symbolic functioning. Therefore, for experiences to be of value for a young hearing-impaired child, they should have sensorimotor involvement, they should concern the child's immediate environment, the "here and now," and they should have the appropriate linguistic symbols attached (Simmons, 1967). These experiences should be selected to stimulate the child to communicate, to engage in cognitive activity, and to promote creative expression. An activity in which the children make paper boats, sail them in whatever water is available (bucket, bathtub, or pond) by whatever power (breath, electric or hand fan, or wind) will induce the children to talk about the experience and to figure out what moves the boats. While this may appear to be an unstructured activity, the teacher knows why she has initiated it, what language she expects the children to gain from it, and how this activity will fit into the development of future concepts to which she plans to expose her students.

ADVANTAGES OF TEACHER-PLANNED EXPERIENCES

There are advantages of teacher-planned experiences over completely spontaneous ones. One great advantage is that teacher-planned experiences permit her to conceive long-range objectives and to plan the activities and materials necessary to afford steady advancement from one developmental level to successively higher ones. Another advantage is that by observing the children's behavior and participation, the teacher can feel fairly confident that she maintains the integrity of the children's thoughts and ideas, a fact that cannot always be assured when she supplies language for an activity the child participated in away from the classroom; often she cannot feel comfortable that she has given the child the words that properly describe the message he was imparting. A third advantage is that the teacher can systematically introduce language structures which have not yet emerged and which the children need and are ready for cognitively. Finally, teacher-planned and initiated activities permit her to systematize the experiences assuring that the language input is compatible with the emerging concepts that the teacher is focusing on, and that the experiences are appropriate to the children's language and cognitive development.

1. Long-range planning. The first advantage listed, that of making possible long-range goals, has broad implications for teachers. For a language curriculum to be productive (and for hearing-impaired children, especially young ones, language is the pivotal component of the curriculum), the teacher must have a well-conceived structure through which she expects to promote language growth. However informally and casually her planned experiences are executed, she must have formulated a rationale for the experiences based on more than intuition, great though her intuitive powers might be. While White's "super mothers" are able to provide stimulating and appropriate environments without knowing how or why they do it, teachers must not only know the how, and why, but the what of their long-term goals. Overall, experiences are the basis of multi-faceted growth, and the wise teacher takes the long view and designs her program to provide a well-balanced, comprehensive language curriculum. To achieve this goal, she will have to know which experiences are to occur at what time and why that is the appropriate time.

2. The match of language to cognitive levels. The advantage of long-range planning is related to, but not

identical with the advantage of integrating emerging concepts into the experiences. Before a child can truly acquire a concept, he must have varied experiences with the many aspects of the concept. The hearing child does this somewhat by trial and error through experience, and he needs a set of working concepts before he can deal with the objects and actions of his world (Hopper and Naremore, 1973). The teacher who builds her students' concepts in a hierarchical manner, providing varied and sufficient contact at all levels (enactive, ikonic, and symbolic), will make it possible for the children first to broaden their too-narrow concepts and then to refine their undifferentiated concepts into accurate and serviceable ones. The label or linguistic symbol that the teacher attaches to the concept is the medium by which the children manipulate the concept. It goes without saying that the order of presentation should be developmentally appropriate and not haphazard. Only the teacher-planned experiences can adhere to such an overall plan.

3. The match of language to the child's thoughts. If one of the goals of a language program is to provide hearing-impaired children with language to use for communication, it behooves the teacher to know what the children are trying to communicate and to provide them with the correct verbal symbols. This feat is not always easily accomplished, and on many occasions both teacher and student experience great frustration when all forms of communication fail. With a planned experience where all the action takes place under the observant eye of the teacher, these frustrations are minimized or eliminated. Such planning does not mean that activities are imposed upon the children and that instruction need necessarily be completely teacher-directed. Children can be encouraged to make suggestions and develop ideas within the spectrum of the teacher's objectives. As the teacher observes the children, she will know what they want to relate, what has excited them, and what has seemed unimportant. As stated by deLaguna (1927), to know what the baby is saying, you have to know what the baby is doing.

4. The language "lift". Finally, there is a very important reason for teachers to structure the experience and the attached language for their students. The linguistic input for hearing-impaired children must always contain some syntactic constructions which the children are not yet using spontaneously. They need a great deal of receptive experience with language more sophisticated than

their expressive levels before they can be expected to use the higher levels productively. Because of their impoverished linguistic input (compared to hearing children), they cannot elevate themselves from immature structures to more mature ones without outside stimulation. The teacher-structured experience with its planning, executing, and follow-up activities is the ideal vehicle for this language "lift." Children from "culturally different" environments face the same difficulty, and compensatory language programs for these children carry the same admonition (Lavatelli, 1971).

SPONTANEOUS EXPERIENCES

The above-stated advantages should not be interpreted to imply that spontaneous activities are not valuable media for promoting language; on the contrary, they are very valuable indeed. A teacher should seize every such opportunity and exploit it to its fullest. The unplanned, but highly exciting incidents that occur in and out of the classroom are excellent sources for language development: the children's interest level is high, the teacher can accurately attach the appropriate linguistic symbols to the activities, and more than likely, the incidents have social and interpersonal implications not easily simulated, in addition to the communication and cognitive skills involved. A teacher who ignores a hail storm outside or a classroom visitor from a distant interesting location is not taking advantage of outstanding opportunities to bring useful real-life situations into her language program. Even in her planned experiences, the teacher must be constantly alert to unexpected incidents which may require her to modify objectives or which may prove to be of more interest and value than the original objectives. If the fuse blows and the popcorn cannot be popped, or if the pet fish purchased the day before die before the chart story can be discussed, it is obvious that the focus of the experience must be redirected, thereby altering the concepts to be developed and the accompanying cognitive and communicative activities. The clever teacher will "shift gears" quickly and smoothly.

EXPERIENCES TO STIMULATE CREATIVITY

Thus far, the communicative and cognitive aspects of language have been explicated. How can language be an avenue for creative expression when hearing-impaired children do well to communicate day to day happenings? It is precisely this limitation of language fluency that in one respect makes creative expression more accessible to hearing-impaired children. They have not internalized all the restrictions of the language; a hearing-impaired child can say that Dr. Max Goldstein, the founder of Central Institute for the Deaf, was the "spark-plug of his life," or that "the jello was nervous," or he can call "a drawer" the "table's pocket," without first having to divest himself of all his linguistic restrictions. Teachers of hearing children are constantly being encouraged to create situations which will stimulate creative activity among their students (Tiedt and Tiedt, 1967; Shumsky, 1965; Torrance, 1962; Wagner, 1965). Strategies are offered which will help these language proficient users to cast aside their conventional verbal symbols and express themselves through other media: poetry, dramatics, creative and imaginative writing, in addition to the other arts, music, dance, graphic arts, among others. Hearing-impaired children, like their hearing siblings and peers should be guided into writing poetry, describing their drawings, dramatizing real and fictional events, creating characters, and writing imaginative tales. Likewise, they should be exposed to the imaginative writings of others, such as nursery rhymes, fairy tales, and poetry and literature. It is important to stress the point that these enterprises should not be delayed until the children have a high degree of language proficiency. Little children can dictate descriptions of their drawings and tell stories before they can write them. Creative language activities need not be postponed until the upper grades, for all children at all ages possess some degree of creativity (Tiedt and Tiedt, 1967) which deserves to be cultivated. Moreover, little children are generally open-minded and receptive to imaginative activities until these qualities become stifled either at home or at school (Reasoner, 1968). Often teachers themselves have been "turned off" poetry by their teachers, a fact which makes them reluctant to include poetry in their language programs (Lord, 1973). Such an omission is highly regrettable. However, children cannot be inspired by vicarious experiences; they will have to have experienced emotions of joy, love, fear, envy, compassion, and others before they can symbolize them in poetry, creative writing, dramatics, and other art forms. If pursuits to encourage creative expression are valuable components of the curricula for hearing children, they are of especial value for hearing-impaired children.

SUMMARY

Language acquisition is an essential aspect of human development. Without adequate command of language, hearing-impaired children cannot achieve their full intellectual and academic potential. Therefore, language programs for hearing-impaired children assume a pivotal position in curricula for these children. The position taken here is that language should serve individuals as a means of communication, as a cognitive tool, and as an outlet for creative expression. Each of these functions of language was examined and found to be a viable component of language. The relationship between cognition and language was found to be a dynamic one with cognition controlling language in the early years (Bloom, 1973; Brown, 1973; Leonard, 1978; Beilin, 1975) and the relative position of the two phenomena being reversed by the time the child reaches the stage of formal operations (Beilin, 1975).

Figure 3-1 shows experiences as the source of all representation. The successive levels of representation are hierarchical, thus involving enactive representation at the ikonic level and both enactive and ikonic representation at the symbolic level. The symbolic level yields various symbol systems, but language is the one of concern here.

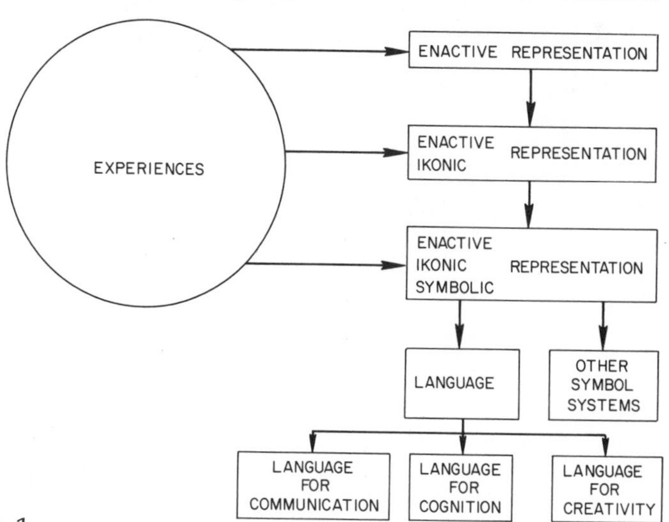

FIG. 3-1
The Role of Experience in Language Acquisition: Levels of Representation After Bruner.

Since experience appears to be the essential element in the ascent to symbolic representation, a child must have an abundance of sensorimotor experiences before he can advance to ikonic and symbolic (language) levels of representation (Bruner et al., 1966). Therefore, it is important for teachers of hearing-impaired children to plan experiences in a hierarchical fashion so that her students can develop concepts that will enhance their communicative, cognitive, and creative abilities. The planned experiences should be part of the teacher's long-term goals, they should match the children's ideas and interests, they should be developmentally appropriate, and they should promote language growth by constantly introducing more sophisticated language structures and concepts.

It is doubtful that such a natural phenomenon as language acquisition can be taught; language is learned, not taught. Therefore, the teacher of hearing-impaired children can best accomplish her goals by creating a stimulating environment and emulating the process by which the hearing child acquires the language of his culture.

REFERENCES

Antinucci, F. and Parisi, D. Early semantic development in child language. In E. H. Lenneberg and E. Lenneberg (eds.), _Foundations of Language Development: A Multidisciplinary Approach_. New York: Academic Press, 1975, _Vol. 1_, 189-202.

Bates, E. Pragmatics and sociolinguistics in child language. In D. Morehead and A. Morehead (eds.), _Normal and Deficient Child Language_. Baltimore: University Park Press, 1976, 411-463.

Beilin, Harry. _Studies in the Cognitive Basis of Language Development_. New York: Academic Press, 1975.

Bloom, Lois. _Language Development: Form and Function in Emerging Grammars_. Cambridge: The M.I.T. Press, 1970.

Bloom, Lois. _One Word at a Time_. The Hague: Mouton, 1973.

Bowerman, Melissa. Semantic factors in the acquisition of rules for word use and sentence construction. In D. Morehead and A. Morehead (eds.), _Normal and Deficient Child Language_. Baltimore: University Park Press, 1976, 99-179.

Bowerman, Melissa. Semantic and syntactic development. In R. L. Schiefelbusch (ed.), _Bases of Language Intervention_. Baltimore: University Park Press, 1978, 97-189.

Boyle, D.G. _Language and Thinking in Human Development_. London: Hutchinson University Library, 1971.

Brown, Rober and Fraser, Colin. The acquisition of syntax. In Charles N.O. Cofer and Barbara Musgrave (eds.), Verbal Behavior and Learning: Problems and Processes. New York: McGraw-Hill, 1963, 158-201.

Brown, Roger and Bellugi, Ursula. Three processes in the acquisition of syntax. Harvard Educational Review. 1964, Vol. 34, 133-151.

Brown, Roger. A First Language: The Early Stages. Cambridge: Harvard University Press, 1973.

Bruner, Jerome S. The act of discovery. Harvard Educational Review. 1961, Vol. 31, 21-32.

Bruner, Jerome S. On Knowing. Cambridge, Massachusetts: The Belknap Press of Harvard University Press, 1962.

Bruner, Jerome S., Oliver, Rose R. and Greenfield, Patricia M. Studies in Cognitive Growth. New York: John Wiley & Sons, 1966.

Cazden, Courtney B. The acquisition of noun and verb inflections. Child Development. 1968, Vol. 39, 433-448.

Cazden, Courtney B. Children's questions: Their forms, functions, and roles in education. Young Children. 1970, Vol. 25, 202-220.

Cazden, Courtney B. Child Language and Education. New York: Holt, Rinehart, and Winston, 1972.

Cherry, Colin. On Human Communication. Cambridge: The M.I.T. Press, 1966.

Chomsky, Noam. Syntactic Structures. The Hague: Mouton 1957.

Chomsky, Noam. Language and Mind. New York: Harcourt, Brace & World, 1968.

Clark, E. V. What's in a word. In T.E. Moore (ed.), Cognitive Development and the Acquisition of Language. New York: Academic Press, 1973, 65-110.

Clark, E. V. Some aspects of the conceptual basis for first language acquisition. In R. L. Schiefelbusch and L. L. Lloyd (eds.), Language Perspectives - Acquisition, Retardation, and Intervention. Baltimore: University Park Press, 1974, 105-128.

Clark, E. V. Knowledge, context, and strategy in the acquisition of meaning. In D. Data (ed.), Developmental Psycholinguistics: Theory and Applications. 26th Annual Georgetown University Roundtable. Washington, D.C.: Georgetown University Press, 1975.

Critchley, Macdonald. Language. In E. H. Lenneberg and E. Lenneberg (eds.), Foundations of Language Development. New York: Academic Press, 1975, Vol. 1, 3-16.

Cromer, R. F. The development of language and cognition. In B. Foss (ed.), New Perspectives in Child Development. Baltimore: Penguin, 1974, 184-252.

Cromer, R. F. The cognitive hypothesis of language acquisition and its implications for child language deficiency. In D. Morehead and A. Morehead (eds.), Normal and Deficient Child Language. Baltimore: University Park Press, 1976, 283-333.

Dale, Philip S. Language Development: Structure and Function. New York: Holt, Rinehart, and Winston, 1976.

deLaguna, Grace Andrus. Speech: Its Function and Development. New Haven, Connecticut: Yale University Press, 1927.

Edmonds, Marilyn H. New directions in theories of language acquisition. Harvard Educational Review. 1976, Vol. 46, 175-198.

English, Horace B. and English, Ava Champney. A Comprehensive Dictionary of Psychological and Psychoanalytical Terms. New York: Longmans, Green and Company, 1958.

Feldman, Carol F. Two functions of language. Harvard Educational Review. 1977, Vol. 47, 282-293.

Fillmore, C. J. Types of lexical information. In D. D. Steinberg and L. A. Jakobovits (eds.), Semantics: An Interdisciplinary Reader in Philosophy, Linguistics and Psychology. London: Cambridge University Press, 1971, 370-392.

Gardner, Beatrice T. and Gardner, R. Allen. Two-way communication with an infant chimpanzee. In Allan Schriver and Fred Stollnitz (eds.), Behavior of Non-human Primates. New York: Academic Press, 1971, Vol. IV, 117-184.

Ginsburg, Herbert and Opper, Sylvia. Piaget's Theory of Intellectual Development. Englewood Cliffs, N.J.: Prentice-Hall, 1969.

Good, Carter V. (ed.) Dictionary of Education. New York: McGraw-Hill Book Company, 1959.

Greenfield, Patricia Marks and Smith, Joshua H. The Structure of Communication in Early Language Development. New York: Academic Press, 1976.

Groht, Mildred A. Natural Language for Deaf Children. Washington, D.C.: A.G. Bell Association for the Deaf, 1958.

Hockett, Charles F. Logical considerations in the study of animal communication. In Wesley E. Lanyon and William N. Tavolga (eds.), Animal Sounds and Animal Communication. Washington, D.C.: American Institute of Biological Sciences, 1960, 392-430.

Hopper, Robert and Naremore, Rita C. Children's Speech: A Practical Introduction to Communication Development. New York: Harper & Row, 1973.

Hunt, J. McVicker. Intelligence and Experience. New York: The Ronald Press Company, 1961.

Jakobson, R. Kindersprache, Aphasie, und Allgemeine Lautegesetze. Uppsala: Almgvist and Wiksell, 1941. (English translation by A. Keiler, Child Language, Aphasia and Phonological Universals. The Hague: Mouton, 1968.)

Lavatelli, Celia Stendler. A systematized approach to the Tucson Method of language teaching. In Celia Stendler Lavatelli (ed.), Language Training in Early Childhood Education. Urbana, Illinois: University of Illinois Press, 1971, 101-118.

Lenneberg, E. H. The natural history of language. In Frank Smith and George A. Miller (eds.), The Genesis of Language. Cambridge: The M.I.T. Press, 1966, 219-252.

Lenneberg, E. H. The concept of language differentiation. In E. H. Lenneberg and E. Lenneberg (eds.), Foundation of Language Development. New York: Academic Press, 1975, Vol. 1, 17-34.

Leonard, L. B. On differentiating syntactic and semantic features in emerging grammars: evidence from empty form usage. Journal of Psycholinguistic Research, 1975, Vol. 4, 357-364.

Leonard, L. B. Cognitive factors in early linguistic development. In R. L. Schiefelbusch (ed.), Bases of Language Intervention. Baltimore: University Park Press, 1978, 67-96.

Lilly, J.C. Man and Dolphin. Garden City, New York: Doubleday, 1961.

Lord, Berman. (Preface) Literature, Creativity and Imagination. Washington, D.C.: Association for Childhood Education International, 1973.

Marler, P. and Hamilton, W.J. Mechanisms of Animal Behavior. New York: Wiley, 1966.

McCawley, James. (Dialogue with) James McCawley. In H. Parret (ed.), Discussing Language. The Hague: Mouton, 1974.

McNeill, David. The capacity for language acquisition. In Jean Utley Lehman (ed.), Selected Readings in Language for Teachers of the Hearing-Impaired. New York: Simon and Schuster, 1966, 47-63.

McNeill, David. The Acquisition of Language: The Study of Developmental Psycholinguistics. New York: Harper & Row, 1970.

Moerk, Ernest L. Pragmatic and Semantic Aspects of Early Language Development. Baltimore: University Park Press, 1977.

Nelson, K. Concept, word, and sentence: Interrelations in Acquisition and Development. Psychological Review. 1974 Vol. 81, 267-285.

Nelson, K. Structure and strategy in learning to talk. Monogr. Soc. Res. Child Development. 1973, 38, Serial No. 149.

Olson, David R. On conceptual strategies. In Jerome S. Bruner, Rose R. Oliver, and Patricia M. Greenfield (eds.), Studies in Cognitive Growth. New York: John Wiley & Sons, Inc., 1966, 135-153.

Piaget, Jean. The Origins of Intelligence in Children. (1st ed., 1936), New York: International University Press, 1952.

Premack, David. Language in a chimpanzee? Science. 1971, Vol. 172, 808-822.

Premack, A. J. and Premack, D. Teaching language to an ape. Scientific American. 1972, Vol. 227, 92-99.

Read, Katherine. The Nursery School. Philadelphia: W. B. Saunders Company, 1960.

Reasoner, Charles. Releasing Children to Literature. New York: Dell Publishing Company, 1968.

Rees, Norma S. Pragmatics of language. In R. L. Schiefelbusch (ed.), Bases of Language Intervention. Baltimore: University Park Press, 1978, 193-268.

Rosenzweig, Mark R.; Bennett, Edward L.; and Diamond, Marian L. Brain changes in response to experience. In The Nature and Nurture of Behavior - (Readings from) Scientific American. San Francisco: W. H. Freeman and Company, 1972.

Schlesinger, I.M. The production of utterances and language acquisition. In D. I. Slobin (ed.), The Ontogenesis of Grammar. New York: Academic Press, 1971, 63-102.

Shumsky, Abraham. Creative Teaching in the Elementary School. New York: Appleton, 1965.

Sigel, Irving. Language of the disadvantaged: the distancing hypothesis. In C. S. Lavatelli (ed.), Language Training in Early Childhood Education. Urbana, Illinois: University of Illinois Press, 1971, 60-76.

Simmons, Audrey A. Motivating language in the young child. Proceedings of International Conference on Oral Education of the Deaf. 1967, 11, 1592-1616.

Simmons, Audrey A. Language and hearing. In Leo C. Connor (ed.), Speech for the Deaf Child. Washington, D.C.: A. G. Bell Association for the Deaf, 1971, 280-292.

Simmons-Martin, Audrey A. Early management procedures for the hearing-impaired child. In Frederick N. Martin (ed.), Pediatric Audiology. New Jersey: Prentice-Hall, 1978, Chap. 10.

Sinclair-de Zwart, H. Developmental psycholinguistics. In D. Elkind and J.H. Flavell (eds.), Studies in Cognitive Development. New York: Oxford University Press, 1969, 315-336.

Sinclair-de Zwart, H. Sensorimotor action patterns as a condition for the acquisition of syntax. In R. Huxley and E. Ingram (eds.), Language Acquisition: Models and Methods. New York: Academic Press, 1971, 121-130.

Sinclair-de Zwart, H. Language acquisition and cognitive development. In T. E. Moore (ed.), Cognitive Development and the Acquisition of Language. New York: Academic Press, 1973, 9-26.

Slobin, Dan I. Psycholinguistics. Glenview, Illinois: Scott, Foresman & Company, 1971.

Slobin, Dan I. Cognitive prerequisites for the development of grammar. In C. A. Ferguson and Dan I. Slobin (eds.), Studies of Child Language Development. New York: Holt, Rinehart, and Winston, 1973, 175-208.

Spire, Andre. Plaisir Poetigue, Plaisir Musculaire: Essai sur Evolution des Techniques poetiques. New York: S. F. Vanni, 1949.

Tiedt, Iris M. and Tiedt, Sidney W. Contemporary English in the Elementary School. Englewood Cliffs, N. J.: Prentice-Hall, Inc., 1967.

Torrance, E. Paul. Guiding Creative Talent. Englewood Cliffs, N.J.: Prentice-Hall, 1962.

Torrance, E. Paul. Scientific views of creativity and factors affecting its growth. In Jerome Kagan (ed.), Creativity and Learning. Boston: Beacon Press, 1967, 73-91.

von Frisch, K. Bees: Their Vision Chemical Senses, and Language. Ithaca, New York: Cornell University Press, 1950.

Vygotsky, L.S. Thought and Language. Translated by Eugenia Hanfmann and Gertrude Vakar. Cambridge: The M.I.T. Press, 1962.

Wagner, Jearnine. A Place for Ideas. San Antonio: Principia Press of Trinity University, 1965.

Warren, Howard C. (ed.), Dictionary of Psychology. Boston: Houghton Mifflin Company, 1934.

Whetnall, Edith and D. B. Fry. The Deaf Child. London: Whitefrairs Press Ltd., 1971.

White, Burton L. and Watts, Jean Carew. Experience and Environment. Englewood Cliffs, N.J.: Prentice-Hall, 1973.

BURTON L. WHITE, Ph.D.

Senior Research Associate
Harvard Graduate School
of Education
Cambridge, Massachusetts

4

The Special Importance of Hearing Ability for the Development of Infants and Toddlers

The position taken in this chapter comes from an uninterrupted twenty years of research on the details of development in the first six years of life, with special focus on the role of experiences in the development of abilities. The first eight years or so of research involved studies of physically normal children in the first six months of life growing up in an institution while awaiting placement for adoption. The later work has featured week-by-week observations of children in their own homes, especially children from all levels of society developing unusually well. We have studied the development of excellence and, of course, we have seen much of less fortunate outcomes as well. We have also, in the course of these studies, worked quite extensively with families, because they, rather than the professionals, are the prime educational child-rearing mechanism.

We have come to the following rather strong conclusions:

1. Intact hearing during the first three years of life is surprisingly important. Prior to the execution of our research, we had no awareness of how important it seems to be in this period.

2. It is quite easy to identify the deaf infant or the nearly-deaf infant.

3. It is equally easy to overlook the infant with a moderate hearing loss, 20-30 dB for example, and the results can affect his or her entire future in harmful ways.

4. Techniques exist to avoid the harmful consequences of undetected moderate hearing loss, and are feasible. These are being used here and there, but are only reaching a very small number of children.

5. A program of identification and treatment from birth should be implemented as soon as possible.

Why is intact hearing ability in the first three years of life so important in our view? First of all, from birth to six to eight months of age there seems to be no substantial language development. Let me underline that and expand on it slightly. Children vocalize and they hear, but they do not seem to be able to process the meaning of words. There is some dispute as to whether their vocalizations and early experiences affect the later acquisition of meaningful language. However, the most conservative point of view that seems to be adopted by language specialists is that there is no language development in the first six to eight months of life. From six to eight months on to three years of age, tremendous growth in language takes place. So much growth occurs that my colleagues who specialize in the process say that by three years of age, the typical child can handle (receptively) something approaching three-quarters of all language he will be exposed to in ordinary conversation for the rest of his life.

A very important distinction, which has not been adequately made in the field of education over the years, is that between receptive and expressive language development. A 13-month-old child who says no words at all is, as far as we can tell, behaving normally. There is as yet no reason for concern, even though some other child down the street may be speaking in short sentences. The onset of speech is extraordinarily variable among children. It can appear as early as eight or nine months of age with a word or two, or it can be as late as two years of age. The variability can be as great as sixteen months, and still the child in question can be developing nicely. If however, that 13-month-old child does not understand at least three dozen words, then he may be in serious trouble.

If you look at the history of assessment of early language skills, you will find that the focus has been on speech, rather than on understanding or language reception. (Bernard Friedlander has done excellent work in this subject area.) The means by which we have assessed language development traditionally have been to keep track of what a child says during a general examination and to ask the child's mother to fill in the rest. Unfortunately, mothers are notoriously inaccurate when it comes to reporting what their children say. The problem, of course, is that testing an infant or toddler for receptive language ability can be a very difficult process.

Whereas the onset of speech, as was said earlier, differs among children, the onset of receptive language ability is not variable to such a substantial degree. By eight or nine months of age, all children generally understand one or two simple words, and by ten or eleven months of age, they can respond to simple instructions, like, "Wave bye-bye," or "Throw me a kiss."

These distinctions between the onset of speech and the onset of the understanding of language are terribly important. If one is going to go into an early detection program, it becomes very important to do a good job of monitoring the growth of receptive language from the age of six months on.

During the age range of six months to three years, the child is in a sensorimotor period. The experiences of this period lay the groundwork for the development of higher intelligence. The best introduction to those processes is in the brilliant work of Piaget. Frequent interplay with caring and talking adults seems to be required for the best results in those processes. I use "interplay" rather than sessions with a Doman-Delacato kit! Frequent interplay must be with caring adults who get more excited about that child's utterances, understandings and discoveries than anybody else in the world. These adults, providing good language models, are required for the most successful children.

Social development between six months and two years of age is an absolutely beautiful process to watch, particularly when it goes well. It is even fascinating when it does not go all that well and you see a totally innocent eight-month-old baby develop into a manipulating 13-month-old. Human innocence disappears between eight and thirteen months of age. To see a 25 pound two-footer controlling a grown woman with a college degree is an impressive tribute to the rapidity of growth of human ability. And it is happening in homes all over the country every day.

Five social skills emerge during this period of life. I will list them, but will not discuss them in detail here:

1. <u>Gaining attention in a variety of socially acceptable ways</u>. One way of gaining attention is present from birth on; that is, just making noise when something hurts. But as children go through these two years, they learn to be much more deliberate and intentional with their sound-making, to raise and lower the volume depending on the ambient noise, and to use light touch when it is likely to be more effective.

2. <u>To express hostility and annoyance easily to people when it is appropriate for the situation</u>. Interpersonal expressions of feelings surface during this period, especially from eight or more months on.

3. <u>Use of an adult as a resource after first determining that you can not do it yourself</u>. Use of an adult as a resource is most easily identified when it first surfaces with a child holding out a piece of a cookie towards his mother and going "Uh! Uh!" which translates to, "You, special person, I seem to have been running low on this material that I'm enjoying very much. I know that you could get me some more. Would you mind?" With nine- and ten-month-old children, who are especially attractive for the most part, it is the most natural thing in the world for the adult to provide what is needed. It can go wrong in the years that follow. Children can, by two years of age, learn that asking for help can be an all-purpose way of manipulating and controlling an adult in order to avoid doing something for yourself.

4. <u>Pride in Achievement</u>. The first time that a child gets down from a table without falling, often around 12 or 13 months of age, she may turn to somebody special, smile and applaud herself, or in

some other way indicate that she knows that you think that was special.

5. Early role play. The first signs of role play or "make believe" most commonly involve either doll play or a telephone. With the receiver, either toy or real, hung over the shoulder, the child engages in conversation knowing full well there is nobody at the other end of the line.

In our research with beautifully developing children, all five of these behaviors are distinguishing characteristics of the socially competent three- to six-year-old. They are all surfacing during the eight to 24 month period. A two-year-old is quite old socially.

Two other facets of development are worth mentioning at this point. They are: discipline and negativism, and are very important. Discipline is not required before a child can crawl. By "discipline" I mean setting limits. I do not mean punishment, I mean controlling the child. Once the child starts to crawl about the home, between seven- and nine-months of age, some of the things he is going to reach will inevitably cause problems for the parents. They will have to move the child some times, and objects at other times. Still other times, they may actually have to curb what the child is trying to do.

Once a 10-month-old has destroyed in five minutes a plant that you have been nurturing for over two years, your first response is likely to be some sort of noise indicating you are unhappy - a loud noise. The response of a 10-month-old to that loud noise is predictable. He has already moved to something else, but he will stop what he is doing. He will turn to look back at the source of the noise, and if it is you, he will smile. This is because there was nothing personal involved in the destruction of the item. By 16 and 17 months of age, the situation changes - there is everything personal in his actions because at that point the child is into the beginning stages of the negativism of the second half of the second year. By then, he has accumulated an inventory of activities and places you have forbidden for the previous six months. They are the ones he will now choose in order to determine whether you really mean business or not. Discipline gets stressed under such circumstances.

Helping social skills develop, disciplining in an effective way, and handling negativism well is the entire social development system. It can only proceed best when there is intact hearing. The means by which the process works are words. People do not socialize their children by gestures.

They talk to them...a lot. If the child cannot hear well, the process does not go well.

Why is it that it is possible to identify the deaf infant so readily? When a child is a week old and a loud noise disturbs everyone in the room but the baby, the parents are very likely to notice such unusual behavior. Also, profound hearing loss is easily detected in routine well-baby exams.

Why do we so easily miss the infant with a moderate hearing loss? A moderate hearing loss is considerably more common than a very severe loss. Furthermore, it can exist even with an intact auditory system because of the greater likelihood of congestion and respiratory illness during infancy. If a child's auditory nerve cells and conduction mechanisms are normal, but his middle ear passages are chronically full of viscous fluid during his first two years, he will not hear well.

An adult with a moderate hearing loss is not as quick or as sharp when it comes to verbal situations. He may misunderstand brief messages, or he may not respond at all when somebody speaks to him. He may speak slightly louder than other people, at times too loud for the situation. He may have diction problems, or his pronunciation may not be quite as good as that of a normally hearing person. Interestingly, in infancy those primary cues do not apply. The early warning system does not work. You do not expect an infant to be quick and sharp in regard to language. You do not expect him to understand everything you say well. You do not expect him to adjust his speech level with any precision. You do not expect his diction to be first-rate. The result is, while we have an effective early warning system for children who cannot hear much at all, we do not really have one for children with a moderate loss. Furthermore, the pediatricians of the country do not seem to have come to our assistance with more sophisticated early detection procedures. Through media, which we are developing, we are urging all parents to screen their infants for moderate hearing loss in the first year of life. Importantly they need to know that the consequences of a moderate hearing loss are:

1. <u>Less genuine interest in language</u>. Language is a source of great fun for children, especially in the second year as they try out different sounds approaching speech. Normal hearing is a prerequisite for such play.

2. Less progress in language development, less progress in intellectual development, and disturbances in social development. A two-year-old who has had a chronic moderate hearing loss is much more inclined to be more physical in his social interchanges. He is much more inclined to pull at you to get your attention than use speech to get your attention. Also, parents usually have more difficulty raising a child with a moderate hearing loss, especially during the 15 to 21 month age range, the peak period of negativism for children. If a child does not hear well, it just makes everything more difficult. Such a loss can lead to an adult attributing resistance and defiance to the baby when there is not any. The child may seem to ignore his parents at times. Adults do not like to be ignored by anybody, especially their own child. The results can be unpleasant or worse.

Useable techniques for the detection of a moderate hearing loss are available. There are effective audiological history questionnaires being used in several sites around the country: Colorado and Massachusetts are two. They seem to be quite effective in identifying the child who is likely to have a moderate or severe loss on the basis of pregnancy and family characteristic data. There are techniques available for pediatric audiometry which allow us, by the time the child is four or five months of age, to do reasonably reliable differential diagnosis. Treatment is sometimes possible then. Minor surgery on conduction mechanisms, and the use of hearing aids, are often quite effective. At the very least, parents have to be made aware of whether or not their child has a loss. The parent, as the prime educator, can adjust what he does if he knows what is going on. If nobody points out the existence of a loss, they may be oblivious to it. Bear in mind that first-time parents are self-taught most of the time.

What we have to have, and I do not think it is too far away, is a universal early detection and treatment program for hearing ability. It should begin during pregnancy and continue through the preschool years. Checking for and dealing with hearing losses is probably the least expensive and least complicated process. It is likely to benefit a substantially larger number of young children than any other encapsulated approach to the problems of early human development.

LOVENGER H. BOWDEN, Ed.D.

Professor
Department of Communications
Howard University
Washington, D.C.

5

Self-Concept: A Determining Factor in Language Development

Inherent in the concerns of this conference is the challenge to provide "quality," "individual," "specific," and "relevant" education for those who are forced to learn compensatory ways of managing life situations. The educational team of parents, teachers, administrators, and support personnel has a major responsibility for maximizing the potentials of our children. This challenge has acquired a new urgency, as we face the increasing demands of a changing society, of modern technology, and of the anticipation of life in the 21st century. All of us are forced to learn new ways of relating effectively to these new environments.

Research in education and related fields has repeatedly demonstrated the importance of early perceptual and cognitive experiences and the development of a positive self-concept, in an atmosphere of love and acceptance. It has been stated that two-thirds of an individual's total life learning takes place during the first six years of his life;

it has been stated further that the average individual utilizes less than one-sixteenth of his total mental power. (Montessori, 1963.) It is also known that 93% of communication is non-verbal and 7% is verbal. (Trupo, 1963.) These three premises should stimulate a sense of challenge in the efforts of every early childhood learning team, for they seem to provide a spirit of unmatched opportunity to assist in shaping the lives of the young children who enter their life spaces. Whether one believes the fullest extent of these premises or not, it must be accepted as fact that: 1. a person's experiences during his early childhood years are of fundamental importance to his growth and development, 2. few individuals experience the actualization of their fullest potential, and 3. too much emphasis is placed on one's physical or psychological liabilities, rather than on one's collective potential and assets.

A well-organized and efficiently operated early childhood program for handicapped children must be exceptional in its goals. The children must be taught to become citizens who are prepared to live and participate fully in the affairs of life. Each child must learn to communicate with himself and with others. The establishment of a program with an enriched curriculum for its children, relevant continuing open-minded educational experiences for its staff, and relevant and effective parent involvement that is pleasant, mutually respectful, and informative should be the goals. Each child should be encouraged and stimulated to become aware of himself and others, to think creatively, to express himself clearly by whatever means possible, to be eager to experiment, to explore, to discover, to have confidence in his own abilities, to solve problems, to share his ideas with enthusiasm, and to grow with others in an atmosphere of warm companionship. Care should be taken by the staff and by parents to assist each child to learn not to view himself as "handicapped." Instead, he should be led to view the facts of his physical, psychological or environmental circumstances or condition, and to develop the capacity to compensate for these conditions to whatever extent is possible for each given set of circumstances.

Jacobson et al. (1971) have called into question the continued use of traditional disability labels. In an examination of the effect of disability labels on the attitudes and expectancies of teachers, they said that labelling a child "handicapped" (I believe "disadvantaged" should be added) reduces the teacher's expectancy for him to succeed. It is probable, also, that such a label has a serious debilitating effect on the child's own self-image or self-concept. Research on this hypothesis is limited but supportive of this contention. Bruner contends that "failures are program and instructor failures, not pupil failures." (Bruner, 1967)

The most innovative and effective trends in education for children with special needs seem to be towards more: 1. individualized, specific, differentiated programming for each child, based on the needs of specific family, local, neighborhood, school and community-oriented and involved insights, 2. continuing education for complete departmental personnel, and 3. greater utilization of the local resources of the family, other schools, communities, and federal and local agencies and institutions.

There is a consensus among many leaders that the team approach is a most beneficial method of teaching; the team approach must involve the child, the total environment of his home, school, and community, and the actual creative utilization and implementation of the knowledge gained in research and in previous educational efforts. Above all else, these endeavors must be set up in an atmosphere that promotes communication, understanding, and appreciation of every individual's worth.

Man is a magnificent and fantastic creature who has the capacity to live simultaneously in two realms of experience, the physical and the symbolic. Some various schools of thought label the two realms the physical and the psychological. Others further divide the latter into the psychical or spiritual and cosmic, man is not viewed as a "tabula rasa" but as having "cosmic continuity." Others label the two realms as the finite and infinite. (Drennen, 1962) The sound, sight, taste, smell, and touch of people, events, and objects comprise the raw data of our physical world: man can neither create nor destroy matter: we were, we are, we will always be. Only our form will change. The composite assumptions, hunches or intuitions about the way things "really are" make up our sense of the symbolic world. It is not man's nature to participate totally in either the physical world or the symbolic world, to the exclusion of the other. In neither world can he be an aloof bystander. Physical facts do not speak for themselves; they carry no automatic or proper significance. We have no way to divorce our participation in the physical realm from the way we represent our experience in the abstract, for the two are inexorably intertwined. Similarly, symbolic meaning does not spring full-blown from the sheer course of events; it must be created. In human affairs, meaning is created only by placing the particulars into some larger frame of reference, an image or model through which the specifics can be interpreted in abstract form.

Because of our extraordinary uniqueness, man has the

capacity to create images of our experiences and to communicate to (and with) others about those experiences. Out of the accumulation of social encounters, we form and share common images. Every encounter adds to the developing and assumptive biases that each man has about himself and about the possibilities of entering into another's thought world. Images are acquired so automatically, and with such pervasive regularity, that most people are only vaguely aware of their constancy and their profound effect. Though formed for the most part in an unconscious way, the assumptive biases, taken together, dictate the meaning we attach to events, and determine what we will see, how we will feel, what we will think, and how we will respond. The images men share about communication and its possibilities - about teaching methodologies - even about the deaf - will largely regulate what sort of encounters each person will seek or avoid.

Birth signals the arrival of a human being into this life experience; a fantastic being, who forty weeks earlier was a single cell. Each person is in constant and creative interaction with the forces of his environment from the moment of conception. It is this dynamic exchange that determines what each individual becomes, mentally, physically and emotionally. In the process by which a person comes into being, four steps are especially significant: The <u>first</u> is conception (the sparking of human "this life" existence); the <u>second</u> is prenatal development; the <u>third</u> is the process of being born, setting each of us apart physically from others. These first three steps constitute a more or less "passive phase" of development. The more "active phase," the development of selfhood, is the <u>fourth</u> step, involving all the experiences through which each of us becomes aware of his existence as a person, distinct from all others. (Borstein, 1973)

What we presently know about development of human beings is vast and impressive; what we do not know is even more vast and overwhelming. But our current knowledge exceeds our application. Collins and Nobbit (1976) refer to the President's Commission on Mental Retardation, 1972, which claimed that our current knowledge of child development needs to be incorporated into medical and health care. Then child rearing practices, social planning, and all other procedures known to affect the quality of life for the child, the socio-economic burden of the handicapped and the disadvantaged would significantly decline and the quality of life for all of society would be tremendously uplifted.

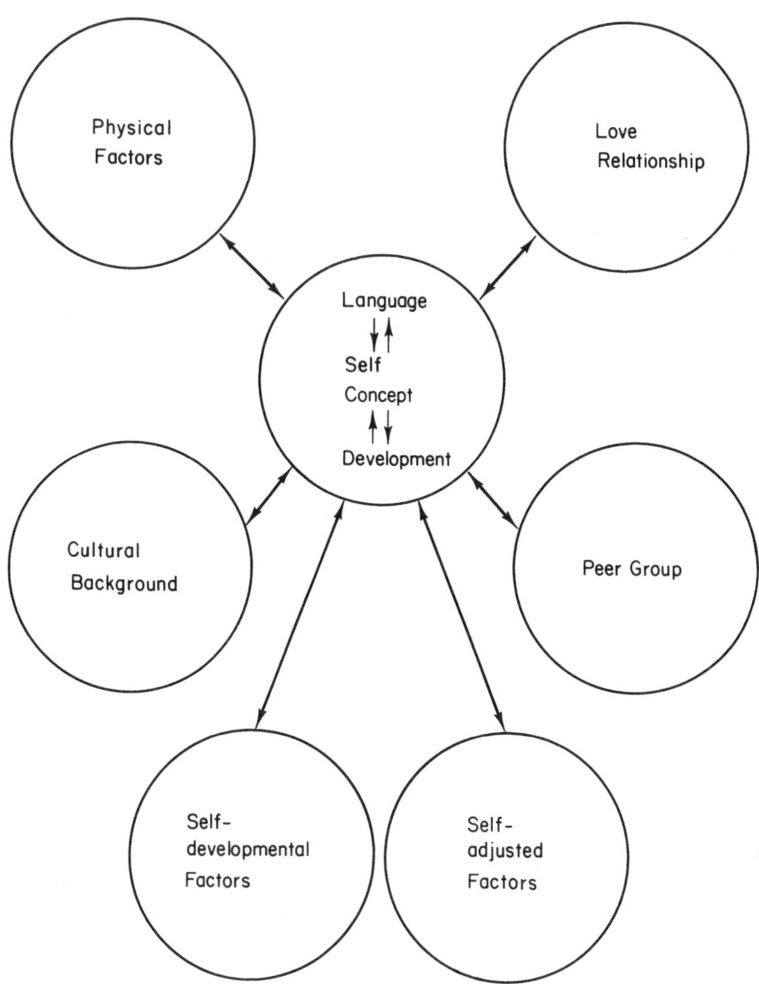

FIG. 5-1
Self-concept and language development.

In studying children, we can focus either on the overt and objective aspects of development and experience or upon the subjective and personal meaning to the individual; the latter deals with a person's ideas, feelings and attitudes regarding himself and is labelled "self-concept." Self has been defined as the organizing function by means of which one human being can relate to another. A person's self comprises his experience of his identity as a distinct individual. Early in his life, exactly where we do not know, a child recognizes that he is a participant in, and yet someone apart from, events in the physical and social world in which he lives. 1. He experiences as his own the sensations arising from within his own body, and 2. he becomes aware of the properties and boundaries of his body. As time passes, 3. he comes to know himself as one who can perceive, 4. as the author of his own thoughts, 5. as one who harbors feelings and desires, and 6. as one who can weigh alternatives and make decisions. (Lewis, 1963)

Eventually a child's self embodies many components:

1. Cognitive components through which he is aware of himself as one who is able to think; their cognitive components include his perception of:

    a. his physical attributes

    b. his conception of himself - who he is and what he is

    c. of his qualities as a person

    d. his abilities

    e. the purposes, beliefs, moral commitments and values that he knowingly embraces

    f. his conception includes his view of his present situation and eventually his view of himself in the perspective of time--as one who also has roots in the past and is able to project himself into the future

    g. toward the end of childhood--the cognitive component includes not only a state of knowing by a capacity of reflection (this enables a person to make his ideas, feelings, impulses and choices the object of his own thought.)

2. The self also includes affective states, embracing the full range of human feelings, sentiments, and moods. The affective sphere not only includes awareness of feelings that are directly precipitated by conditions that impinge upon a person but also feelings pertaining to himself, sometimes described

as positive or negative feelings toward the self, such as pride and shame.

3. These cognitive and affective states are often linked with another property of the self, namely a capacity for self-evaluation, of viewing oneself with approval or disapproval.

4. When affective states of approval or disapproval, combined with knowledge of what is approved or disapproved, become relatively stable and constant they constitute another component of the self, the attitudinal component. Attitudes toward self may be particularistic, or they may be also global and pervasive, falling on a continuum ranging from serene self-acceptance to bitter self-rejection.

The self has many other characteristics embodying in various ways cognitive, affective, evaluative, attitudinal processes. When once a view or attitude regarding self has been established, there is a tendency to preserve and defend it; this tendency reflects what seems to be a universal need to maintain a degree of stability, a conviction of certainty regarding who and what one is. A person's craving for certainty is often stronger than his craving for truth.

But there is a paradox here, for while a person strives to preserve a cherished view of himself, he is never (as long as he retains his vitality) completely immune to circumstances of his life, the pressures from within and reminders from without that challenge this view and threaten to modify or dislodge it. When these occur the machinery for rationalizing and shutting off the threat may be thrown into gear. But there always remains the possibility that a person will use his reflective capacities and will take stock of himself.

It is estimated that the child develops an awareness of himself as a distinct individual sometime during the first year. The development of self involves, among other things, a process of differentiation:

1. differentiation between physical self and environment (limitations of his physical self.)

2. differentiation between persons and things (the human and non-human parts of his environment.)

3. differentiation among categories of people (this is dependent on the difference in appearance, and in their differentiated responsiveness to the child's needs.)

4. differentiation of types of responses - finer distinctions are also made relative to expressions (smiles, scowls, tones, gestures.)

5. differentiation among characteristically organized acts or roles, and patterns of activity.

6. differentiation among individuals--potent sources of pain or pleasure -- significant persons in development of self-concept.

7. child learns to develop a social behavior (in the presence of others.)

Other evidences of increasing self-awareness:

1. Localization of "self" with reference to various body points, including head, face, eyes, heart, the genitals.

2. Recognition of differences between boys and girls and clear identification of the sex to which they belong; this is an important step in self-concept.

3. Assertion of self in opposition to others. (Around age two he seems to be testing his power of self-assertion in his relationship with others.)

4. Comparison of self with his peers and testing of self in competition with others.

5. Curiosity and self-esteem interact, seem to be positively related and probably grow and develop together; positive reinforcement to initial active, curious behaviors tend to build a wealthy repertoire of environmental experience that develop capabilities, develop confidence and build high self-esteem. Conversely, the child who is punished when he reaches out and has new experiences tends to restrict his activities, limits his experiential world and fails to develop those capabilities that contribute to his self-esteem.

6. The Social World influences the child's view of himself. A child's self-evaluations are dominantly influenced by the "significant others" in his social world. The young child initially considers the social world as a single, fairly consistent one

within which obligations are straightforward and simple.

However, in later childhood and adolescence (earlier, with the increased TV viewing,) the child's social world branches out into two parallel worlds with his parents and his peers. The impact the parents have on a child depends not only what they <u>actually</u> feel or think or do, but in the <u>child's perception</u> of what they think, feel and do. The child also comes to evaluate himself and his worth as an individual in terms of the reinforcements (positive or negative) given to the social group to which he belongs. Social class, defined by the prestige of his culture, plays a significant role in the development of self concept. A child who is abused because of his ethnic origins bears an extra burden in the processing of forming ideas and attitudes pertaining to himself, especially if he is made to feel ashamed of his background; studies of Bowden (1970) indicates that many black children as early as preschool level are being affected negatively by the prejudices of the larger society.

I have dealt with the uniqueness of man to creatively interact with his environment. This process of interaction is very complex and involves one's total self in a myriad number of non-verbal experiences before the development of meaningful (as we perceive it outside of the self of another) utterances. It is obvious that language is related to self-development; upon careful scrutiny the question may be asked, is the foundation for self-concept laid prelinguistically - through the myriad non-verbal encounters that have been stored in the child's subconscious or psyche? The self appears to be based, in part, on others' attitudes toward the developing organism, and in part, on the developing organism's attitudes towards itself.

REFERENCES

Borstein, Robert E. <u>Nature of Human Consciousness</u>. San Francisco: W.H. Freeman, 1973.

Bowden, Lovenger H. Unpublished Doctoral Dissertation from the University of Maryland, 1970. <u>Specific Learning Experiences for the Language Development of Culturally Different Preschool Children</u>. University of Maryland, College Park, Maryland.

Bruner, J. S., Goodnow, J. and Austin, G. <u>A Study of Thinking</u>. N.Y.: Science Editions, Inc., 1967.

Collins, Thomas W. and Nobbit, George W. The process of interracial schooling: An assessment of conceptual frameworks and methodological orientations. In _The Desegration Literature: A Critical Appraisal_. 1976, _July_.

Drennen, D. A. _Modern Introduction to Metaphysics_. New York: Free Press, 1962.

Jacobson, Leonard I., Berger, S.E., Bergman, R.I., Millham, J., and Greeson, L.E. Effects of age, sex, systematic conceptual learning, acquisition of learning sets, and programmed social interaction on the intellectual and conceptual development of pre-school children from poverty backgrounds. _Child Development_. 1971, _Vol. 42_, 1399-1415.

Lewis, Morris Michael. _Language, Thought and Personality in Infancy and Childhood_. N.Y.: Basic Books, 1963.

Montessori in the Home: A Preliminary Study - Practical Application of the Principles and Method of Maria Montessori for the Use of Parents in the Home. (2nd edition), Bethesda, Maryland: Elad Enterprise, 1963.

Trupo, Anthony. _The Million Dollar Secret that Lies Hidden Within Your Mind_. Englewood Cliffs: Prentice-Hall, 1963. (by Anthony Novelli, pseud.).

SYLVIA RICHARDSON, M.D.

Associate Clinical Professor of Pediatrics
University of Cincinnati Medical Center
Cincinnati, Ohio

6

Myth—Communication

Since each of us perceives events in relation to his or her own frame of reference, I would like to present my view of the world as a certified speech pathologist who "grew up" in special education, as a pediatrician in an academic and multi-disciplinary clinical setting, and as a certified Montessori directress. My primary and constant concern is for the child -- particularly the child with language and learning problems.

Ten to fifteen years ago most of us tried to convince educators and physicians that there really were children with learning disabilities, children of normal intelligence who for a variety of reasons, couldn't learn the basic skills of reading, writing, spelling and arithmetic in a regular academic program. Today, if you read the "professional" literature such as Good Housekeeping, Reader's Digest, etc., you might assume that a good 50% of the school population is learning-disabled. Children with learning disability are called by many names (over 50 labels have been documented), depending upon the current vogue in their school system and community. In some areas they are called children with neurologic impairment. In other areas they are called children with minimal brain dysfunction or minimal brain injury, which is like having "a touch of pregnancy." They may be called dyslexic and they may be called hyperkinetic. For some obscure reason we seem to have an inordinate need to categorize or label children. Possibly this is because we place the burden of learning on the child instead of accepting the responsibility for appropriate teaching.

In 1966 the United States Department of Health, Education and Welfare appointed a Task Force to define "minimal brain dysfunction." In 1977 the United States Congress asked the Bureau of Education of the Handicapped to define learning disabilities. There is still no universally accepted definition, yet everyone seems to agree that these children are of normal intelligence; they do not have sensory impairment; they have no physical handicap; but they can't manage to learn the basic skills of reading, writing, spelling and arithmetic in a regular class. The HEW Task Force described 99 signs and symptoms of "minimal brain dysfunction." All 99 signs and symptoms can be subsumed under four major headings: disorders of coordination, disorders of language, disorders of the functions of attention, and disorders in the functions of perception. It is quite apparent that this is a very heterogenous population of children and many etiologic factors can be responsible for the variety of problems that these youngsters demonstrate.

In discussing the categories of disorders associated with learning disabilities, I plan to elaborate chiefly on disorders of coordination and attention in order to dispel some of the myths in these areas. Such myths include, "visual-motor incoordination causes learning disabilities," and "all learning-disabled children are hyperactive."

1. Disorders of Coordination: Gross motor incoordination is not much of a problem for an adult. There are many clumsy adults who have never had any trouble in school. As a matter of fact, some of my clumsy patients often come to the office followed by their even clumsier fathers, but if father is a physician or the chairman of the Board or a college professor he has evidently managed to get along in school. However, clumsiness for a child can be a serious problem. If you are a little boy, a clumsy little boy, and you are unable to play tetherball with the other youngsters and you can't play foursquare and nobody wants you on the team it can be devastating for your self-image. If you don't feel very good about yourself, you may not learn anything very well, but that in itself doesn't mean that you are learning-

disabled. Certainly clumsiness is not the cause of learning disabilities, but it is frequently associated with school problems.

One of the myths that we communicate and perpetuate is that Americans are a child-centered people. We do a lot to children but I wonder how often we provide for children the means for them to obtain optimal development. For example, we abound in team sports for youngsters but we no longer provide old-fashioned calisthenics. We minimize gym and emphasize team sports because we want our children to learn to compete. Yet there are a lot of clumsy children who can't possibly compete. They are the bench-sitters by the time they are old enough for the competitive sports programs. However, they could have had a lot of assistance in their preschool and earliest school years if we would provide gyms and parks where children could learn to climb trees and ladders, walk walking beams, and partake in all of the activities that we now call body management. When I grew up we could walk the railroad tracks. There was a lot of empty space in the neighborhood where we could play and explore. Today there are no sand lots where children can play ball for fun. The six- or seven-year-old child playing ball is not interested in the rules of baseball or the fine art of throwing a curve -- he is too busy developing the basic neuromuscular control requisite for just getting the ball in the general vicinity of an arbitrary target.

Fine motor incoordination can be more of a problem than general awkwardness. If a little boy has fine motor incoordination, that means he is not very good at buttoning and unbuttoning, zipping and unzipping, dressing and undressing. The child with fine motor incoordination has difficulty cutting, coloring inside the lines, and doing other kinds of handwork when he first enters school.

Most mothers tend to do more for their children longer than they really need to, and the mother of a child with fine motor incoordination tends to do a great deal more for him than she does for her other children because she knows that he needs help. Instead of teaching him to help himself, it is easier to do it for him. A good deal of this relates to ignorance. We don't teach mothers-to-be about child growth and development and how a child needs to learn on his own. Most mothers are loving and try very hard to do the right thing, but they don't always know how to help children to help themselves. A child with fine motor incoordination may have been overly protected. He may not be able to assume the responsibility for his own learning when he enters school. Thus, incoordination can provide many problems which may not be related to learning disability as such, but which can provide obstacles to learning. If a child is not taught appropriately and helped to compensate for this difference, he can easily be labelled as learning-disabled and placed in a special class.

2. Disorders of Language: We know that one of the earliest indications of possible school difficulty is delay in the acquisition and use of language. Many youngsters come to school with a mild language disorder. A language disorder, not a language difference. A language difference may be a handicap also but it simply means that the child's first language is not standard American and may be some other language such as Chicano, Puerto Rican, Black English, Indian, etc. The language of these children is not impaired, it is different. They need a different kind of teaching. However, we often impose standard American on them as soon as they enter school and then consider them damaged if they cannot learn immediately.

The child with a language disorder generally does not have the rules of his language built in by the time he gets to school. I believe that if a child has not internalized rules of his language by the time he gets to school, he will not learn to read with any facility. It doesn't matter what his language is as long as he has internalized the rules of his own language, whether that be Chicano or any other language. If he has the rules and structure of his language built into his system, the rest will come with good teaching.

3. Disorders of the Functions of Attention: These children are often called hyperkinetic or hyperactive but the primary symptoms are distractibility, extremely short attention span, low frustration tolerance, poor impulse control, irritability and hyper-excitability. Many people seem to believe the myth that all children with learning disabilities are hyperactive and vice versa. The etiology of this entity is usually ascribed to brain damage, indeed so much so that the behavioral syndrome itself is considered by some to be sufficient evidence to make a diagnosis of "minimal brain dysfunction" even in the absence of history or clinical evidence of neurological impairment. More mythology.

Hyperactivity is not a disease. Hyperactivity is an adjective and it is relative to the person who uses the term. When someone tells me that a child is hyperactive, I want to know a lot about the person who uses the word before I accept the label. To automatically equate "hyperactivity" with "minimal brain damage" or LD is ridiculous. For example, I'm Italian. If you know Italians, you know that they are not exactly the most quiet people. If you were to come into my home when the whole family was together you'd find everyone talking at the same time, knives and forks waving through the air, people getting up, sitting down, coming in, going out, all talking at the same time. You could easily say, "For Heaven's sake this is a brain-injured family!" But by the same token, I could walk in an Anglo-Saxon home and assume that everyone is dead.

Hyperactivity is a relative term. There are many teachers and other adults who don't like moving targets. Anyone that moves much is called hyperactive. We tend to gauge a child's behavior according to our own expectations, our own definition, and our own personality.

Many children, called hyperactive, are very quiet when they are doing things that are of interest to them or when they are doing things that they *can* do. In a doctor's office we don't see very many hyperactive children. I don't think anyone in an examining capacity does see very many hyperactive children. We see a lot of hyperactive parents, mothers and fathers who are uptight about their child. We also see many *hyper-reactive* children. Children who react to stress, either at home or in school, by excessive activity and acting-out behavior.

Innumerable mothers have been unjustly burdened by being held entirely responsible for their children's problems. In fact, this is one of the most dreadful myths that we have continued to communicate: that a child's behavioral disturbance is probably the direct result of maternal pathology. This is ridiculous. Each mother should be taught to recognize temperamental differences and how to adapt child-care practices most appropriate to her own child's specific qualities of individuality.

To combat this myth that the course of an infant's development is determined primarily by maternal needs, attitudes, and motivation, I would recommend to you the work of Chess and Thomas in their last book published in 1977, *Temperament and Development*. Chess and Thomas view temperament as a general term referring to the *how* of behavior. It differs from ability and from motivation, the *what* and the *why* of behavior. Temperament is the behavioral style of an individual child and deals with the *way* in which he behaves. For example, two children may each throw a ball with accuracy and have the same motives to do so. However, they may differ considerably in the intensity with which they throw, the rate at which they throw, the mood which they express, the readiness with which they shift to a new activity, and the ease with which they will approach a new situation or a new playmate.

Chess and Thomas observed temperamental differences

that are demonstrated from birth. Similar studies have been done in relation to infant's activity levels as early as the 1930's. However, Chess and Thomas delineated nine categories of temperament in infants and followed them for seven or more years to observe the kinds of interactive processes which occur when children with specific temperamental patterns are exposed to different environmental influences. In brief, they described three essential types of children: the easy child, the difficult child, and the slow-to-warm-up child. The "easy child" is characterized by biologic regularity, a preponderence of approach reactions to the new, positive mood of mild to moderate intensity, and easy adaptability. The "difficult child" has biologic irregularity, a preponderance of withdrawal reactions to the new, many negative mood expressions of marked intensity, and slow adaptibility. The "slow-to-warm-up child," like the difficult child, has withdrawal responses, negative mood, and slow adaptibility, but by contrast, has mild reactions and may or may not have irregularity of biologic functions. As might be expected, individual children vary widely in the degree and sharpness with which they exhibit one or another of these constellations.

If a mother believes the middle class conventional myth that the course of an infant's development is determined primarily by her maternal attitudes, motivations, and needs, she will be delighted with an "easy child" who will reassure her that she is an adequate, healthy, and loving mother. However, if the baby is a "difficult child," the special child-care demands made by such an infant can create several types of parental responses, depending on their own personality structures and the socio-cultural pressures of their group. The mother may feel threatened and anxious or she may believe that she is unconsciously rejecting her child, unloving or just plain inept. On the other hand, the mother may blame the infant and resent the extra burdens and demands he puts upon her. Of particular importance, most parents of difficult children responded positively in the Chess and Thomas study once they understood that their child's temperament existed independently of their own attitudes and functioning, and that a specific type of management was required.

When I was a young girl I asked my Italian grandmother how I would learn to be a mother. Grandmother told me not to worry because she said there is a maternal hormone. I accepted this statement because she was usually right. However, nobody mentioned a maternal hormone when I was in medical school and I guessed that it was not something that could be measured in a test tube. However, I later learned that there is, indeed, a maternal hormone and I was suffused with it as soon as I saw my first baby. The maternal hormone is guilt. As soon as you see your first baby you know that you're going to do it wrong. And if you are not totally convinced of that, you can find an article in any of those professional journals mentioned earlier stating that all mothers are responsible for their children's problems, or that child-raising is a "task not easily achieved by the average mother in our culture." Usually those articles are written by spinsters or men. The psychiatrist, Fritz Redl, commented (Redl and Wineman, 1965) that he had never seen a generation of mothers so intent on achieving the impossible and avoiding the inevitable. Women want to be perfect mothers, each wants to be the best. If a mother has a very different temperament from that of her baby, if the mother for example is very quiet and passive and the child has high intensity temperamental attributes, it can make for very difficult interpersonal relationships between that mother and baby from the very beginning.

To simplify further, when a mother has a child with whom she can't cope, whose activity level is such that she cannot deal with it, she usually assumes that it is her fault, it is her failure as a mother. When we feel guilty we behave in appropriate ways. We utilize what I call apologetic behavior. For example, if mother yells too much one day and feels guilty about it, the next day she may give the child something he doesn't need or she may allow him to do something that she normally would not allow. This is apologetic behavior. It does not help a child to learn that he can control his parents' behavior by such manipulation. The pattern of frequent punishment or threats followed by indulgence or remorse can only lead to enslavement of the parents by a tyrannical child. Also, when we feel guilty about our relationship with the child or our inability to cope with him, we tend to behave differently with that child than we do with the other children in the family. This in itself can create additional behavior problems.

Teachers must also be aware of the myth that a child is a "tabula rasa," a clean slate on which the family and society can inscribe the ultimate behavioral patterns and outcomes. He is neither an inert and malleable mass to be shaped at will by the environment, nor is he an homunculus, a rigid structure whose characteristics are fixed and unchangeable over time. A child with an initial pattern characterized by frequent negative reactions may shift to a more frequent expression of positive mood if his life (home or school) experiences are benign and favorable. A very adaptable child who is repeatedly faced with impossible demands and expectations may, after a time, become increasingly less adaptable in his behavior. An older child may learn to modify or control certain temperamental reactions when their expressions would be undesirable -- or he may simply let it all hang out, if he is under sufficient stress. Parents and teachers, all adults, must learn to acknowledge and respect the individual differences among children even as we demand that recognition for our own individual differences.

4. Disorders of the Functions of Perception: Perceptual problems in children are a subject of discussion and debate, possibly because in this area we know the least. We know more about visual perceptual problems because they are the easiest to detect. There are many tests for visual perception and visual-motor performances. Many techniques have been devised for teaching children with visual-motor problems or visual perceptual problems. However, these devices are designed primarily to improve visual-motor functions, not to teach a child how to read. If the visual-motor problem is such that it interferes, then certainly the child needs help in that area but visual-motor training should not be given indiscriminately or in place of reading instruction. Auditory perceptual problems are of great concern. However, these are less often recognized and/or treated. The functions of perception include: figure/ground discrimination, short and long term memory, temporal solving power or perceptual speed, and closure. Each of these different functions must be analyzed to help a child with perceptual problems so that learning experience can be designed to meet his individual needs.

Many children in the preschool and kindergarten age group deviate markedly from what might be called "normal" development, and the extremes within the range of normal variation are quite far apart. Remember that a child under six or seven years of age may have normal intelligence, but his perceptual maturation or neurologic integration may not be precisely at chronologic or mental age level. Such a child may well be crippled more by inappropriate teaching (dyspedagogia, if you like) than by any intrinsic problem.

At this point perhaps we should explore (and explode) the myth that all children develop and mature at the same rate, that all children are ready for first grade at the age of six years. It has been estimated by Shirley (1963) that 15% of children reaching school age are not yet ready for reading instruction because of immaturity. Ilg and Ames (1962) found that approximately 50% of children in an upper middle class community were "overplaced." They stated that "possibly the greatest single contribution which can be made toward guaranteeing that each individual child would get the most possible out of his school experience is to make certain that he starts that school experience at what is, for him, the right time." This should be when the child is sufficiently mature to embark on his academic career, not a time arbitrarily decided upon by external forces such as school law or custom.

Can anyone tell me why the age of starting school in the United States is six years? The usual answer to that question, on each occasion that I've asked it, has been "because it's the law." It is difficult to believe that the lawmakers in our country know more about child growth and development than anyone else, but we do have that law. In other countries children start school at different ages. I learned recently that the Americans adopted this system from the Swedes, who determined that six years was the best age for children to start school because it is by the age of six that the average child can make his way through the snow to get there.

Reading readiness tests have been devised to assist the schools in selecting the students. In some communities school entrance has been determined by the child's IQ rating, due to the belief that a child's higher intelligence would insure his ability to succeed. However, neither intelligence nor readiness tests have proved a reliable evaluation of the child's true potential or educational prognosis. "Readiness" has been a controversial subject in education and is rarely discussed in pediatrics. We give lip service to the notion that it is desirable to match teaching methods to a child's specific developmental needs. It is incumbent on us in medicine, education and psychology then, to provide diagnostic information that will define the child's developmental needs. It should be possible for us to send a child to school with a good deal of information, perhaps speculation, about how that child goes about learning and about his "ripeness" for particular kinds of tasks. We should be able to locate his position on a maturational scale and we should be able to define when a child is more than two standard deviations from the mean in any single area of performance.

When I was the Director of the Child Study Center at the University of Oklahoma in the early 60's, we reviewed 817 consecutive cases of children who were referred there because of possible mental retardation. We found that only 50% of these children were retarded. The other 50% comprised a rather motley crew. Thirty-nine percent were children with specific reading disabilities. When we reviewed the histories of the non-retarded children we found that 98% of the mothers of the children with reading disabilities had been told by kindergarten teachers that their children were immature and not ready for first grade. However, nobody seemed to pay any attention to this and the children went right on into first grade. The average mother has been waiting for six years to get her child into school and, if the child is obviously intelligent, she certainly isn't going to hold him back. The average father simply can't understand that his child could possibly flunk sandbox. Most parents will say, "I don't care whether he can cut with a pair of scissors. I don't care whether he can color inside the lines. He is supposed to learn how to read." Most parents do not recognize that there is a progression in growth and development so that hand skills such as cutting with scissors and coloring inside the lines are very important activities, especially if the child is going to learn how to manipulate a pencil.

At any rate, we asked a dozen kindergarten teachers, all from schools of white middle-class socio-economic level, to write their descriptions of the "immature child." We were amazed and troubled by their responses. For example, one teacher wrote, "these children are clumsier than the other children"; another said, "these youngsters tend to be closer to the ground than the others"; another wrote, "these children tend to bring the playground in with them." They described clumsiness, but didn't always use that word. They gave us illustrations. They didn't say fine motor incoordination but "these children can't cut with scissors; they can't color inside the lines; their handwork is messy and sloppy." The teachers didn't use terminology such as language disorders or language differences. However, they wrote "the immature children tend to be very verbal, but you can't follow the line of their thought. They get their syntax all mixed up. They show syntactical kinds of differences in their language rather than articulation problems." My favorite response in this regard was, "the immature children don't seem to have the rules of their language built in." None of the kindergarten teachers, bless their hearts, used the term hyperactive. One teacher wrote, "These youngsters are never where you last saw them." The term "disorganized" in behavior was used rather than hyperactive. The teachers also wrote that these children couldn't match shapes, couldn't tell differences between various geometric forms, etc. All in all, the most outstanding behavioral characteristics of the "immature" six-year-old, as described by these kindergarten teachers, appear to be inadequate language skills, immature gross and fine motor performance, insufficient attention span, and visual-motor immaturity. Most frequently the immature child's behavior was described as disorderly or disorganized. His vocal and motor output was thought to be excessive and without syntactical or contextual structure. Teachers also reported that the immature child tends to speak and act without thinking and, when compared with mature peers, this child seemed to require more auditory, visual, tactile and kinesthetic reinforcement. He was also described as clinging and overly dependent on the teacher. In general, he seemed to lag behind his mature classmates in terms of performance in school activity, physical appearance, social and emotional interactions and learning ability. Kindergarten teachers also noted that the immature child was usually male.

I'm sure it has occurred to you that the kindergarten teachers' description of immature children are quite similar to the characteristics attributed to children with learning disability. Does this mean that immature kindergarten children may be learning-disabled? Or does this mean that by pushing immature children through the primary grades in regular classrooms along with their mature peers we are creating children who look learning-disabled? The answer to both of those questions may be affirmative. It seems to me that we have created a diagnostic dilemma and that some of the problems may rest in the educational system rather than in the children. We must destroy the myth that all children are ready for first grade at the age of six years, and we must accommodate for children with varying maturational schedules. We are too quick to label some children as disabled, and we often miss those whose learning disabilities are real.

We know that there is a wide range of normal variation in motor development, language development, even temperament. We can plot a child's height and weight on a growth chart, for example, and we can determine that, even though he may look very large, if he is in the 98th percentile he is within the normal range of variation. We determine pathology, or abnormality, when the child is more than two standard deviations from the mean. Do we know the mean and two standard deviations from the mean for the various functions of perception? What are the upper limits of normal for auditory closure? For auditory figure/ground discrimination? For high intensity temperamental attributes? We are still unable to determine each child's state of perceptual organization or "ripeness." Diagnostic teaching should be a continuing enterprise from kindergarten through the primary. If we demand that all children must go to school, then we must provide appropriate education for every child and we must also accept, in fact as well as in theory, the concept of individual differences. We should withhold labels until we know what we are talking about.

Once a child gets into the first grade he is expected to learn in the same way as all others and with the same speed. We give all children 27 months to learn the basic skills of reading, writing, and arithmetic -- that's all. First, second and third grade. It seems to me that it is the height of disrespect for us to assume that all children are exactly the same and all ready for what we think they should do, when we think they should do it. When we say that children do not learn we often mean that they are not learning what we want them to learn. Some of them are learning that they are stupid. Many of them are learning how to fail but they are certainly learning every minute of the day.

We also should remember that a great deal of learning, especially in the young child, occurs "underground." Do you know anything about the bamboo plant? It's really a fantastic organism. The bamboo spends four to seven years developing its entire underground root system before any of it appears above ground. The bamboo works underground developing its own root system in order to have the water and nourishment it needs to provide its own environment for growth -- and <u>then</u> it appears. Isn't this like our children? So much goes on underground that we don't see in the way of language development and all developmental skills. Then all of a sudden the child walks and talks, as though he had learned it all last night. But the root system was growing and developing underground. So it is with our children before they are ready for the world of academics. It takes years to build the root system of "readiness."

The asparagus also has remarkable characteristics. A friend of mine planted some asparagus and waited and waited and waited for it to come up. Being an optimist, he continued to water and tend the ground and he continued to wait, but nothing happened. Finally he decided to forget it and laid down a driveway, some of which went over the area where he had planted the asparagus. Suddenly -- you guessed it -- the asparagus came up! Right through the concrete driveway, up came the asparagus! He couldn't have pulled it up, nor could he have prevented its growth. It may have been bent, but it grew up through the driveway! Many of our children are just like the asparagus. We wait and wait, we tend the ground and water it. When we see no results we become despondent and decide they just can't make it. Then they come through, and when they do, <u>nothing</u> can prevent their progress. You can't force them to "come up" early. You can't force them to develop, but give them time and when the time is right for them, nothing will hold them back. Learning-disabled children are often like the asparagus that came up through the driveway, bent, but they came through. And so will our youngsters if we learn how to help them develop the skills to enable them to live successfully in the everyday world. After all, isn't this what education is all about?

The importance of parent education has been discussed at length. I'm sure it is important provided that it is appropriate. There are ample studies now to indicate that whether a family is strict or permissive in child-rearing practices does not alone explain the variation in behavior that we observe from child to child. Most children can adapt to a relatively wide range of child-rearing practices without developing symptoms of malfunction. However, some children may develop difficulty unless the practices are modified to better "fit" the type of child. A good example of this would be the child with temperamental traits making up the "difficult child" described by Chess and Thomas (1977). Such a child will encounter trouble with either a strict or permissive approach unless it's modified enough to take these characteristics into account. Chamberlin (1974) and others have noted that the child's development is enhanced by a "positive contact," which refers to the amount of praise, reassurance, affection, companionship and intellectual stimulation that occurs between parent and child. There is considerable evidence that children who have been talked to, read to, and otherwise stimulated in the home do better in school than children not receiving this kind of attention. Parent education, to me, should include considerable discussion of temperamental differences as well as how to provide the kind of emotional support and intellectual stimulation that will influence the long-term development of the child. (Like making sure that the soil is in the best possible condition while the bamboo plant establishes its root system.) Of course, this kind of support must be continued in school as well as at home.

The need to revise teacher education is quite as important as parent education. I believe that the best trained and highest paid teachers in the school system should be the teachers of kindergarten through grade three. All primary teachers should have thorough training in early childhood education and language development, as well as regular and special education techniques. It shouldn't matter to anyone whether a child is able to complete the primary in four years or in six years as long as he has learned the basic skills of reading, writing and arithmetic by the time he goes to middle school curriculum.

Here we come to another myth: "Competition in class is good for children." I think competition is good but I don't know that it belongs in a classroom. I think that each child can enjoy competing with himself, taking joyful pride in his accomplishment when each successive step is better than his last achievement. Education is not the place for a pari-mutuel. As you know, the parimutuel is a form of betting on horses in which those who bet on the winners share in the total stakes. Too often we parents seem to be concerned with the child's position in the class -- whether he comes in win, place or show. We act as though we actually have a share in the stakes, as though having a "winner" gives us some kind of status. To carry the analogy a bit further -- the child's chief purpose in education is simply to get all the way around the track, not just to win, place, or show. If he feels that our only interest is in the winners and that he can't finish among them, he may well lose spirit and stop trying to get around the track at all.

The school child wants to learn, and his joy and self-respect grow as he masters each new skill. He is not concerned with how long it takes him; it's the adult who likes to complete a task and see the results quickly. Learning takes time and each child will learn according to his own "ripeness" for particular kinds of tasks and according to his particular learning style and rhythm. The task of the adult is to develop flexible methods of instruction that will meet each child's needs rather than to search for ways to make the child fit a particular method or curriculum -- like putting him into a Procrustean bed and chopping off his feet if he's too long. Too often we try to rush nature, to push the child into activities for which he is not ready, to try to make him fit a mold of our design, not his. This leaves him with little recourse; he can try dutifully and halfheartedly to please us; he can rebel actively (or hyper-reactively) or by passive resistance; he can withdraw into a world of day-dreams, or he can just quit. Children can develop many kinds of deviant behavior in their reactions to pressure at home or at school, but in doing so their valuable constructive energies are dissipated. Learning is no longer a source of joyful discovery and mastery but a painful striving to meet adult-imposed standards. To return to the analogy: every child must be given the time, help and encouragement he needs to get around the track at his own best speed -- never mind who comes in win, place or show.

What is "normal" child growth and development? Who is this child who is going to be the adult of tomorrow, whose major job is the creation of tomorrow? You have forgotten all about the child who created you. We all have. We all must learn not only to prepare the home environment for the children, the school for the children, but also the community for the children -- to establish a climate where children can grow and thrive according to their needs, not according to what we want to impose on them. We must learn to respect children, to respect the work of the child. As parents we must learn how to provide the necessary emotional support and intellectual stimulation for each of our children. In the schools we must learn how to be more responsive to the individual needs of all children, recognizing the enormous variations among individual differences, and respecting them. Schools and entire communities should be designed and built for children as well as adults. Instead of arguing about labels, perpetuating ridiculous myths, and constantly putting the onus for learning and behaving on the child, we must learn to create an environment, a climate, in which all children can learn and thrive and produce a new generation of better adults.

REFERENCES

Chamberlin, L. J. Improving School Discipline. Springfield: C.C. Thomas, 1974.

Chess, Stella and Thomas, Alexander. Temperament and Development. N.Y.: Brunner and Mazel, Inc., 1977.

Ilg, Frances and Ames, Oouis. Parents Ask. Chicago: Harper & Row, 1962.

Redl, Fritz and Wineman, D. Controls from Within: Techniques for the Treatment of the Aggressive Child. N.Y.: MacMillan, 1965.

Shirley, Hale. Pediatric Psychiatry. Cambridge: Harvard University Press, 1963.

MICHAEL HANES, Ph.D.

Director, Preschool Education Department
High/Scope Educational Research Foundation
Ypsilanti, Michigan

7

How Curriculum Choice Affects Child Management

Child management, perhaps more than any other aspect of education, continues to be a popular topic for discussion in preservice teacher education and is frequently requested as a topic for inservice training. Teachers openly share problems and willingly experiment with new ideas for improving classroom and child management. The problems typically included in these discussions include a diverse range of situations and behaviors. Equally diverse is the variety of techniques that teachers use in dealing with child management concerns. In many ways, approaches to child management have become devices of art as Dewey (1938) described the multitude of approaches to motivating, encouraging and modifying children's behavior. Distinct management problems are isolated and associated with the child or the teacher-child relationship or the child's relationship with classmates. Rarely is the curriculum examined as the source of child management problems.

The separation of curriculum issues and child management concerns is common in many training materials used in early childhood education. Many curriculum texts only discuss child management in terms of a set of recommendations. Ways of organizing the classroom, developing a warm and affectionate teacher-child relationship and scheduling blocks of time for specific content are typically discussed as ways of avoiding child management problems. While some curricula do provide suggestions for handling personal conflicts that may arise, there is a great deal of variation in the degree to which recommendations specify the manner in which a curriculum is to be implemented in an actual classroom setting. In some cases, curriculum designers do not specify actual instructional strategies, preferring instead to allow the teacher to interpret the curriculum through a personal teaching style. In a similar manner, texts on child management rarely discuss the relationship between the curriculum and specific child management techniques. Consequently, the explanation or rationale for implementing a particular approach to child management may be unclear and may even contradict the rationale for the general curriculum approach employed in a classroom.

MAKING DECISIONS ABOUT CHILD MANAGEMENT

The decision to implement a particular child management strategy appears to be based on two criteria. First, is a particular approach effective in resolving a management problem? The question of effectiveness is not uncommon to American education, especially with the current trends emphasizing accountability in education. Effectiveness is clearly related to the pragmatic concerns of education, a concern for techniques that have been proven to be related to significant changes in children's behavior and a concern for efficient methods of producing behavioral change. In fact, the contemporary heritage of the general field of curriculum is characterized by the pragmatic tasks of design, implementation and evaluation (Pinar, 1975) as well as a major ameliorative function of solving the immediate problems of the school.

A second criterion for selecting child management strategies is whether the proposed strategy fits with the teacher's view of appropriate ways of working with children. While this decision may be determined on empirical grounds, teachers frequently rely on an implicit system of values about children, teachers, education and teaching as they make decisions about child management problems. Interestingly, both questions rely on value decisions. That is, even the selection of the criteria for effectiveness ultimately depends on a value orientation in terms of the important outcomes in a particular situation.

Subsequently, the actual bases for making decisions may be implicit in the teacher's behavior rather than a set of explicit principles. In a similar manner, curricula may include implicit psychological and philosophical positions which are the bases for decision making. Whether the bases for making decisions about classroom management are implicit or explicit in the teacher or the curriculum, the significant point is that these bases can be translated into a set of behavioral expectations for the child. Indeed, all classrooms operate with a set of behavioral expectations which may be directly related to the basic philosophical and psychological positions of the curriculum. The following discussion focuses on the positions inherent in different curricula and their relationship with behavioral expectations for the child. Throughout the following discussion the assumption is that the behavioral expectations for the child are a major source of child management problems.

ALTERNATIVE CURRICULUM APPROACHES

The task of differentiating early childhood curricula has been approached in a variety of ways. The best known efforts have included papers which distinguish curricula in terms of instructional objectives, materials and techniques (Mayer, 1971); teacher-child interaction patterns (Weikart, 1971); theoretical differences in child development and the nature of structure in the classroom (Anastasiow, 1977); and distinctions based on ideological differences (Kohlberg and Mayer, 1972). The following discussion draws on each of these analyses, but is focused on a central set of concerns which must be addressed by all curricula. The point being that clear distinctions between curriculum approaches are difficult to identify without some common reference point for comparison.

In analysis of curricula, Kliebard (1977) has suggested that all curricula must be responsive to a common set of questions. That is, curricula must provide some means of determining:

1. What should be taught?
2. What is the rationale for selecting content?
3. Who should have access to what knowledge?
4. What are the guidelines for governing the teaching of what has been selected?
5. How should parts be related to create a coherent curriculum?

As a basis for differentiating curricula, these questions require an examination of the underlying assumptions as well as actual classroom organization and operation.

Even with this focus, the variety of early childhood curricula is not easily categorized. The following discussion is limited to two distinct approaches which represent opposing ends of the continuum of curricula. These curricula are differentiated by Kohlberg and Mayer (1972) as representing two different educational ideologies: cultural transmission and progressive-developmental.

What should be taught? Most early childhood education programs agree on the content for the curriculum. The content is defined generally in terms of actual subject areas, such as reading, math, language arts, science and art. In some programs which emphasize the child's development, the content areas may be categorized in terms of different aspects of development, such as social development, language development, motor development and cognitive development. The feature that distinguishes these seemingly different approaches from the progressive-developmental position is the emphasis on teaching skills which are thought to be prerequisite for reading, writing and mathematics, the foundations for acquisition of more complex knowledge. The cultural transmission ideology and behavioral learning psychology which underlie these curricula suggest that the child needs to have direct experience with the specific skill content. These experiences are aimed at mastery of specific skills such as reciting the alphabet, acquiring a specific vocabulary and acquiring letter-sound correspondence.

In contrast to the cultural transmission ideology, the progressive-developmental position views skill acquisition as a function of the development of cognitive processing. For example, the cognitive processes related to understanding spatial relations, temporal relations, representation and logical relations provide the framework for organizing the curriculum content. In the progressive-developmental position, skills are developed as a result of the child's experiences and developing abilities in the different areas of cognitive development. Therefore, the progressive-developmental position emphasizes classroom experiences which challenge the child's developing thought processes, such as comparing and discriminating differences and similarities. As a result, the specific content of the curriculum may vary to the extent that experiences are provided which stimulate and challenge the child's developing abilities.

What is the rationale for selecting the content? Early childhood classrooms that focus on the acquisition of the prerequisite skills, as stated above, are based on an ideology which places the transmission of knowledge as the most important task of education. The identification and organization of specific content is based on two types of information. First, educators have identified content areas which appear to be important factors for successful membership in society. Second, the behavioral learning psychology inherent in the cultural transmission position suggests that complex information is best learned in a sequential manner. New information is hierarchically arranged so that previously learned information provides the basis for more complex learning. That is, information is sequenced in terms of a logical analysis of the content. Subsequently, letter names, letter-sound correspondence and blending, leading to decoding and word spelling, are isolated skills which are taught in a prescribed sequence leading the child to becoming a successful reader.

A basic assumption of the progressive-developmental position is that each child reconstructs knowledge through interactions with the social and physical environment. In addition, this position argues that children progress through stages of development in which the child's thought processing qualitatively changes. The progressive-developmental position focuses on the child's interactions with the environment as the important factor in supporting the development of each child's cognitive development. The organization and content of the curriculum is judged appropriate in terms of an understanding of the child's level of development. Therefore, curriculum content is derived from an understanding of the way children develop and the types of experiences which support development.

Who should have access to what knowledge? At this point it should be clear that the two positions on early childhood curriculum contain different views of the concept of knowledge. The commitment to skill acquisition in the cultural transmission position carries a basic assumption that the significant knowledge in early education can be defined as a finite set of information. An additional assumption is that the teacher has mastered the knowledge and serves as the knowledge source for the child. In order to gain access to that knowledge, the child must successfully master a hierarchy of skills as they are presented in the classroom. Consequently, more advanced forms of knowledge are available only to those children who successfully master each step in the sequence. Those children who do not master a particular step with other children must receive remedial help, but most importantly, each child is expected to proceed through the same sequence until they have acquired the prescribed outcome.

The progressive-developmental position emphasizes a view of knowledge as progressively developing cognitive processes. The information gained through interactions with the environment is valuable to the extent that the interactions promote cognitive development. The task of early education in the progressive-developmental position is to promote the child's cognitive development and to broaden the range of experiences for the child. Since a variety of experiences are appropriate in promoting each child's cognitive development, each child will have equal access to knowledge in terms of progressively more complex thinking. In summary, the progressive-developmental position is that all children must be exposed to experiences which challenge cognitive development; it is not important that all children acquire the same pieces of information in the same sequence.

What are the guidelines for teaching? The diagnostic-prescriptive and instruction by objectives methods, as they exist in early education, are clear examples of the instructional approaches which are consistent with the cultural transmission position. Since the teacher and the materials are the primary sources for the curriculum, the child is placed in a basically responsive role. In some early childhood classrooms, certain periods of the day are devoted to allowing children to select an activity. In most cases, however, the selection is limited to teacher-directed or materials-directed activities. In general, the cultural transmission position places the child in a responsive role with the content and organization of the classroom being directed by the teacher and/or prescribed curriculum materials. Instructional strategies include practice on isolated skills until mastery is demonstrated, at which time the child is given practice in applying mastered skills in context. Much of the instruction follows the sequence of teacher presentation, child practice, mastery testing and application.

In contrast, the progressive-developmental position emphasizes an active decision-making role for the child. By allowing the child to select and design personal learning experiences, the teacher is able to assess the child's level of development and determine what might be appropriate learning experiences for the child. The teacher's role is to arrange the elements of the environment (for example, physical objects and materials, opportunities for child-child and teacher-child interaction) so that the child's developing abilities will be challenged and supported. The teacher must rely on an understanding of the child's interests and level of development as well as developmental theory for designing appropriate experiences for the child. That is, the guidelines for teaching are derived from child development theory and an understanding of the kinds of experiences that promote development.

How are the parts related to the whole curriculum? Integrating distinct units of information to make a coherent curriculum is generally a difficult task for most early childhood curricula. The cultural-transmission position must rely on the teacher or the curriculum materials to provide a means of integrating distinct units into a coherent curriculum. In either case, the integrating factors are focused on the content or other sources external to the child. Factors which relate to the child are given a secondary emphasis in the integration of content. Since the information to be acquired by the child is typically presented as isolated units, the task of integrating curriculum components is critical in the cultural transmission position. In fact, the basic position holds that specific skill areas need not be integrated until the child has reached a particular level of mastery. For example, subjects such as science and social studies receive very little emphasis until the child has clearly mastered prerequisite skills in reading and writing. The end result can be seen in a number of classrooms where children see no relationship between reading, math and science.

The progressive-developmental emphasis on the child's development of cognitive processes also relies, to a certain extent, on the teacher's ability to design an integrated curriculum. The task is much less complex in view of the fact that the integrating factor is the child's developing cognitive abilities. Since the emphasis is not on distinct information units, the teacher can focus on the range of developing abilities in the children and the sequence in the development of cognitive stages for designing consistent and coherent experiences for the classroom. Similarly, the child's daily experience is not segmented by instruction in specific content areas, but instead, the day is represented as a total experience in which the child's range of cognitive abilities are applied througout the day. For example, in the Cognitively Oriented Curriculum the young child is asked to employ discrimination and representation abilities throughout each aspect of the classroom day (Hohmann, Banet and Weikart, 1978).

TABLE 7-1
A SUMMARY OF TWO CURRICULUM POSITIONS AND THEIR RELATED EXPECTATIONS FOR CHILD BEHAVIOR

ALTERNATIVE CURRICULUM POSITIONS

CULTURAL TRANSMISSION POSITION

1. Curriculum content consists of specific information; sequenced skills arranged in a hierarchical structure; child receives direct experience with skill content.

2. Transmission of knowledge is the focus; knowledge consists of pieces of information; information to be acquired is considered as prerequisites for successful membership in society.

3. All children are capable of learning information presented in a particular sequence; the acquisition of complex information is based on the cumulative acquisition of smaller pieces of information.

4. The teacher and the curriculum materials are the sources for organizing the curriculum content. Information is best acquired through the practice of isolated skills.

5. Integration of curriculum components is dependent on the teacher and the materials; curriculum content is the source for integrating components.

PROGRESSIVE-DEVELOPMENTAL POSITION

1. Curriculum content focuses on the development of cognitive processes in the child; experiences are judged appropriate in terms of an understanding of the kinds of experiences which promote and support cognitive development.

2. Cognitive development is the basis for constructing an understanding of the world.

3. All children must be exposed to experiences which promote cognitive development.

4. The teacher is responsible for organizing the classroom environment to include opportunities which challenge and support each child's development.

5. Curriculum content is integrated in terms of the child's development of cognitive processes.

BEHAVIORAL EXPECTATIONS FOR THE CHILD

1. The child's task is to acquire a prescribed set of information units.

2. The child will acquire information in segmented units. If the child masters the information presented, the child will have greater success in society (i.e., succeed in later schooling and ultimately as a member of adult society.)

3. The child will practice skills presented until mastered. Children who are unable to master skills are deficient and require remedial assistance.

4. The child will respond to the direction and content of the curriculum. The child will follow the teacher's directions in learning new information.

5. After mastering prerequisite skills, the child will be able to apply those skills to new problems. The child is not expected to integrate newly acquired information, the cumulative effect of acquiring information provides for the integration of separate information units.

---

1. The child is expected to progress through a sequence of cognitive stages as a function of classroom experience and normal development.

2. The child is expected to interact with the environment in developmentally appropriate ways and to utilize those experiences in the development of cognitive processes.

3. Each child is expected to progress through a developmental sequence, but each child may respond differently to different experiences.

4. The child is expected to actively respond to the structure of the environment and seek new experiences.

5. Each child is responsible for selecting and developing personal learning experiences. The child will be actively involved in a variety of learning experiences.

RELATING CURRICULA AND CHILD MANAGEMENT

The previous discussion indicates that early childhood curricula differ in basic assumptions, rationale and classroom operation. These differences are briefly summarized in Table 7-1. A basic assumption has been that the premises for each of the positions were related to behavioral expectations for the child. The rationale for examining behavioral expectations is that child management problems are seen to exist as a result of the discrepancies between the characteristics inherent in the child and the behavioral expectations of the curriculum. In view of the fact that education is the process of assisting children in acquiring or developing new knowledge, all early education curricula contain the behavioral discrepancies. The critical decision is to determine which discrepancies are most desirable and which discrepancies are counter-productive to the goals of the curriculum. Table 7-1 also presents some of the behavioral expectations that result from the two alternative positions for curricula.

To summarize the behavioral expectations of the cultural transmission position, the child is expected to respond to the directions of the teacher and the content of the curriculum. As the recipient of information, the child is expected to accumulate information as the result of presentations by the teacher or from direct experiences with curriculum materials. A typical child management problem that exists in this setting has been labeled lack of interest, lack of motivation, or the inability to attend to the task. Teachers frequently comment that a particular child has a short attention span or that a child is unable to attend to a task while in a group setting. The problem may be seen as inherent in the child (e.g., the child is immature) or in the situation (e.g., large groups are difficult to control). Child management techniques which are consistent with the behavioral orientation and are appropriate for the problem include isolating the child from group activities or assigning tasks which require less time for completion. Since the curriculum content and organization are fixed, teachers rarely view the curriculum as a source of the child management problem. When, in fact, the curriculum represents an imposition on the learner and the behavioral expectations may be developmentally beyond the abilities of the child. The small percentage of children who are unable to <u>conform</u> to the behavioral expectations of the curriculum are labeled as problem children.

The progressive-developmental position presents a distinctly different set of behavioral expectations for the child. In essence, the child is expected to actively interact with the social and physical environment. The child is held responsible for selecting and developing personally meaningful learning experiences. With these expectations, the major child management problems involve the expansion of the child's experience beyond a particular self-selected activity. For example, many children are fascinated by the block area and will consistently prefer to build the same structure day after day. According to the basic position, the teacher's task is to generate opportunities for the child to apply developing cognitive processes to new situations. In this case, the teacher may suggest to the child that the block structures can be represented in other media in the art area (e.g., the child may want to paint a house). In other words, the teacher is constantly evaluating the curriculum content to determine if the child's development is being stimulated and supported. Children may also have difficulties in maintaining interest in an activity. Accordingly, the teacher will examine the learning opportunities available in the classroom and the child's developmental interests to design appropriate opportunities for the child. The significant point is that the curriculum content is based on the child's interests, so that maintaining an attention span is the joint responsibility of the child developing self-control and the teacher initiating interesting opportunities.

Even though the relationships between early childhood curricula and child management problems are often abstract and quite subtle, the implications for classroom operation should be quite clear. All curricula are based on some fundamental assumptions about children, learning and teaching. These assumptions influence not only the content and organization of the curriculum, but also the kinds of behavioral expectations for the teacher and the child. Ultimately, the teacher must make a value decision about the kinds of behavioral expectations that are desirable. In this process, the teacher needs to consider the short term or immediate effects of these decisions as well as the long term outcomes. That is, do these behaviors represent the kinds of behaviors that will be essential for the child to develop optimally and function successfully in society? From one perspective, some of the important long term questions include: How do children best develop a sense of self-discipline and how do children learn to solve new problems and make decisions?

As Bernstein (1975) suggests, educational curricula communicate a great deal about society and social order beyond the explicit knowledge content. Conceptually, the implicit knowledge inherent in the organization, content and operation of a curriculum may have the greatest impact on what children actually learn. All too often, education focuses mistakenly on the explicit content in the curriculum as the source of problems and concerns. The previous discussion of child management reflects the complex relationships that may exist between implicit assumptions of a curriculum and the actual behaviors that children are expected to acquire. Early childhood educators and special educators in particular need to carefully analyze the implicit and explicit content of curricula for the purpose of clarifying child management concerns and understanding the full impact that a selected curriculum may have on the child.

REFERENCES

Anastasiow, N. J. Strategies and models for early childhood intervention programs. In Guralnick, M. (ed.), *Early Intervention and the Integration of Handicapped and Non-handicapped Children*. Baltimore: University Park Press, 1977.

Bernstein, B. *Class, Codes and Control (Volume 3)*, *Toward a Theory of Educational Transmissions*, London and Boston: Routledge and Kegan Paul, 1975.

Dewey, J. *Experience and Education*. Collier, 1938.

Hohmann, M., Banet, B. and Weikart, D. P. *Young Children in Action*. Ypsilanti: High/Scope Educational Research Foundation, 1978.

Kliebard, H.M. Curriculum theory: Give me a "for instance." *Curriculum Inquiry*. 1977, *6*, 257-276.

Kohlberg, L. and Mayer, R. Development as the aim of education. *Harvard Educational Review*. 1972, *42*, 449-496.

Mayer, R. S. A comparative analysis of preschool curriculum models. In Anderson, R. and Shane, H. (eds.), *As the Twig Is Bent*. Boston: Houghton-Mifflin, 1971, 286-314.

Pinar, W. (ed.). *Curriculum Theorizing: The Reconceptualists.* Berkeley: McCutchen, 1975.

Weikart, D. P. Early childhood special education for intellectual subnormal and/or culturally different children. Prepared for the National Leadership Institute in Early Childhood Development in Washington, D.C., October, 1971.

Part II

Practice and Procedures

Many countries share their concern over the development and implementation of programs for early intervention. This international perspective is reflected in papers of this section which discuss the orientation and administration of individual programs. Practices and procedures include the social, emotional, educational, and psychological interaction between parent, child, and teacher. The chapters also discuss the role of parent involvement programs. They stress how such programs influence the effectiveness of teaching strategies to foster and enhance the overall development of the child, specifically for language.

A.M.J. vAN UDEN, pr., Ph.D.

Director
Institute for Deaf Children
St. Michielsgestel
Netherlands

8

How to Converse with a Speechless and Languageless Child

Conversation is an exchange of thoughts. The term "conversation" is preferred to the conventional term "communication," with its often unilateral theory of sender or receiver, encoding or decoding processes, and is preferred to "language" with its often one-sided formal training. A real conversation is always two- or more-sided, always receptive and expressive, integrated into one whole, always spontaneous and creative from all participants. Conversation is the original form of language, and it is "the full form of language" (van Ginniken, 1909). Poems, novels, textbooks and other forms of language are merely "derivatives," developed from the beginning and always central form of language: conversation. Too, conversation is the beginning and central form of our thinking. We think in that language in which we converse (van Uden, 1977). Yet, conversation is just one aspect of the education of a deaf child. Other important aspects which will be discussed in this chapter as they relate to conversation are: cognitive development including mathematics, auditory training, physical training, music and dance, drawing and the arts, development of socialization and mainstreaming.

THE SEIZING METHOD

One of the main problems that educators of the deaf face is how to converse with a speechless child. Many parents and teachers of the deaf use an approach which requires a foundation of basic language forms and vocabulary before short, very often formal, conversations can be started. In this way, they hope to develop slowly that spontaneity and creativity essential to real conversations. Yet, the best approach is easier. We begin to converse by the "seizing method" and by "playing the double part" (van Uden, 1977).

Let us study this approach in normally hearing children and their mothers, since every mother manages to converse with her speechless and languageless baby from the very first day after birth. Different observations have revealed some important facts about how this conversation takes place. The following is an example:

> Mother hears her baby making some noise, and goes to the crib. The baby is moving his arms and legs, and is half-crying, half-smiling. The mother understands these expressive movements, these non-verbal utterances of "body language" (Piaget, 1955, 1935; Birdwhistel, 1970; Fast, 1970; Wood, 1976) and says,
>
> "Are you hungry?"
> "Come here, my darling."

Those two sentences represent a conversation: the first sentence responds to the words the baby would probably say if he could speak, "I am hungry." The second sentence is mother's personal contribution to the conversation, "Come here my darling." In the first sentence, mother "seizes" (or grasps) what the child wants to say and suggests to him the right words. This is called the "seizing method" in which mother speaks for the child as well as for herself. The child does not yet understand the second sentence, but mother makes herself understood by the situation; she picks her child up from the crib. Very soon the child will understand "Come here!" and will open his arms as soon as he hears it.

All of us follow the seizing method, in essence, when we encounter a person whose language we do not know. Here is a personal experience:

> Some time ago I was in the waiting room of the railroad station at Rosendaal in Holland. A Frenchman sat down in the coffee shop and started to talk to the waiter in French. The waiter didn't understand him, but when the Frenchman opened his wallet, the waiter looked in and said, "Oh, you don't have any Dutch money? You can change it over on that platform." He pointed to the exchange booth where the Frenchman was then able to change his money.

In this anecdote we see again how one participant in the conversation, the waiter, followed the "seizing method": his first sentence expressed what the Frenchman probably wanted to say - the waiter played the part of the Frenchman. The second sentence was his own contribution to the conversation: he played his own part, thus he played the "double part."

The mother continues playing the double part as long as the child needs it, until about four years of age. Some mothers of retarded children stay with this approach for an even longer period of time, but instead of pulling the child's immature utterance up to the model of normal language, the mothers imitate the child's immature speech and soon develop a kind of idioglossia. This is very dangerous because at this point the child's linguistic development stops. In addition, it has been shown (Schmahlohr, 1968; Hurley, 1965; for deaf children, Greenstein, 1975), that when parents have difficulty accepting their child, his language development is impeded. These parents do not "listen" enough to their child's utterances, and so they do not adopt the "seizing method." Consequently, they do not converse well with their child. Still, parents can learn this art of listening. I often allow parents to watch their child during his intelligence test in order to demonstrate the richness of his communication abilities as well as his inventiveness and creativity.

A special aspect of mother's personal contribution to the conversation is her description of or comments about what she or the child are doing. This occurs during such activities as eating, walking, or cooking. Especially while bathing or dressing can the mother develop in the child body awareness as well as teach the names of body parts. Furthermore, the mother can expose the child to difficult, yet commonly used, language structures such as figurative meanings, the language of feelings, and idiomatic expressions. The mother also trains the auditory memory by speaking very melodiously, by progressively expanding her own as well as her child's sentences, and by singing rhymes and songs. Every normally hearing child has an excellent "individual teacher" of his own, for at least three to four years!

THE ROLE OF BODY LANGUAGE IN CONVERSATION

Body language is the first language we acquire. A long time before a child starts to use words, he is already expressing, non-verbally, subject and predicate with object: actor-actio-actum (cf. for deaf children Maesse, 1935; Schlesinger, 1971; Goldin-Meadow and Feldman, 1975; Schlesinger and Namir, 1978). By body language we mean any movement of the body, including facial expression, clapping or rubbing the hands, stamping the feet, positions (distances) and postures of the body, all used as a conscious or unconscious message to someone else. That message can be emotional and/or informational and/or attitudinal. Man has a strong, original, innate, spontaneous, creative ability both in inventing non-verbal motor-iconic emblems of body language, and in understanding them. Hirsch (1923) found normally hearing German adults using as many as 853 of these emblems, about 500 of which were already being used by infants. At two years of age a normally hearing child can express twelve different feelings non-verbally (Bridges, 1932, quoted by Wood, 1976). A child changes over to mainly verbal communication at about 2.5 years of age. Here is an example taken from this transitional period.

> A boy 2.4 years of age said, "Mama, lemonade!" while pointing to the kitchen. There, he shaped his hand as for a glass, and pretended to pour from the imaginary bottle with his other hand. While rubbing his hand across his belly, he said, "Nice."

We have a marvelous mode of expression with body language, with many of its emblems very difficult to translate purely into words. Some examples of emblems noted from deaf children (not exposed to sign language) which seem to be universally understood and used are:

"Never mind."	"Let me see."
"I dare you."	"Hold me."

As mothers see their hearing-impaired children using these non-verbal expressions, they should "seize" every opportunity to verbally translate and respond to that body language. It should be obvious that there are countless opportunities for using the "seizing method" every day.

An interesting topic relating to body language concerns the dividing line between speech and sign. How an esoteric sign originates can be illustrated by the following experience:

> One of the instructors in our home-training service came into the home of a congenitally deaf child 2.5 years old. The child came to mother and made a strange sign, turning his right hand over his left one. The instructor, astonished, asked what was the meaning of this gesture. "Oh, he wants a cookie," the mother said. Then she told how this sign had originated. Some time ago the child had dramatized the following: he pulled his mother by her skirt to the cupboard, shaped his hand as for the cookie jar, pretended to open the lid with his right hand, pretended to take out the cookie, put it into his mouth, and nodded, "Yes" with a happy face. The mother understood him and gave him a cookie. The effect was such that a little bit later he came back for another cookie, again dramatizing and pretending, but with a shorter version this time. Eventually the child could easily convey his want by just turning his right hand over his left one!

This mother made the same mistake as many mothers without expert guidance: she had started "playing the deaf mute." She stood on the dividing line between manualism and oralism. Instead of reinforcing the child's dramatization into an esoteric sign, she should have requested him to say "cookie," or at least should have made him protrude his lips into an /u/ <u>before</u> he got a cookie. That cookie then would have reinforced this beginning of speech, and would have kept his hands free for the natural body language. Happily enough, our hometraining guidance usually prevents such a dangerous development from occurring.

The mother in this example did more than just reinforce the development of the esoteric sign; she responded to the first dramatizing expression of the child (his body language) with her own body language expression. The danger is not so much that the child expresses himself with body language. This is natural, and remember that the normal-hearing child first begins to communicate in this way, too. A deaf child needs it much longer, however, and most profoundly deaf children don't change over from mainly body language to mainly oral language in spontaneous conversation until about age seven (age nine among peers in a dormitory setting). Oral language is encouraged and developed by application of the "seizing method"; the children are offered words again and again at the moment they need them, even if they cannot imitate them. No, the danger in this development of body language between mother and child arises when the mother starts to use body language more than she would with a hearing child. Then what occurs is a conversation in body language, with an increase in use of esoteric signs which are understood by no one else. It may be difficult at times to manipulate the situation in such a way that the child will understand the speech of his mother. In these instances, the mother may have to employ progressively more concrete levels of communication (i.e., from verbal language to body language) in order to get her meaning across. Later on, written words can also be helpful in avoiding an excess of body language.

The deaf child spontaneously intersperses his speech with body language, in much the same way as a young normal-hearing child. This is quite appropriate and makes his speech functional. The mother, though, is instructed to always request the words from him in the corresponding situations, and is never to "play the deaf mute." For the young child who still does use body language in a creative, dramatic way, esoteric signs would be an impediment to his communication. It is, after all, impossible to use one's hands in both ways at the same time. Speech, on the other hand, neither impedes nor disturbs the natural body expressions. It is understandable, then, that Northcott (1975) found that there was no need for an esoteric means of communication in the programs of parent guidance. It would be worthwhile to start a careful differential investigation on the effectiveness of spontaneous communication between children in a total communication hometraining program, and those in an oral one.

EARLY SPEECH TRAINING

When not exposed to speech, even a normal-hearing child will become speechless, speech-mute and speech-deaf. This has been clearly shown by a few exceptional cases of so-called "wolf-children" (Lane, 1976). Deaf children are very much endangered in this respect. The major objective of early hometraining is to prevent "mutism" and "deafism." "Prevention" is the key word, because a congenitally deaf child as such is not born mute; he babbles (Mavilya, 1969) and this babbling can be transferred into speech. Nor is a deaf child born totally deaf; he perceives at least vibrations, which can be transferred into sound awareness. Oral hometraining guidance must be started as early as possible, however. We found the following significant relationships in 73 profoundly deaf children (losses of 95 dB +) six months to five and a half years of age (van Uden, 1974):

a. the later the hometraining starts, the more deaf children are found to have lost their original face-directedness and vocalizing behavior

b. deaf children who had kept their original face-directedness, vocalized more and came to lipread better than those deaf children who had lost their face-directed behavior and had to relearn it

c. deaf children who were face-directed reacted better to hearing aids, than non-face-directed children

d. deaf children who got their hearing aids before 2.6 years of age reacted better to those aids by becoming sound-conscious sooner, by vocalizing more, and by developing better oral-aural understanding, than those deaf children who got them after 2.6 years of age.

A formal, consciously controlled manner of developing early speech seems to be inadequate and almost impossible in young children below three years of age. Speech training by an expert speech therapist is at least possible from 2.5 years of age, for exceptional cases. Speech training is more than "articulatory training." The one-sided technical approach by some speech therapists has been criticized by Reichling (1949, also van Eijndhoven, 1978). Speech is an informative behavior, asserting, asking, appealing (Buhler,

1934), towards listeners, in essence a dialogical behavior. Articulation is a manipulation of speech organs and is formal, not functioning in a conversational way. It happens too often that a deaf child has been taught to speak very intelligibly, but he simply does not use his speech in daily living. Of course, it will be necessary <u>sometimes</u> to work formally, e.g., to correct "baba" into "mama," but the word should be integrated immediately after that into a conversation.

Non-verbal imitation games may be one of the starting points of developing early speech. Man has an imitating capacity which has already started working by two weeks after birth. Babies have demonstrated imitation of tongue and lip movements as well as finger gestures (Meltzoff and Moore, 1977). This capacity for imitation can be developed through mirror games, preferably together with the sound in the hearing aid. It is also important to develop an identification of sound and object; i.e., the horn of a car, the "meow" of a cat, the "bow wow" of a dog. More important than requesting the child to imitate the adult, is for the adult to imitate, "seize," and expand upon what the child says. For example, if a child suddenly babbles "car," the speech therapist or mother should immediately imitate "car" and then show a photograph of father's car. That "operant" (a behavior by chance, Skinner, 1957) was reinforced into a word. A clever adult will "seize" and reinforce a lot of words with difficult phonemes in this way. Operant conditioning, then, is another technique which is important in the development of early speech.

A third technique is that of classic conditioning. The example of "cookie" told above was one of classic conditioning; the child learns to use a signal (speaking at least /u/) in order to get a cookie. Lipreading and sound-perception can also be taught even before the first birthday, using both classic and operant conditioning techniques.

Lipreading and speech must be a <u>pleasure</u>, for only by pleasure are they reinforced. Mother can play games with the child which reinforce certain language forms or words--for example, she can hide his ball and as she helps him look for it behind every piece of furniture, she can ask, "Where is the ball?" When the ball is finally found, she can exclaim, "There's the ball!" The repetition of certain daily activities also provides a natural opportunity for developing lipreading and language skills. Mother should <u>verbally anticipate</u> the activity rather than <u>physically identify</u> it; for example, mother can tell the child "We are going to take a bath now," and only if the child does not understand this should she gradually give more clues (by getting out the soap, towel, etc.).

One of the greatest difficulties deaf children have in learning language is their memory function, including memory for lipreading and/or auditory and/or spoken forms of the words, and memory for series of words, both for short-term (immediate perceptual memory) and long-term memory (intermediate apperceptual memory). One of the best teachers in our institute has said that deaf children will "oralize" (lipread, hear and speak) those words best, which they can also read and write. This does not mean that the written form should be presented to the child first. Rather, the oral form is always presented first (for deaf children with no other handicaps), and is possible much earlier than the written presentation. Once the graphic form is introduced, it reinforces the already known and used oral form. We follow the Ewings' (1964) practice of introducing the written form of words for those words which the child already knows through lipreading, and sometimes through speech. This link is formed by using speech balloons. For example, if the child understands and/or can say, "No," we draw it for him this way:

FIG. 8-1
A Speech Balloon

Even at the higher levels the same order is followed: first a new word is spoken, imitated from "mouth to mouth" (van Uden, 1977), and then written down. Ling (1977) believes that teaching new words through the written form is very often confusing to deaf children. We support this belief, and at our school we ask the child to write down the new word only after he has imitated it. If he has spelled it incorrectly, we show him how to spell it and make him aware of the difference between the pronunciation and the spelling.

Our studies have shown that prelingually profoundly deaf children can correctly identify more than twice as many words known through both lipreading and reading, than through lipreading alone. This difference can be largely attributed to the effect of the words as figures against a vague background. Indirectly, the written form reinforces the memory. For these reasons, we start reading at about 3.5 - 4 years of age, following the methods described above. Deaf children selected for mainstreaming, then, start out one step ahead of normal-hearing children in that they can already read and write. There are deaf children, usually those suffering from dyspraxia (van Uden, 1974) who need the reinforcement of the written word more so than others. For those children who learn to lipread slowly and with difficulty, the written form should be used at a still earlier age, by classic and operant conditioning techniques, as Premack (1971, 1975) did with chimpanzees. In the beginning, the shapes of words can be contoured in this way (cf. Hart, 1963):

FIG. 8-2
Contouring words.

The best and most direct reinforcement of oral memory for deaf children, though, is rhythmic speech. We found (van Uden, 1974) that prelingually profoundly deaf children are able to retain a short-term memory for spoken sentences of seven to nine words at 13 years of age by rhythmic training throughout their education.

In essence, the same method is followed for introducing conversation with deaf children as for normal-hearing children: that is, the "seizing method" and "playing the double part." These methods require some attitudinal prerequisites in order to work for the deaf child, however. Deaf children, in contrast to normally hearing children, must be kept face-directed. As long as the deaf baby is lying on his back in the crib or playing in the play-pen, his attention is directed to his mother's face almost naturally by his position. This changes the moment he starts to crawl (Ewings, 1947) and later, walk. While a normal-hearing, walking child maintains his relationship with his mother by means of his hearing, a mobile deaf child loses that contact. Furthermore, when the mother is careless about her child's focus of attention, the child can lose his person-or face-directedness and become object-directed to the point of near autism. (Recall how difficult it is to regain that lost face-directedness, and the consequences thereof for lipreading and hearing development). This face-directedness is a prerequisite for starting a conversation, and can be reinforced from infancy through games and play. An important first face-to-face game is peek-a-boo, mentioned in all courses of parent guidance. Other games which involve turn-taking and face-to-face contact include bouncing on the knee, imitating facial expressions (with appropriate sounds) in the mirror, throwing and retrieving objects, and puppet shows (with hands at the sides of the face). Conversational attitudes can also be created with team-like games. Mother and child can play alternately with a tower of rings: the child puts the first ring on the pin, and the mother puts the second one on, or the child puts on the blue rings, and the mother puts on the red ones. Or, the mother can cut magazine pictures into large pieces for the child to assemble, and then have the child cut out a puzzle for her to make. By ages four to five, further suggestions include picture-completion games, picture-arrangement games, and quiz games, all with speech. In auditory training, the mother should again reverse the roles, making the child give auditory training to her.

It is important that children learn sentences that can be part of a conversation. The following story illustrates this point. A teacher once taught her children to clearly articulate many sentences describing their activities or experiences. A few days later, the parents of one of the children came to visit. The child entered the guest room in which his parents were staying and demonstrated the language he had drilled to perfection, "The table has four legs." "The cupboard has no legs" and so on. The parents, instead of being pleasantly surprised, stood bewildered; had their child lost his mind? The teacher saw the disappointment in their faces, and soon after adopted more natural methods. There is an essential difference between the sentences quoted above, and sentences like the following:

> "Can I come in?"
> "I want to wash my hands."
> "Comb my hair, please."
> "Help me button this, please."

To put it boldly, "A word or a sentence which is no part of a conversation, is no language at all!"

"Visualized conversations" can be the basis of first reading lessons for young deaf children. Experience-based, the dialogue between mother and child originates from the "seizing method" and by "playing the double part." Its visualization is composed afterwards in a series of speech balloons recorded in a "diary." We use just one picture for the whole reading lesson as an aid to help the child remember the whole event (such as blowing bubbles, making popcorn, etc.). Our rationale is that when every sentence is accompanied by a picture, the language becomes picture-language. Reading skills can be practiced using these diaries in different ways. For example, the diary can be photocopied twice, the sentences can be cut out from the balloons on one page and pasted into the correct balloons on the other page. Or, the sentences can be cut out in strips, which the child must put into the proper sequence. These visualized conversations can also be used to train lipreading and listening. The mother reads one of the sentences of the conversation, and the child must use his lipreading and auditory skills to identify the correct sentence. It should be clear that the teaching of language, reading, and conversation are one whole, even at the hometraining and preschool level.

These reading lessons present an ideal opportunity to teach some difficult <u>semantic aspects</u> of language. These include language of feelings (glad, surprised, satisfied), language of contrasts (empty-full, hot-cold, same-different), relative language (more than enough, not yet), and figurative meanings and illusions (my leg fell asleep, raining cats and dogs). The mother will not formally teach these as such, but will "seize" them as they occur normally and spontaneously, and use them often in the speech balloons and reading lessons. Any opportunity to teach some necessary, everyday language must be seized immediately and recorded in the diary. It may be helpful to display a chart on the wall where new expressions, or those from the natural situations which are not so easily understood, can be written and practiced. Some examples are:

> Please, look over here!
> On time--too late--tomorrow
> How kind of you--How smart you are!
> May I?--Help me!--I'm ready.
> All gone!--Wait a minute!
> No, thank you.
> I know it.--I forgot.
> Pick it up!

In conclusion, it is quite possible for a prelingually profoundly deaf child who is not multiply handicapped, to have mastered a vocabulary of 600 or more words by the time he is six years of age. It is also possible that he is able to pronounce all phonemes and phoneme combinations, that he can recognize all letters and analyze and synthesize words graphically and phonetically, and that he can read many of the reading lessons in his diaries from school and home. The range of this language growth among children is very broad, however, even among deaf children who are not multiply handicapped. There are many reasons for this difference but much depends upon the quality and the dedication of the teachers. Very important, too, is the work of the parents. Most important, however, is that the conversational method makes deaf children <u>happy</u> because they are accepted as persons with thoughts, ideas, and desires as unique as those of anyone else.

REFERENCES

Birdwhistel, R. Kinesics and Context: Essays in Body Motion Communication. Philadelphia: University of Pennsylvania Press, 1970.

Buhler, K. Sprachtheorie. East Germany: Jena, 1934.

Eijndhoven, J. van. Speech for the deaf child. The AOEHI Journal. 1977-78, Vol. 4, 44-54.

Ewing, A.W.G. and Ewing, E.C. Teaching Deaf Children to Talk. Manchester: University of Manchester Press, 1964.

Ewing, I.R. and Ewing, A.W.G. Opportunity and the Deaf Child. London: University of London Press, 1947.

Ewing, I.R. and Ewing, A.W.G. New Opportunities. Springfield: Charles C. Thomas, 1958.

Fast, J. Body Language. New York: M. Evans, 1970.

Ginneken, J. van. Het gesprek. Nieuwe Taalgids. 1909, 86-96.

Goldin-Meadow, S. and Feldman, H. The creation of a communication system: A study of deaf children of hearing parents. Sign Language Studies. 1975, 8, 225-234.

Greenstein, J.M. Methods of fostering language in deaf infants. Final report to Health, Education and Welfare Department, Grant OEG-0-72-539, Washington, D.C., 1975.

Hart, B.O. Teaching Reading to Deaf Children. Washington, D.C.: A.G. Bell Association for the Deaf, 1963.

Hirsch, A.P. Die Gebardensprache der Horenden und ihre Stellung zur Lautsparche. Im Anhang eine Sammlung von Horendengebarden. Selbstverlag des Verfassers, Charlottenburg, 1923.

Hurley, G. R. Parental acceptance-rejection and children's intelligence. Merrill-Palmer Quarterly. 1965, Vol. 11, 19-31.

Lane, H. The Wild Boy of Aveyron. Cambridge: Harvard University Press, 1976.

Ling, D. and Ling, A. H. Speech and the Hearing-Impaired Child. Washington, D.C.: A.G. Bell Association for the Deaf, 1976.

Maesse, H. Das Verhaltnis von Laut-und Gebardensprache in der Entwicklung des taubstummen Kindes. Langensalza, 1935.

Mavilya, M.P. Spontaneous vocalizations and babbling in hearing-impaired infants. Unpubl. Doct. Diss., Teachers College of Columbia University, 1969.

Meltzoff, A.N. and Moore, M.K. Imitation of facial and manual gestures by human neonates. Science. October 1977, 75-78.

Northcott, W. H. Hearing-Impaired Children, Birth to Three Years, and Their Parents, Curriculum Guide. Washington, D.C.: A.G. Bell Association for the Deaf, 1975.

Piaget, J. Le Language et la Pensee Chez l'enfant. Delachaux et Niestle, Neuchatel, Paris, 1930. The Language and Thought of the Child. New York: The World Publishing Company, 1955).

Piaget, J. Les Debuts de l'Intelligence. E. Flammarion, Paris, 1935.

Premack, A.J. and Premack, D. Teaching language to an ape. Scientific American. October 1972; Also in Atkinson, R.C. and Pinel, J.P.J. (eds.), Psychology in Progress. San Francisco, 1975, 173-180.

Premack, D. Language in chimpanzees. Science. 1971, 172, 808-822.

Reichling, A. A new method of speech-training. In Rapport du IIe Congres International Pour la Pedagogie de l'Enfance Deficiente. Amsterdam, 1949.

Schlesinger, I.M. The grammar of sign language and the problem of language universals. In Morton (ed.), Biological-Social Factors in Psycholinguistics. London: Logos Press, 1971, 98-101.

Schlesinger, I.M. and Namir, L. Sign Language of the Deaf: Psychological, Linguistic and Sociological Perspectives. New York: Academic Press, 1978.

Schmahlohr, E. Fruhe Mutterentbehrung Bei Mensch und Tier, Entwick-lungspsychologische Studie zur Psychohygiene der Fruhen Kindheit. Munchen, 1968.

Skinner, B.F. Verbal Behavior. New York: Appleton-Century-Crofts, 1957.

Uden, A.M.J. van. Dove Kinderen Leren Spreken. Rotterdam, 1974.

Uden, A.M.J. van. A World of Language for Deaf Children. Part I: Basic Principles. A Maternal Reflective Method. Lisse, 1977.

Wood, B.S. Children and Communication: Verbal and Non-Verbal Language Development. Englewood Cliffs: Prentice-Hall, 1976.

JEAN S. MOOG, M.S.

Instructor in Education of the Deaf
Washington University
Central Institute for the Deaf
St. Louis, Missouri

9

Listening: A Critical Aspect of Communication

Listening, really listening, to a child can be a powerfully motivating factor in stimulating that child to talk. Certainly no one would disagree that verbal communication encompasses both talking and listening. However, most of us who have worked with language-handicapped children have for too long a time stressed the importance of our talking and the child listening. "Language bombardment" and "bathing the child in language" are terms that have been used for this TALK TALK TALK-to-the-child approach. We have given little or no attention to our listening and the child talking. Now it is time that we, the parents and teachers of children who need help in learning to communicate, begin to decrease our talking and increase our listening. I am suggesting that as we increase our listening efforts, our children will increase their talking efforts. Listening, in particular an adult listening to a child, is a critical aspect of conversing with or communicating with that child. Most of us, at any age, talk more readily when we are with someone who wants to listen. In the same way, most of us are inhibited and talk less when we are with someone who is talking a great deal or who seems uninterested in what we have to say.

We, as parents or teachers, must learn to be ready listeners when the child wants to talk, and ready talkers only when the child wants to listen. This sounds simple and obvious, but all too often the reverse takes place: we expect the child to listen when we want to talk and we expect him to talk when we want to listen. With the emphasis now on LISTENING, let us consider the following ways that our listening can help the hearing-impaired or language-impaired child develop and improve his ability to communicate.

LISTEN TO THE CHILD'S IDEAS--------then-------RESPOND
LISTEN TO THE CHILD'S LANGUAGE---then-------EXPAND
LISTEN TO THE CHILD'S SPEECH------then-------MODEL
LISTEN TO THE CHILD'S TOPIC--------then-------TALK
LISTEN TO THE CHILD'S EXPRESSION--then-------ENJOY

LISTEN TO THE CHILD'S IDEAS--------then--------RESPOND

Listening, especially to a hearing-impaired child, implies more than simply being attentive when that child is telling you something. Listening, in the sense that I use it, means taking the necessary time and effort to figure out what the child is trying to communicate. This is no small task. However, if the child realizes that we are making an effort to understand him, he in turn is likely to put forth great effort to make himself understood. In this way, our efforts as listeners in trying to understand can be effective in encouraging that child to talk.

Sometimes, no matter how hard we try, we may not understand the child. When this happens, we should encourage him to do everything he can to clarify his meaning. Not being understood is a frustrating experience. But remember, although we may be frustrated, discouraged and upset, the child is even more frustrated, discouraged and upset. Be understanding - not impatient. Some of the following techniques are suggested to clarify communication:

> Repeat what you think the child said and confirm it with him. See if he can make any corrections or additions in order to further clarify his idea.
>
> If you understood only part of what he said, restate the words you did understand. Then use

gestures and/or physical prompts such as pictures or objects to determine the meaning of the other part.

If you did not understand, encourage the child to use pictures, pointing, gestures or anything else to get across his idea.

If you still don't understand even after both of you have exerted effort, then you may have to admit to the child that you just do not understand. Most of the time it is better to admit this than to "fake it," especially if the child expects a response. A child usually knows when we really do not understand and pretending that we do might be interpreted as a lack of genuine interest in what he is saying. Such well-intended dishonesty may backfire and discourage the child from further communication attempts.

Such a communication exchange with a child can be tiring and exasperating. It is important that we, as listeners, make a conscious effort to remain calm and patient as we try to help that child make himself understood. If he senses that we are impatient, disgusted or "too busy," he will be less likely to try to talk to us.

Once we have figured out what the child is trying to say, we can then give him the words he needs to say it. He should first listen to a clear speech model, and then he should be encouraged to repeat. This procedure will not only help him learn how to verbally express himself, it will also help the listener recognize his speech patterns so that the next time she will be more likely to understand him. We will thus become more competent listeners, and the child will soon become a more effective talker.

Responding to the content of what a child has said is another important aspect of listening. We should always respond to the child when he does communicate. However, responding does not necessarily mean doing what the child wants, nor does it always mean giving him what he wants. Responding to a hearing-impaired child, or any child, is usually a two-step procedure. First, we must let the child know that we have understood what he has said. Then we must decide on our response to what he said and convey that response to him. It is important to respond to the child if we want him to continue his communication efforts.

LISTEN TO THE CHILD'S LANGUAGE------then------EXPAND

As the child talks and communicates his ideas, we must listen carefully to the words and the language structures he uses, especially noticing the words he omits. We often can predict so well what the child will say that we "hear" words that he did not actually say. We sometimes become such good listeners that we "fill in" and modify what the child says without being fully aware that we are doing so. Often we think the child is using language structures correctly, when, in fact, his language is still quite elliptical. So once we understand the idea the child is trying to communicate, let us think back to the form and the actual words he used to express himself. For example, the child may be talking in sentences but omitting function words, such as articles and prepositions, or auxilaries. When this happens, we can repeat what he said, putting in the omitted words or endings and, if possible, emphasizing them in order to draw the child's attention to what he has omitted. An example, such as, "I play baseball school," should be modeled, "I was playing baseball at school," with the emphasis on the underlined parts. Sometimes when words are omitted, just the phrase in which the omission occurs can be repeated. An example might be, "I'm going outside play baseball." To this you might simply say "to play baseball." It is often helpful to spend a day or two writing down word-for-word precisely what the child says. This can give an idea of the direction in which the child's language can be expanded.

A child is usually interested in learning the names of the things in his environment that are meaningful. We can assist him in this process by labelling things for him when he is interested and attentive. He should also be given an opportunity to try and say the name himself to help him remember it. This word building must be fun and informal, though. We should not test him, nor become discouraged when repetition is necessary. It is not easy to learn new words and a hearing-impaired child, as all children, has a large vocabulary to acquire. Clothing, food, toys, games, activities - all of these offer possibilities for such vocabulary development.

Because deaf children tend to use little variety in their language production, they need to be given training in flexibility. We should sometimes use language that is different from that which he uses spontaneously. Synonyms for very familiar and over-used words are another way to introduce flexibility. If the child is speaking in sentences, then the sentence structure might be varied. For example, if the child says, "I watch T.V. Then I go to bed," you might rephrase it to, "After I watch T.V. I will go to bed." Other possibilities are:

"When this T.V. show is over, I will go to bed."
"I want to watch T.V. before I go to bed."
"May I stay up and watch this show instead of going to bed now?"
"If you let me watch one more show, I'll go to bed when it's over."

At a simpler level, if the child is comfortably using one-word utterances, we should start expanding them to two- or three-word utterances to express the same idea. For example, if he is using mostly nouns, then noun-verb or adjective-noun combinations might be introduced. If the child says, "ball," we can expand that to "big ball" or "that ball" or "red ball" or "throw the ball," depending on what he is trying to express.

Just as the child needs enrichment in vocabulary, so also does he need variation in phrase and sentence structure. Not only do we need to utilize phrase structures of place, manner and time, but we need to vary those phrases, and repeat them often enough that they become part of his language repertoire. Let us consider the time phrase signaled by "after." There are endless possibilities for using "after" plus the future tense, once we become aware of trying to use it. For example:

After dinner, we will go for a ride.
After your bath, I'll read to you.
After the T.V. show, we will go to the store.

The same principle applies to any sentence structure or expression that the child is not presently using. Once we begin using a particular structure, we need to try to find more occasions to use it again until the child knows it and is using it spontaneously.

Structure may often cause the child difficulty. He may confuse the word order in the sentences he uses. When this happens, we should provide the correct word order for what he is trying to say. If he says: "I have at home a ball," we need to say for him instead, "I have a ball at home."

LISTEN TO THE CHILD'S SPEECH--------then-------MODEL

We need to listen carefully not only to what the child says, but to how the child sounds when he talks. If we have trouble understanding him, we first have to figure out what he wants to say. Once we know that, we can express that thought for him with a good, clear speech model. When a child has difficulty making himself understood, it's a good idea to pick out one or two of his words and say them clearly for him to imitate. We need to analyze his speech in order to determine which features are unintelligible. If he has omitted sounds which we know he can make, we might remind him or show him the written symbol, or we might emphasize the aspect we want him to change. If he repeats after the model, we should listen carefully to how he says the words in order to recognize his speech patterns in the future. The spirit in which we approach this task is critical. Corrections as described should be presented in an informal, good-natured way. We should refrain from nagging the child. Our approach should be one of positive helpfulness rather than negative criticism. Let us first listen to him. Then we can provide a good, clear model (and the written symbol if that is helpful). If he attempts to imitate the model, we should let him know we are pleased. By no means should we force him to imitate. Getting him to watch and listen is worthwhile even if he does not immediately attempt to change his own production. By not insisting that he imitate, we often will find him attempting and practicing on his own.

LISTEN TO THE CHILD'S TOPIC----------then---------TALK

Our job as parents and educators also requires talking to the child and helping him learn to listen. Our talking often occurs in response to the child. Ideas for topics of conversation then, should emerge from listening to the child. By listening, we can learn about the child's interests. Simply observing his attentiveness can also provide a great deal of information. If he is not paying attention, he might not be really interested in "hearing" what we have to say. When talking to a child, we must talk about things in which that child is interested. Remember, also, the distinction between talking with the child, and talking at the child. Our talk can turn the child "on" or it can turn him "off." Sensitivity to the child's ability to listen, to understand, and respond to what we say, is important. When talking to the child we should try to:

> Get the child's attention before trying to tell him something.
>
> Talk at a rate at which the child can understand. This will probably be a little slower than the rate

used when talking to another adult.

Enunciate our words clearly in order to provide the child with a good, clear speech model.

Keep the language at a simple enough level for the child to be able to understand what we are talking about.

Included in the task of talking to a child, is making sure that the child understands what is being said. We need to look for signs of comprehension from the child. If the child seems confused or seems not to understand, we must do whatever we can to make our meaning clear. A little understanding goes a long way in motivating him to try harder to understand even more. Confusion may force him to give up altogether trying to understand. Evaluation of the child's comprehension of what has been said can sometimes be made objective by having the child demonstrate his understanding in some way. However, often such a judgment may remain quite subjective. Facial expression or the "look" in his eyes often indicates comprehension. However, it is frequently difficult to ascertain whether the child has grasped the meaning. When in doubt, we should assume that he did not understand, rather than that he is being stubborn or difficult. Sometimes, no matter how hard we try, the child will indicate, or we will suspect, that he does not understand what was said. Here are some things to try:

Repeat more slowly and, perhaps, more clearly. If necessary go where there is less interference from noise and other distractions.

Rephrase in simpler or more familiar language, emphasizing key words when necessary.

Restate, using a combination of gestures and words.

Clarify using physical prompts such as pictures or objects, in combination with gesturing, if necessary.

Demonstrate what you want done by doing it yourself.

Physically involve the child in relating the language to the idea being expressed.

We often have to do whatever is necessary in order to make ourselves understood. Communicating with the child in a way that is meaningful to him often requires a good deal of effort on both sides. But the child needs your help in learning to understand your speech and the speech of others.

Listening is a vital aspect of conversation. Listening is important for us. Listening is important for the child. We must first expect the child to "listen" and to understand, and then do whatever is necessary to help him live up to that expectation. We want to listen to him, but also want to be sure he becomes a good listener too.

LISTEN TO THE CHILD'S EXPRESSION------then------ENJOY

Children can be quite delightful in their thoughts and methods of expression. Listening to a child allows a glimpse of the world from his point of view. A child's perceptions of happenings and objects in the environment are often different from our adult perceptions. A child's naive and innocent view of the world can be quite refreshing if we take the time to listen and understand what he is telling us. If we have fun and keep our sense of humor, we can more thoroughly enjoy the individual "specialness" of each child.

Let us always remember:

> Children can be fun when they aren't being stubborn, grouchy, demanding, unreasonable, troublesome and totally exasperating.
>
> Parents and teachers can be fun when they aren't being stubborn, grouchy, demanding, unreasonable, troublesome and totally exasperating.

JOAN GODSHALK, M.A.

Infant Center and Preschool
Lexington School for the Deaf
Jackson Heights, New York

10

Putting the Parents on the Teaching Team

Many programs for the hearing-impaired infant from birth to about three years of age are parent-oriented or family-focused. These programs for the youngest children acknowledge the parents as the child's most influential teachers. The more effective infant programs reflect this belief: they give top priority to the quality of parenting and their goal is to develop caring, nurturing parents. In other words, the staff responsible for programs for infants and toddlers see their major role as supporting and helping parents to develop the gift for nurturing.

In the more effective infant programs, the staff also realize that language development is interwoven with all aspects of the child's development; how the child feels about himself, how he plays, how he interacts with his family and how the family feels about and responds to the child. Knowing that the parents are the child's most influential educators, and that parents have more impact on the child's language development than teachers, the staff use a team-teaching approach in designing programs for deaf infants. The parents and teacher plan together and share their knowledge. The parents share with the teacher their knowledge about their child, and the teacher shares with the parents her knowledge, not only about that individual child, but the knowledge she has gained from her experience with many hearing-impaired children. Both parents and teacher work together to develop a program to meet the child's and family's needs.

Child-oriented preschool programs seldom give top priority to helping parents develop more competence in parenting or nurturing their child. Daily preschool programs that hearing-impaired children enter when they are three or four years of age need to continue to provide the support parents experienced in infant programs. The child in preschool will develop better language skills if parents can feel competent and confident in their role. The parents continue to be the child's most influential teacher, and if the staff hopes to influence the child's language development, the preschool must include parents on the teaching team. The parents' participation and active involvement in educating and interacting with their own children, in both the home and school environment, is important if the parent is to feel competent in the parenting or teaching role. Dramatic changes need to occur in preschools to implement a program that truly includes parents. Unfortunately, many teacher training institutions provide little or no help to teachers in preparing them to work with parents. The staff of the more effective infant programs usually learned this aspect of their work on the job, and in most instances it was the parents who taught the teachers.

Most programs for deaf infants have developed during the past twenty years. The staff who pioneered the early programs had little experience working with parents and their hearing-impaired infants and toddlers. There were few programs in existence to provide models for the new infant programs. My experience as an infant teacher at the Lexington School for the Deaf, and the changes introduced in the program over the years, are probably similar to the learning process teachers in other infant programs experienced. Describing the changes that occurred may provide insight to the staff of preschool programs as to how they can support parents in their parenting role.

In 1960 at the Lexington School for the Deaf, a program for toddlers was introduced, consisting of tutoring sessions in speech and language. I worked with the toddler while the mother or father sat waiting in the background. These sessions occurred two to three times a week, and each lasted a half hour. Little thought was given to the child's developmental level, family interactions, the parents' feelings and attitudes toward their deaf child, the role of parents as language models or the relationship between language growth and other aspects of the child's development. Few of the toddlers successfully learned language. A tutoring program that had been successful with older hearing-impaired children was being imposed on the toddler. But this kind of tutoring was not appropriate for the toddler's developmental level, and the example the staff set for the parents when using such a tutoring approach confused the parents in their struggle to gain competence in nurturing their deaf child. Parents' questions and comments, and the brief opportunity I allowed myself to observe the parent and toddler interacting, resulted in a program change. The parents taught me that they needed to be involved if their children were to develop any language skills, and the children's response - or lack of response - helped me realize that the content of the program had to be changed so as to be more appropriate to the child's developmental level.

As a result, we changed the program from tutoring the child to demonstrating for the parents, language development techniques that the parents could use at home with their child. This demonstration method was successful for the children whose parents had feelings of competence in nurturing their child. But most of the parents of deaf infants and toddlers did not have such feelings of competence, and the demonstration method frustrated these parents and deepened their feelings of incompetence. As a result, they lost interest in their child and the program, and gradually became less responsive to their child's communications and overtures. The parents taught the teacher that they had feelings and attitudes toward their hearing-impaired child that made it impossible for them to model themselves after her. When the staff realized that the demonstration approach was effective only with the small number of parents who already had feelings of competence and the ability to nurture, they re-evaluated their roles as teachers. They redefined their role to be facilitators of more adequate parenting as well as supportive, nurturing persons to the parent. In order to implement a program whose goal is caring, nurturing parents the staff realized they needed more training. They also saw the need for support programs for parents dealing with their feelings and attitudes toward their hearing-impaired children.

Staff training focused on three areas: teacher's feelings and attitudes toward parents, better understanding of infant and toddler development and the parenting role in that development, and greater insight into parents' feelings about their handicapped child. Teachers attended a series of meetings in which they freely expressed and sought to resolve their feelings and attitudes toward parents that interfered with their ability to support the parent. The quality of parent-staff relationships is vital for a parent-teacher team approach. Without the opportunity to explore their feelings and attitudes toward parents, teachers will not be sensitive to the subtle messages they communicate that may prevent the development of competence in parents.

Weekly play sessions with a group of hearing infants and toddlers and their parents were also scheduled. These provided the staff with the opportunity to observe how hearing children and their parents interacted. The staff gained more insight into infant and toddler development, the role of parents as educators of their children, and they gained more knowledge of language development and how it relates to other aspects of the child's growth and experience.

Another addition to the program was psychiatric supervision for the teachers. Teachers need this supervision and support when the goal of a program is to develop caring, nurturing parents. There are many issues that involve the parent and child with which the teacher cannot deal adequately without such supervision. There are other issues which teachers are not trained to handle, and they need to develop the sophistication to know when and how to make a psychiatric referral. Psychotherapeutic counseling provided by trained personnel became an important part of the Lexington School program for parents. The staff strongly believe that if parents are to experience success in nurturing their child, they must have the opportunity to deal openly with their feelings about their handicapped child. Only if parents have an opportunity to resolve their feelings of denial, loss, sorrow, anger or guilt in relationship to their handicapped child will they be able to feel fulfilled in their parenting role.

THE PARENT-TEACHER TEAM IN THE PRESCHOOL

The preschool classroom teacher can develop a program that gives top priority to helping parents nurture their child. Ideally, the classroom teacher needs to be given time, outside of the classroom, to meet with parents both individually and in groups. Until the administration can find ways of providing this time for teachers, other aspects of a parent-teacher team approach can be implemented. The success of the team-teaching approach depends on the quality of the interaction between all the staff in the preschool and the parents. To improve the quality of parent-staff communications, the staff should be given the opportunity to meet as a group to express freely and seek to resolve those feelings and attitudes toward parents that interfere with their ability to assume their role as facilitators of more adequate parenting. A person trained in psychotherapy should lead the group.

The child's and parent's first year in a school program is the most important. If the parents get no support during their first experience of separation from their child, they frequently withdraw from their child and the program. Teachers have observed that parents come to school often during the child's first few weeks in attendance, but within a short period of time they are seen less often. Have parents gotten the message that their role as parents is not very important, and that the preschool staff will take over the education of their child? The issue of parent-child separation is important to parents as well as to children. Both have feelings of anxiety and uncertainty during this period. A program that encourages the parent to attend the class full time until both the child and parent are able to separate comfortably is ideal. During this period the parent and teacher will have many opportunities to share information and plan together. The parents will have the opportunity to observe and interact with many hearing-impaired children and learn teaching techniques that they can modify and use in their parenting role. Most important, the parents will feel that they are able to support their child during the difficult period of transition from parents and home to school and other caring people - the teachers.

When a comfortable separation has been achieved, the parents should continue to be actively involved in their child's school experience by working as class assistants on a rotating schedule throughout the school year. Parents will continue to feel satisfied as educators of their children and the children in the class benefit by having an additional language model during the school hours. Parents should be encouraged also to serve on school committees and advisory groups. Not only will parents contribute good ideas but they will learn that they are listened to and that their contributions to such decision-making groups are significant. Parents need to know not only that they are welcome in the preschool, but that the the staff considers parents essential to the success of the school program. Provision of an attractive lounge for parents in the preschool area and encouragement of parents to volunteer throughout the school can reinforce parents' belief that they are important.

Group therapy should be available to mothers and fathers. If psychologists, psychiatrists or other appropriately trained personnel are not available to lead such groups, teachers need to urge the administration to provide this support service for parents.

Preschool programs should help parents develop the confidence and skills they need to have success in their parenting role. Parents need to know they will be listened to and respected by the staff. Teachers should encourage parents to be actively involved in their child's school experience during the preschool years. When this occurs, families will have more success in dealing with the responsibilities of parenting as their children grow, and children will have more success in learning language and fulfilling their own intellectual and social potential.

WINIFRED H. NORTHCOTT, Ph.D.

Associate Professor
Mankato University
Department of Special Education
Mankato, Minnesota

11

The Young Hearing-Impaired Child in a LEA Sponsored Pre-School Program

In the fall of 1975 the UNISTAPS Project, a family oriented regional preschool program for hearing-impaired children, birth to four/five years, was validated by the Joint Dissemination Review Panel of the U.S. Office of Education for national dissemination. In the First Chance network are 185 model programs currently funded under the Handicapped Children's Early Education Program (P.L. 91-230, Title VI-C) which are monitored directly by the Bureau of Education for the Handicapped U.S. Office of Education. Only 7 programs to date have received what might be likened to the coveted "Good Housekeeping Seal of Approval" for consumer products. The Parent-Infant Program at Central Institute for the Deaf, St. Louis, Mo., under the direction of Dr. Audrey Simmons-Martin, as well as the UNISTAPS Project, is among this small group.

The acronym UNISTAPS identifies the agencies and institutions which participated in the development of the

TABLE 11-1

1969-1977: AN OVERVIEW

EARLY PHASES	EVOLUTION	OUTREACH

1969-70 Hearing
1973-34 Vision
	1970....Hearing
	- University coursework
	- Conferences: statewide parents; professional staff
	- Workshops: deaf blind
	- Inservice training: Minneapolis staff
	- Inservice: staff of private nursery schools; day care centers; Head Start
		Speech, hearing, language: 1971...
		- 1973 OCD/BEH Collaborative Project (Head Start)
		  - State Advisory Committee
		  - Pilot projects (Head Start and LEA)
		- Host, site visitors
		- Inservice training, site visitation: nursery schools

1973 Head Start (OCD-BEH Collaborative Project)		State Guidelines: Preschool Handicapped, 1974.

1973-74 Noncategorical parent program: low incidence handicaps	1973....Vision
	- Inservice training, Minneapolis staff
		Noncategorical programming, 1974 ...
		- P.S. Administrators; teacher educators; staff preschool prog.
		  - Workshops
		  - Miniconferences
		  - Special study institutes
		  - University/state college

1974 - Noncategorical		

OPERATIONAL	TRANSITIONAL STAGES	TRANSFERRAL
program (Mpls. P.S. [lab]) severely disabled children, 0-4/5 years	- Reading lists - Demonstration teaching - Parent Program (individual) - Group Parent: noncategorical (low incidence handicaps) West Metropolitan (District #287) Regional Vision Services	- Lectures Slide/tape: state/laboratory - Conference/convention presentations (National;State) - Journal articles (1969-1977=19) - Monograph chapters (5) - Consultant services (state, other state; national) - Co-sponsor: University of Minnesota Early Childhood Conferences - Curriculum Guide (0-3): hearing-impaired - Book: Hearing-Impaired Child in regular Classroom: Preschool, Elementary, and Secondary years

Source: Northcott, W.H. and Erickson, L.C. The UNISTAPS Project. A family oriented noncategorical program for severely handicapped children, birth to four/five years. Final Report. 1969-1977. Minnesota Department of Education, St. Paul, Mn. Available: ERIC Clearing House- Handicapped and Gifted Children. The Council for Exceptional Children. 1920 Association Drive, Reston, Virginia 22091.

Project, 1969-1977, as follows: UNIversity of Minnesota; STAte Department of Education; Minneapolis Public Schools. The Project operated in two separate locations: the Minnesota Department of Education, Division of Special and Compensatory Services, St. Paul and the direct service, laboratory program conducted by the Minneapolis public schools under the direction of Lou C. Erickson, Coordinator.

The UNISTAPS Project evolved from a program in 1969, which served only hearing-impaired children. It extended its enrollment in 1973 to visually-impaired children, and in 1974, initiated service on a noncategorical basis. It is an exemplary model (not the model) of early intervention through parent involvement for severly handicapped children, birth to four or five years. It is a prototype of that described in the State Guidelines (1974). It has internal consistency in terms of written goals, objectives, activities to reach them, and a formal evaluation plan designed to improve the system of individualized educational programming for each child and family according to their lifestyle and values. The basic premises are the following: 1. Preschool education for the child and his family should be offered without cost as soon after birth as the diagnosis of handicapping condition is established, 2. The center of learning for any young child is in his home, where his parent(s) or surrogate parents are his first natural, informal teachers, 3. The public school district of the child's residence must find the case, and, through the mandated census law, manage the case, and coordinate the family-oriented educational services in partnership with parents and the health care system, and 4. The multiplicity of causal factors relating to the handicapping condition(s) mandates a. multi-agency involvement (health, education and welfare) b. a multidisciplinary team of specialists to serve the child c. cooperation and coordination among the representatives of institutions responsible for major educational decisions concerning the child and his family.

The directive of the State Guidelines is that services should be available to children without the necessity of labelling the child with a specific term for a disability or handicap. Developmental and behavioral needs of individual children in essential life-skill tasks, are classified into four basic areas: 1. Communication (receptive and expressive language), 2. Psychomotor, 3. Cognitive/linguistic, and 4. Social/adaptive behavior. The focus is on identifying the specialists required to support the child and his family, not on labelling the child with special needs. However, categorical criteria of handicap (medical label) is still required for child count and state funding purposes.

The Regional Program for the Hearing-Impaired: Minneapolis Public Schools, 1969-1974

Change in Entrance Characteristics: 1969-1974

Laboratory program statistics were not kept on hearing-impaired children as a separate category after 1974, when a noncategorical direct service program was introduced. However, from 1969-1974, entrance characteristics revealed encouraging trends for those children having a severe or profound hearing loss. The mean age of diagnosis of children with profound hearing loss (91 dB+) dropped from 23.6 months in 1969 to 12.4 months in 1973-74. In 1969, the mean age of enrollment of children with profound hearing loss (N=29) was 35.2 months. Five years later, the mean age at enrollment dropped to 19 months for audiometrically deaf children. Specific project efforts to increase the awareness of the medical and general community with regard to early identification and treatment of significant hearing loss tend to be underscored as contributing to this trend.

Shattering Myths About Deafness: Field Research Studies

There is nothing inherent in the condition of deafness that makes special class placement automatic. An examination of Table 11-2, showing the educational placement of "graduates" of the laboratory program, highlights the fact that no one setting or method of instruction (<u>oral</u> <u>simultaneous</u>*) is appropriate for all hearing-impaired children. Twenty-five of the 32 children in regular class placement as of 1974 had a severe or profound hearing loss. The "graduates" of the laboratory program with severe or profound <u>congenital</u> hearing losses, who were receiving their education in regular classes with support services, are significant. They serve to highlight the fact that given an intact sensorineural system, a great many children who are labelled "deaf" by audiological assessment have become <u>functionally</u> hard of hearing or partially hearing, as a result of early educational intervention, and are making active use of residual hearing when fitted with binaural hearing aids. They can speak for themselves and can be understood by non-handicapped class-

---

* <u>Oralism</u> and <u>total communication</u> are philosophies, not methods. The <u>simultaneous method</u> adds a form of sign language to speech, speechreading and use of residual hearing which are presented under the <u>oral method</u> of communication.

TABLE 11-2
INFANT-PRESCHOOL PROGRAM:
HEARING IMPAIRED CHILDREN, 0-4,
MINNEAPOLIS PUBLIC SCHOOLS,
EDUCATIONAL PLACEMENTS, FALL 1974

	CHILDREN FIRST ENROLLED IN 1968-1969 (N=65)		ALL CHILDREN ENROLLED 1968-1974 (N=167)	
	N	%	N	%
Total enrolled	65	-	167	-
Number multiply handicapped*	11	-	25	-
Number misdiagnosed (i.e., not hearing impaired)	2	-	4	-
Number for whom deafness is primary disability	52	100	138	100
Infant-Preschool	0	0	19	14
Integrated Program	23	44	40	29
Full day integration in home school	(19)	(37)	(35)	(25)
Full day integration at Lyndale or Hamilton	(4)	(8)	(5)	(4)
Partial integration	3	6	13	9
Lyndale or Hamilton	(3)	(6)	(11)	(8)
Anoka	(0)	(0)	(2)	(1)
Self-contained program				
Aural-oral classes	6	12	28	20
Lyndale or Hamilton	(6)	(12)	(28)	(20)
Total Communication Classes	15	29	24	17
Lyndale or Hamilton	(11)	(21)	(13)	(9)
St. Paul	(2)	(4)	(5)	(4)
Wright County	(0)	(0)	(3)	(2)
Minnesota School for the Deaf	(2)	(4)	(3)	(2)
Moved or no information+	5	10	14	10
TOTAL	52	100	138	100

*Two are EMR children now functioning as regular members of EMR classes; one has been diagnosed as a learning disabled child and is partially integrated at Lyndale School.
+Three were known to be integrated before they moved.

mates. These facts were ascertained in the following field studies:

> Kennedy (1974) examined the peer acceptance and self-perceived status of one group of severely-to-profoundly deaf children enrolled in regular public school classes over a three-year period, compared to a random sample of normal-hearing classmates. The findings were that these hearing-impaired children were as socially acceptable as their classmates and as perceptive as their normally hearing peers in estimating their own social status.
>
> McCauley, et al. (1976) indicated that the overall quality of behavioral interactions of the hearing-impaired children was not significantly different from that of a random sample of their hearing peers, as far as positive/negative and verbal/nonverbal behavior were concerned. However, the amount of positive and verbal interaction with teachers was significantly greater for the hearing-impaired subjects. The normal-hearing group interacted positively and verbally with a larger number of peers than did the hearing-impaired group. Later, Kennedy (1976) involved three language achievement measures and the Key Math achievement test. No significant differences were found among the hearing-impaired group and a randomly selected, equal-sized, same-sex sample of their normally hearing classmates, except for the MAT Word Knowledge where normally hearing pupils scored significantly higher.

Historical Perspective

From the beginning of the Project in 1969, two basic dimensions of educational services were provided for each child and family: 1. An individual parent/child teaching session weekly and 2. Enrollment in a community nursery school around the age of three. Binaural hearing aids were prescribed, when necessary, and individual or small group instruction by a teacher of the deaf was offered once or twice weekly as a supplement to the nursery experience with non-handicapped peers (Northcott, 1977). This pattern of services mirrors the individualized educational preschool programs offered in England and the Scandinavian countries as observed by the author while on a traveling fellowship in 1967. The value of play was universally recognized as being paramount in motivating a young hearing-impaired child to develop good speech attitudes and increased use of residual hearing. Thus, in 1969, two classrooms in a school building in Minneapolis were remodelled to provide a home living center where parent and child, under supervision, made active use of the natural times of interaction - toileting, bathing, feeding, and laughing together - for auditory, cognitive and linguistic stimulation of the toddler. The second portion of the weekly one-to-two-hour parent teaching session was set aside for response to parent questions about daily management of the child. Reports were also made on observed change in activities related to specific behavioral objectives (jointly written by parent and adviser).

Ratio of Hearing to Hearing-Impaired Children in the Integrated Nursery School.

In the state of Victoria, Australia, the ratio of the three-year-olds with hearing loss is three to every seven hearing children; at age four, the ratio is changed to two to 18 normally hearing children. In Stockholm, Sweden, one nursery chair is reserved for a hearing-impaired child among every 20 with normal hearing. At Lexington School for the Deaf, in New York, neighborhood children were enrolled in the special nursery class in an effective "reverse mainstreaming" pattern of integration, with a ratio of even numbers of hearing and hearing-impaired children (Rankhorn, 1974). In Minneapolis, where more than 35 nursery schools have been available in the city and suburbs, generally speaking only one child with hearing loss is placed in each integrated setting.

Across countries and sponsoring agencies or institutions there is clear agreement, regardless of the ratio, that the integrated nursery program offers valuable exposure of a hearing-impaired toddler to models of natural peer group language and behavior in the context of play; it permits creative exploration and development of cognitive awareness on the part of a child, as well. It requires a structured teacher, however, who is attuned to the developmental needs of each child. The practical effect for the hearing-impaired child is the increased use of verbal expression, however imperfect, as a means of gaining attention, assistance and companionship. The focus is on a developmental and inductive approach to language learning - natural (functional) language, natural learning, natural listening: in other words, a developmental and inductive approach to concept learning embedded in language learning through the child's active exploration of his immediate environment.

CHANGES OVER TIME

In the orderly expansion of educational services to severely handicapped children birth to four or five years of age in the Minneapolis public schools, significant changes occurred in the programming of children diagnosed as hearing-impaired (deaf or hard-of-hearing) by medical specialists. These changes have been grouped under major program impact areas within the comprehensive, noncategorical, service delivery system.

Administration and Management

1. The concept of limited responsibility. By 1976-77, no children were served by only one staff member, nine children representing all handicaps were served by two staff persons (the area of professional competence varying), sixteen children representing all handicaps were served by three staff members in different disciplines, and 56 children were served by four or more specialists. The staff had expanded over a period of eight years from one family advisor/teacher to five. A full-time social worker, a speech and language clinician, physical therapist, an occupational therapist, two teacher aides, a Family Education Coordinator, and a Coordinator of the Family Oriented Program were added. A half-time educational audiologist was moved from half-time staff member to a continuing consultant role. This assured multidisciplinary team involvement in the assessment process and direct or indirect educational service thereafter.

Thus, children who demonstrated poor response to auditory learning and a natural approach to language learning could be accurately diagnosed. Children who gave evidence of educationally handicapping conditions beyond the deafness or home conditions where response-ability of essential care-givers was low, also could be assessed.

2. A formal evaluation plan based on a modified discrepancy evaluation model. (Provus, 1971) This approach required 1. the defining of program standards, 2. comparing outcomes to standards to identify discrepancies and, 3. using this information to assess the extent to which, in this instance, hearing-impaired children, families and the program achieved specified standards. Significant educational options were added for children with receptive and expressive communication disorders and/or delays.

3. The seasoned teacher of the hearing-impaired was recognized as central to the transfer of confidence and competence to parents. She took the central role in parent training for modelling and expansion of language and stimulation of listening skill development within the parent teaching and individual guidance sessions.

4. Rearrangement of the professional work week schedule. With a majority of hearing-impaired children programmed into regular nursery schools (tuition being paid through the federal project and supplemented by state special education aids) a family advisor/teacher was assigned to make regular visits to the regular nursery school to observe. She did demonstration teaching and consulted with the teachers about the hearing-impaired child's progress in an integrated setting. These occurred at a minimum of once a month, a full morning each. Evening meetings or participation in periodic family workshops meant a staff member could schedule her next day's appointments to begin at noon.

Services to Hearing-Impaired Children

In addition to the individual weekly Parent-Teaching session for each hearing-impaired child and family, several options were available in a group educational setting. The five alternative settings in which hearing-impaired children could be found are (Northcott and Erickson, 1977):

1. Prescriptive Nursery. There was a short-term assessment stay or sustained-period placement providing a nursery experience three afternoons a week for children. Team observation and individual service from specialized staff members was required prior to other programming decisions. These, in turn, were based on identification of short and long term goals and objectives for each child.

2. Kindergarten Readiness Nursery. This was an option for language-delayed children, including the hearing-impaired child who was a candidate for regular kindergarten class placement at age five. The nursery was structured to provide children with readiness experiences that included the language, concepts and gross and fine motor activities used in the Minneapolis Public School kindergartens. Among these was highly individualized emphasis on specific areas of developmental delay which might interfere with optimum functioning in the regular classroom. Two half days weekly were devoted to to this enterprise.

3. Sensori-Motor Nursery. Parents and infants of young children who could not sit independently or move around in their environment were enrolled in this if their needs were greater than can be provided for during intermittent home therapy sessions. Based on a Piaget framework of cognitive development, this nursery operated twice weekly for one-and-a-half hours each. The physical therapist was in charge of the nursery, with consistent involvement of the occupational therapist and speech clinician, and other staff members as appropriate. Four infants and a parent for each comprised a maximum nursery group. Parents also attended monthly parent meetings on child development and parenting topics jointly determined by staff and families.

4. Special Nursery: Hearing-Impaired. A teacher pursued a highly structured, sequentially developed, auditory/oral approach to language learning, which was chosen by the vast majority of parents of hearing-impaired children enrolled. This included placement in a regular nursery school in the community around the age of three (regardless of the degree of hearing loss). However, it was deemed necessary for some children to add a more visual language through the simultaneous method of instruction, under the philosophy of total communication. In 1976-1977, four children were enrolled in this special nursery. By definition, total communication in this nursery refers to the use of audition, speech, speechreading (lipreading plus body language), formal signs, natural gestures and some simple written language. Fingerspelling and most written language were not appropriate at this early maturational level. A highly individualized approach to language development was used, utilizing some or all of the above. For one child, (a retarded deaf child) single words were the most appropriate interaction tool. For another, a child with auditory agnosia and a moderate hearing loss, language was developed in three steps: 1. sign alone, to reduce sensory input, 2. sign and speech, and 3. speech without the sign. For another child who exhibited no other handicaps, short, simple phrases were used. The main goal for each child was comprehension of language in an experiential setting. The system of sign that was used was SEE (Signing Exact English.) However, it is not a guarantee that the child will understand what is said to him (Anderson, 1977).

Services for Parents

The addition of a Coordinator of the Parent and Family Education, Guidance and Counselling Program in 1974, re-emphasized the dual focus of the partnership of parents and staff in joint design of activities in three-month intervals throughout the year. The dual focus was on the following: 1. attention to the support of the parent (affective and instructional domains) and 2. presentation of factual material concerning the child's handicap, development, management and education. The smorgasbord of offerings included: weekly morning meetings; evening sessions monthly; family workshops on Saturdays, once a month; integrated nursery observation; home visitation periodically; individual parent teaching session weekly as needed; home and agency services coordinated, individually.

Parents of hearing-impaired children signed an individual contract with the primary case manager of their child's program, indicating the amount of participation they could effectively manage in a given three-month period. With the existence of a noncategorical program of educational services, parent interest in cross-cagegorical nuclear and extended family meetings varied sharply. Shared feelings and priorities seemed to relate to the prognosis for special or regular classroom placement upon reaching the formal school years. A second bond among parents in their choice of support meetings was the developmental age of the child in a particular life-skill area (e.g., communication skills of receptive and expressive language). Exploration of all available educational settings for hearing-impaired children of elementary and secondary school age and discussion about the implications of method and degree of functional deafness remained disability-specific, at parents' request.

Staff Development

During the first five years of the UNISTAPS Project, 1969-1974, rich variations in professional growth opportunity were available. They ranged from attendance and leadership roles in workshops, conferences, conventions and seminars, to course work, consultation with specialists and formal inservice training. This last dimension can be categorized as 1. disability-specific, 2. general early child development, 3. normal developmental expectations vs. deviancy vs. dysfunction and 4. practical issues that assure quality control in programming for children and their families. Two of the three consultants judged by the staff to be most valuable among the plethora of specialists engaged over an eight year period, were outside the field of special education. The areas of consultant support were: 1. Directive and nondirective counselling techniques related to three dimensions of the dynamics of interpersonal communication: a. receiving and giving information, b. building a trust relationship, and c. encouraging redirection and responsibility in parents and essential others in the hearing-impaired child's life. 2. Developmental characteristics of young children in essential life-skill areas. First-place "winner," by all criteria of consultant impact directly on the quality of services to child and family, was Doreen Pollack, Director of Speech and Hearing Services, Porter Memorial Hospital, Denver, Colorado. Her workshops in Minnesota and "hands-on" demonstration of the techniques related to the systematic encouragement of a young child to learn to listen, to be aware of sound (environmental and speech), to discriminate, attach meaning and respond appropriately in spontaneous verbal communication, remain vivid in our memory. Subsequent participation by the staff in Mrs. Pollack's seminars and workshops in Colorado resulted in the method of instruction being systematically changed from a visual/oral to an auditory/oral one, in the Minneapolis public school laboratory program of the UNISTAPS Project.

The process of building a cohesive multidisciplinary team of specialists to serve severely handicapped children and their families was painful and slow. A saying "Hell hath no fury as a vested interest masquerading as a moral principle" comes to mind. The shift of individuals in the Coordinator role, from a disability-oriented specialist to one whose training and competencies were in the area of health care delivery and communiversity educational services (non-categorical) facilitated the integrative process.

SUMMARY

The Family Oriented Special Education Preschool Program (birth to four/five years) in the Minneapolis Public Schools includes hearing-impaired children (deaf and hard-of-hearing) and staff members with specialization in the area of deafness. They are responsible, as primary case managers, for the language development program involving all children whose primary developmental delay is in the communication skill area. Each is a serious student of her discipline and a seasoned educator as well. Each feels comfortable in the role of support specialist to other members of the interdisciplinary team, at various times.

The UNISTAPS Project has served well as a prototype and model of implementation of the Minnesota State Guidelines: Preschool Educational Programs for the Handicapped in Minnesota. It is not THE model, but A model of excellence, by objective judgement of the Joint Dissemination Review Panel, U.S. Office of Education (Northcott, 1978). The basic premise that the public school district of the child's residence is the case finder, case manager and coordinator of educational services in partnership with parents and the health care delivery system (State Guidelines, 1974) is highly valid today. Special Education laws state "a local school district may contract with public, private or voluntary agencies." (Section 120.17, Subd. 2. Method of Special Education). The state education agency and local education agency offer a stable tax-base; access to computer services and equipment; community awareness of mandated responsibility to serve handicapped children, 4-21 years of age, all disabilities; and continuity of programming through post-secondary school years. The coordination of city-wide non-categorical services to handicapped children from birth to four years of age (permissive not mandatory by state law in Minnesota) is reality. Federal funds, under the Handicapped Children's Early Education Program, (P.L. 91-230, Title VI-C) provided the "seed" which fell on fertile soil. In 1977-1978, 204 children were provided direct service; 109 were of mandated school age (four years plus); 95 fell in the permissive range, birth to four years of age.

EROSION

The decision not to continue the project in 1977-78 through federal funding signaled some minor and major system changes in the Minneapolis program.

1. Tuition payment for nursery school enrollment in a community-based private nursery school has been discontinued.

2. Audiological and ophthalmological evaluations are no longer underwritten by the school district.

3. Over a five year period the regional program for the hearing-impaired, birth to age four/five, was moved three times to totally different locations, during which the efficiency apartments (remodeled classrooms) were lost and the wing-back chairs, round table for parent coffee cups and discussions, stove and refrigerator which were central to the parent-teaching individual sessions each week, were dispersed as well. The quality of parent guidance has remained sterling, nonetheless.

4. Inservice training funds for consultant services and staff-designed in-house coursework are sharply curtailed. The national outreach which led staff and Project Director to

the four corners of the United States, by invitation, has ended.

5. A formal, printed Evaluation Report was not developed during 1977-1978. This may be restored as a target objective of the program next year.

There are clear pieces of evidence of the enduring impact of the Project and the assurance of sustained high quality of educational services for hearing-impaired children in the future, however. The visitors book this year shows guests from several foreign countries as well as many from nearer geographical areas. Three years ago, parents of children enrolled in the program rallied in protest of an impending cut of two and a half professional positions. They generated responses which included statements from the Governor of Minnesota and key urban legislators, two major editorials in our largest city newspapers; parents as guests on talk-shows; letters to the editor and spontaneous offers of assistance - all of it favorable. The positions were not cut. Parents respond to their child's needs.

REFERENCES

Anderson, D. In W. Northcott and L. Erickson (eds.). The UNISTAPS Project. A family oriented noncategorical program for severely handicapped children, birth to four/five years. Final Report. 1969-1977. Minnesota Department of Education, St. Paul, Mn. Available: ERIC Clearinghouse-Handicapped and Gifted Children. The Council for Exceptional Children. 1920 Association Drive. Reston, Virginia 22091, 1977.

Kennedy, P. and Bruininks, R. H. Social status of hearing-impaired children in regular classrooms. Exceptional Children, 1974, 40, 336-342.

Kennedy, P., Northcott, W., McCauley, R., and Williams, S. M. Longitudinal sociometric and cross-sectional data on mainstreaming hearing-impaired children: Implications for preschool programming. Volta Review. 1976, 78, 71-82.

McCauley, R.W., Bruininks, R.H., and Kennedy, P. Behavioral interactions of hearing-impaired children in regular classrooms. Journal of Special Education. 1976, 10, 277-284.

Northcott, W.H. and Erickson, L.C. The UNISTAPS Project. A family oriented noncategorical program for severely handicapped children, birth to four/five years. Final Report, 1969-1977. Minnesota Department of Education, St. Paul, Mn. Available: ERIC Clearinghouse: Handicapped and Gifted Children. The Council for Exceptional Children, 1920 Association Drive, Reston, Virginia 22091, 1977.

Northcott, W. H. Integrating the preprimary hearing-impaired child: An examination of the process, product and the rationale. In M. E. Guralnick (ed.) Early Invervention and the Integration of Handicapped and Nonhandicapped Children. Baltimore: University Park Press, 1978, 207-238.

Northcott, W. H. (ed.) Curriculum Guide: Hearing-Impaired Children - Birth to Three Years - and Their Parents. Alexander Graham Bell Association for the Deaf. 3417 Volta Place, N.W., Washington, D.C. 2007, 1977.

Provus, M. Discrepancy Evaluation for Educational Program Improvement and Assessment. Berkeley, California: McCutchin Publishing Corp., 1971.

Rankhorn, B. Some Effects of Reverse Integration on the Language Environment of Hearing-Impaired Children. New York: Lexington School for the Deaf, 1974.

State Guidelines: Preschool Education Programs for the Handicapped in Minnesota. St. Paul, Minnesota 55101, 1974. Approved State Board of Education, Dec. 9, 1974.

GERRY McCARTHY

Visiting Teacher of the Deaf
Department of Education
Dublin, Ireland

12

A Visiting Teacher Service—Early Intervention in Ireland

Early intervention in Ireland is carried out mainly by teachers of the deaf who visit the homes of the hearing-impaired children. The purpose of this chapter is to outline the rationale upon which our approaches are based and to present some aspects of the methodology which we find to be effective.

It is appropriate to first give a brief description of the system of education of the hearing-impaired which has evolved in Ireland, and how the Visiting Teacher Service fits into this system. Although the two major schools for the hearing-impaired were established in the first half of the last century, it was not until the 1950's that oral/aural education procedures were adopted. With this development came an awareness of the importance of early intervention, and attempts were made by the schools and clinics to provide parent guidance. While the assistance provided by these was of great value, it was recognized that more continuous training and guidance of parents was necessary if the full potential of young hearing-impaired children was to be reached. In 1972, a Ministerial Committee set up to review the provisions for the education of hearing-impaired children, recommended the establishment of a Visiting Teacher Service. One of the functions of this service was to provide guidance for the parents of pre-school and school-age children with impaired hearing. By 1978, the initial target figure for a full complement of personnel (twenty teachers) for the service had been reached.

In Ireland, the schools for the deaf, as those for the hearing, are operated by a combination of state and private enterprise. While funding is provided by the state, the schools are actually administered by religious orders. The absence of a state/private school dichotomy, as well as general consensus on methodology, results in a reasonably uniform approach to education of the hearing-impaired throughout the country. Oral/aural residential and day programs are provided for hard-of-hearing, profoundly deaf and language-disordered children. The two major schools also provide programs using methods variously described as manual, combined or non-oral, for hearing-impaired children who fail to make progress by oral methods. Mainstreaming, as it is known in the United States, has never been a feature of education of the hearing-impaired in Ireland, though there have been several individual cases in recent years.

THE TASK OF THE VISITING TEACHER SERVICE

Northcott (1973) observed that any hearing-impaired child who functions well in social and academic endeavors, and is developing good speech and language, has exceptional parents. It is neither intelligence nor wealth that makes them outstanding, but rather their dedication to their child's welfare. The task of the Visiting Teacher Service, then, is to develop 'exceptional' parents, for only they can provide the frequency and variety of experiences and interactions, out of which communication skills develop. In addition, the stable parent-child relationship is a vital ingredient in reinforcing and motivating the child toward the development of new skills. The visiting teacher, in conjunction with other appropriate agencies, has to communicate to parents:
1. the parents' important role as language models not only for the hearing child, but especially for the hearing-impaired child, 2. the value of the child's residual hearing and the necessity of appropriate amplification, 3. the hearing-impaired child has all the needs and feelings of a normally hearing child. How the visiting teacher carries out this task

will vary with both individual teachers and parents. The rate at which parents assimilate information and guidance varies, as does the amount of repetition required. Social, emotional, and environmental factors may also influence the nature of parent-teacher interaction. Therefore, it is important for the teacher to program appropriately for each family situation according to parent differences.

THE TASK OF THE HEARING-IMPAIRED CHILD

The task of the hearing-impaired child is the same as that of his hearing peer, to acquire a code or system of symbols which permits the production of unique utterances for the purpose of communication (Kleffner, 1973). Though this is quite an achievement, it is no great chore for the hearing child. Through continuous exposure to and experience with language, he has mastered the code by age three. The auditory channel plays a vital role in this mastery, yet no deliberate efforts are required either from the child or from those around him. How much more difficult, then, for the severely and profoundly hearing-impaired child to acquire something that is transmitted through a channel which, to a large degree, he doesn't have.

The fact that the young hearing child actually does develop very complex language skills leads many psycholinguists, among them Lenneberg (1967), to suggest that children are equipped with an innate capacity for learning language. We, along with Moog (1970), feel that deaf children do not differ from hearing children in this capacity, but they must be given enough examples and be allowed to go through a natural order of grammatical development. The Visiting Teacher Service bases its approach on this rationale. We strive to give the hearing-impaired child such awareness of and familiarity with language that the inevitable outcome will be normal language development. However, the hearing-impaired child does not progress through the stages of language acquisition at the same rate as a normally hearing child, nor is the same precision of articulation expected or demanded of him. Rather, a satisfactory voice quality and natural patterning should be the early goals. In our program, we emphasize the auditory processing of fluent connected language, since the language input from the environment is that of connected language and not single words or phrases (Graham, 1976). This approach, characterized by maximum emphasis on use of hearing, comprehensive intervention and emphasis of connected speech input, is known as the Auditory Global Approach. As described by Calvert and Silverman (1975), it is the initial approach for all of the hearing-impaired children in Ireland.

To assist the child in breaking the linguistic code, then, it is essential that teachers be equipped with all the available information on language and its acquisition. Russell, et al., (1976) proposed that teachers of hearing-impaired children should be expected to know as much about language as a teacher of chemistry is expected to know about chemistry. Only out of a global view of language can teachers institute procedures aimed at encouraging the proper sequence of language development. With this knowledge we can recognize the sequential order of certain skills demonstrated by the child, in his acquisition of overall language competence (Simmons, 1966).

THE TASK OF THE PARENT

In the normal course of events, no one would suggest that the responsibility of rearing children to become well-developed, stable persons belong to anyone but the parents. In the case of the hearing-impaired child, the parents' task is even greater. On them falls the burden of maintaining a strong and stable relationship, of providing sufficient auditory and linguistic stimulation and of providing experiences necessary for cognitive, linguistic, social and emotional development. No amount of supportive services - teachers, social workers or clinicians - can relieve the parents of this responsibility.

Just as parent-child verbal interaction is vital for language development in hearing children, so it is for hearing-impaired children too. But the unplanned approach that works with hearing children must be replaced with an understanding of the hearing-impaired child's needs, abilities and difficulties. Only then can the parent-child interaction be fruitful. The interactions (verbal as well as physical experiences) need to be frequent, continuous and deliberate in order for speech and language to develop satisfactorily. How parents relate to their child is also important: they must see him first as a <u>child</u> who wants to be talked to in a friendly, normal, interested manner rather than in a deliberate, unnatural way. Having developed an understanding of typical and atypical language development, the parents must then become aware of opportunities within the home for language growth. Activities which have a high repetition rate, such as eating, cooking, washing and cleaning, are ideal for giving the child exposure to language in a natural and meaningful way (Simmons-Martin, 1975). Parents must involve their child in the family's daily activities not only for the purposes of language growth, but also for cognitive development. In this way, the child's understanding of language will develop in association with the growth in his cognitive skills.

In normal mother-child interactions, it is almost instinctive that the mother talks about the child's immediate personal experiences. The exact same thing should be done with the hearing-impaired child, in order to expose him to the full range of vocabulary and language structures. The mother is also encouraged to provide language which reflects the child's probable thoughts, thus vocalizing both parts of the conversation. van Uden (1968) stresses the importance of conversation for 'global' language and also as a teaching approach. With the very young child, conversation consists of the mother providing comments appropriate to the child's thoughts, as well as her own comments; she provides the child's answers to her own questions and when the occasion demands, provides the child's questions for her own answers. By encouraging him to imitate <u>his</u> part of the dialogue, she is also helping him develop his oral awareness.

Another opportunity for developing language in the home is through the child's play, especially his pretend play. McConkey (1970) outlines five stages in the development of pretend play: exploratory, relational, self pretend, simple pretend, and sequence pretend. The child progresses from holding, mouthing and examining objects to performing actions in a logical order (e.g., putting a doll in the bathtub, turning on the faucet, soaping the doll, splashing, and drying). This development of play can provide meaningful language input, from the low levels of labelling to the higher levels of complex descriptions of activities.

As for any child, it is good for the parent to encourage an interest in books and pictures. Story-telling, nursery rhymes, and finger games are all fun as well as of value, especially in helping the child to recognize and acquire phrase structure.

An environment which is laden with language-generating activities and experiences is very necessary for the young hearing-impaired child's language growth. In general, it is the parents who have the major responsibility of providing the environment and experiences which will foster the development of communication skills: listening, language, speech and cognition. The affective needs of the child are also included as concerns of the parent.

THE VISITING TEACHER SERVICE IN ACTION

The role of the visiting teacher is clearly oriented toward the parents of the hearing-impaired child. Consequently, the purpose of their visits is to provide support and encouragement, to advise and demonstrate, to answer questions and to give information to the parents. Soon after the diagnosis of the hearing loss, the visiting teacher is the person on whom the parent depends most. The advice given by the audiologist is usually forgotten as different emotions and thoughts overwhelm the parents. The teacher can listen to and relieve some of the often irrational worries about the child's intellectual ability, speech ability, and education. It is the role of the teacher to determine each parent's level of acceptance and knowledge about the handicap, and to adapt procedures to their particular needs.

AUDITORY TRAINING

The ultimate goal of auditory training is to have the child receive the maximum amount of speech input, as his impaired hearing will allow. Once the child is successfully wearing the aid, the next step is to develop an awareness of speech through constant and meaningful exposure to it. Even the child with the greatest hearing loss can develop an awareness of time and intensity patterns. The degree to which he will be able to discriminate features of speech will vary, but early training is a vital factor.

Counseling on the hearing aid is important, especially when parents question the value of even talking to their child. The teacher's own enthusiasm and conviction about the hearing aid must serve initially to motivate the parent in perservering with the aid, since the benefits of amplification may not be immediately apparent. The parents must be taught how to operate the hearing aid, and need to understand the importance of checking it often (especially with younger children) to make sure it is switched on and is at the settings recommended by the audiologist. Finally, the parents must develop realistic attitudes as to the role the aid can play in sound awareness and voice quality (Simmons-Martin, 1978).

LIPREADING

The evidence to support the value of lipreading in conjunction with auditory and vibrotactile reception of speech is conclusive, yet the role of lipreading in early language acquisition is a much smaller one than from school age on.

One reason for this is that a young child does not watch faces often enough or for long enough, so that limiting his exposure to speech to only those times when he does watch would be unwise. More importantly, since the prosodic features which convey so much information in the early years are primarily acoustic patterns, it is important that the child first become "hearing-oriented." Instead of using the term "lipreading" or "speechreading", McCormick (1970) prefers "watching for information" because it embraces the aspects of verbal as well as non-verbal communication. When the child does watch his mother's face, she is encouraged to reward him with a pleasant expression and by speaking to him. This response in turn encourages further face-watching by the child. Parents are also reminded of the effects of angle, distance and illumination for visual reception of information. Generally, hearing-impaired children in Ireland are allowed to develop early lipreading skills naturally and without special instruction.

DEVELOPING SPEECH SKILLS

We believe that the proper emphasis in the early years is on the child's receptive language development. After a period of time during which the child has stored a certain amount of language information, speech and language expression develop. Parental approval of and pleasure in their child's cooing encourages further cooing and babbling. Parents can imitate the baby's babbling and even add to its variety by feeding back different consonant/vowel combinations. The child is encouraged to repeat after the pattern, and his approximations reflect not the precision of articulation, but the rhythm and length of utterance. After learning how to imitate and becoming aware that speech is for communication, the child must experience the need to speak. Parents must not anticipate his needs but rather should demand that he first attempt to vocalize them (Simmons, 1970).

In all of these speech activities, the visiting teacher observes the parent-child interactions and makes practical suggestions that are relevant to that specific situation. In her own interactions with the child, the teacher can demonstrate how best to elicit speech from the child as well as how to reinforce his spontaneous utterances.

WHY A VISITING TEACHER SERVICE?

In a country such as Ireland, where the population is small and sparsely distributed, it is felt that early intervention can take place more efficiently through a Visiting Teacher Service than by establishing clinics or home demonstration centers to which parents and children would come. One advantage in our service is the avoidance of tiresome journeys, and the relaxation of families in their own home environment. In addition, Ross (1972) points out that the teacher can demonstrate speech and language stimulation activities using the raw material which every home provides. More importantly, the mother-child interactions can be observed as they occur in the usual home setting. Home visits also allow for a more confidential relationship to be established with the family and the regular calls help relieve feelings of isolation. Our system also helps to get professional assistance to parents very soon after the intitial diagnosis and there is involvment of the extended family and the community in understanding the needs of the hearing-impaired child. However, it is agreed that a demonstration center would have advantages, such as providing the services of all the professionals under one roof. Also, it would provide parents with a greater opportunity to discuss their problems with other parents, and would allow them a break from the sometimes intense emotional setting of the home. Without a doubt, a combination of both systems would be most beneficial. In practice, homes are visited about once a week and the duration of the visit varies from a few minutes to over two hours. The teacher must be flexible and able to use common sense in deciding how long to remain. There are occasions when the visit is clearly inconvenient to the parent, and other occasions when fruitful discussion with the parent or activity with the child can go on for hours. Almost invariably, the teacher can depend on the normal home situation to provide opportunities for speech and language stimulation for the child, and for demonstration and discussion of approaches with the parent. Naturally, the teacher must be prepared to take the initiative if the situation does not provide the opportunities.

There are some general points of which the visiting teacher must always be aware: Fellendorf (1977) gives Northcott credit for identifying MAFA - mistaking activity for achievement, as a trap into which teachers, but more especially parents, can easily fall. Intelligent behavior must not be confused with linguistic skills. Behavior management of the hearing-impaired child is another problem area. It may become necessary for the visiting teacher to point out instances where the child manipulated his family for his own ends. Teachers can then counsel parents on how to control this. Misunderstandings and frustrations often result when the hearing-impaired child is not informed of the limits, set by the family or society, which must be observed. Consistency and much love is required of these parents. It is often the case that the visiting teacher is only one of several professionals seeing the hearing-impaired child. Close cooperation is then required in order to ensure that counseling and advice remains compatible and complementary. Parents can be very vulnerable, and conflicting information can be an additional source of worry and frustration.

In the relatively short time since its establishment, Ireland's Visiting Teacher Service has become a vital aid to parents and their young hearing-impaired children. Members of the service are concerned with increasing their expertise through study, sharing of knowledge and in-service training. We recognize the need for cooperation with assessment services so that even earlier diagnosis of hearing-impairment, especially in hard-of-hearing children, can take place. We are also concerned about the need to identify as early as possible other factors which may impede the child's language and learning. In summary, in the daily operation of the service, the visiting teachers assist parents to understand their children's development, set realistic goals and to work consistently towards achieving these targets.

REFERENCES

Calvert, Donald R. and Silverman, S. Richard. Speech and Deafness. Washington, D.C.: A.G. Bell Association, 1975.

Fellendorf, George. What when wrong? Talk. 1977, 83.

Graham, A. Catherine. An analysis of chart stories. Unpubl. Study, Central Institute for the Deaf, 1976.

Kleffner, Frank R. Language Disorders in Children. New York: Bobbs-Merrill Company, 1973.

Lenneberg, E. Biological Foundations of Language. New York: John Wiley and Sons, 1967.

McConkey, Roy. Learning to Pretend. Handbook P.I. St. Michael's House Research, Dublin, 1970.

McCormick, Barry. A Parent's Guide. London: The National Deaf Children's Soc., 1970.

Moog, J.S. Approaches to teaching pre-primary hearing-impaired children. A.O.E.H.I. Bulletin, 1970, Vol. 1.

Northcott, Winifred H., (ed.). The Hearing-Impaired Child in a Regular Classroom. Washington, D.C.: A.G. Bell Association, 1973.

Ross, Mark. Principles of Aural Rehabilitation. New York: Bobbs-Merrill, 1972.

Russell, W. Keith, Quigley, Stephen P. and Power, Desmond J. Linguistics and Deaf Children. Washington, D.C.: A.G. Bell Association, 1976.

Simmons, Audrey Ann. Language linguistics for the hearing-impaired. In Jean Utley Lehman (ed.), Disadvantaged Deaf Children Institute Papers. California State College at Los Angeles, 1966, 100-117.

Simmons-Martin, Audrey. Chats With Johnny's Parents. Washington, D.C.: A.G. Bell Association, 1975.

Simmons-Martin, Audrey. Early management procedures for the hearing-impaired child. In Frederick Martin (ed.), Pediatric Audiology. New Jersey: Prentice-Hall, 1978, Chap. 10.

Simmons, Audrey Ann. Motivating language in the young child. In Jean Utley Lehman (ed.), Selected Readings in Language for Teachers of the Hearing-Impaired. New York: Simon and Schuster, 1970.

van Uden, A. A World of Language for Deaf Children. Part I. Institute for the Deaf, Saint Michielsgestel, 1968.

LUISA E. PACHANO, M.S.

Professor, Special Education Department
Instituto Pedagogico
Universitario de Caracas
Caracas, Venezuela

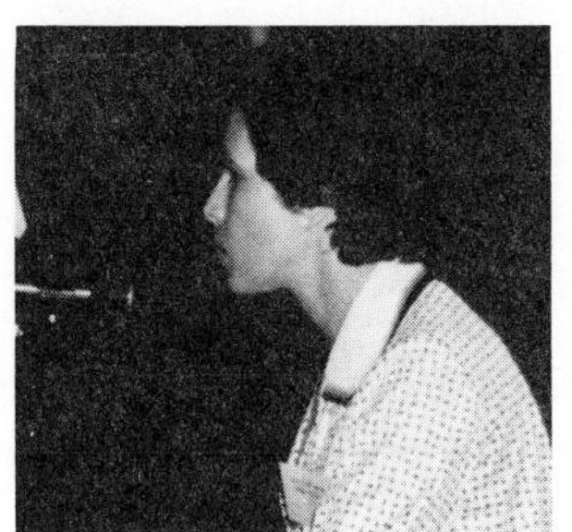

13

A Program for Early Language Development

Speech is one of mankind's greatest achievements. Communication is probably man's most basic need, and it is through the unique media of language that men interact with each other. It is language that enables us to share experiences and culture, and to pass these on to our successors. Language occurs with such spontaneity and ease in our life that we rarely appreciate its importance; rather, we frequently ignore its relevance. Nevertheless, without language, society as it is today could not have been conceived. We acquire language gradually from the moment we are born, apparently with no effort and almost without notice of it.

Recognizing the very important role of language in the satisfaction of one of man's greatest needs (that of communication), it becomes clear that adequate language development in the child is essential. The very early period of a child's life, from birth to the age of five, seems to be the most critical not only for his general development but especially for his cognitive and linguistic growth. Both areas depend upon stimulation for adequate development: language requires an environment that promotes communication, and cognitive skills develop only as a result of interaction with the environment. Among the many skills the child acquires during his preschool years, learning to talk seems to be the most difficult and yet the most marvelous of all.

Our program at the Center for Early Language Development in Caracas, Venezuela recognizes the importance of stimulating the young child's overall learning while emphasizing language development. To this end, experiences are provided which allow richer and more meaningful interactions with the home environment, resulting in a more effective learning.

Parents are directly involved in the stimulation process which takes place in the home during family activities. We feel that parent-child interaction in a home setting is more natural and provides many more opportunities for spontaneous communication than would occur in a clinic or school setting. In this respect, the Center's facilities closely resemble a home setting in design, furniture and other decorative features. The lobby substitutes for a regular living room, "activity rooms" are more like playrooms in the home, bathrooms are similar to a child's bathroom with decorated wallpaper, and so on. Wicker furniture, curtains and cushions decorate all rooms. The warm and informal home atmosphere serves as an important motivating factor for full family participation in the program. The setting has proven to be attractive and comfortable to families belonging to different socio-cultural and economic levels as well. Attention is also given to acoustic aspects in order to provide optimal conditions for oral communication. Features such as wall-to-wall carpeting, acoustic tiles in the ceiling and the wicker furniture all contribute to an environment that promotes conversation and communication among those who attend the Center's various programs.

We provide services in the following manner for children with normal overall development, for children with communication disorders and for children with hearing impairments. We have a nursery program for normally-developing children between one and five years of age. Groups of fifteen children are formed according to their ages. At present, we have five groups divided as follows: one to one-and-a-half years, one-and-a-half to two years, two-and-a-half years old, three to four years, and four to five years of age.

During the school year, these children attend the nursery program for four hours every morning. Preschool teachers in charge of the groups carry out a program of planned experiences which are based on natural situations and are carefully developed to stimulate learning in general and to foster communication in specific. Such experiences include stimulation in motor skill development, cognition, language, and socialization. Because of close family participation during group activities, each child can be given individual attention and additional intensive stimulation in his weaker areas of development. As the child advances in his learning he is progressively incorporated into various activities at different group levels. In this way, each child is allowed to progress at his own rate and manner.

In this nursery program we pay close attention to "high risk" children who are apparently following normal patterns of development but who should be carefully observed during their early learning years. These children are evaluated quarterly in medical, psychological, linguistic and educational areas.

Children with communication disorders or hearing impairment, as diagnosed by a multi-disciplinary team of professionals, also receive training and education at the center. Parent and child come in for individual or small-group sessions in which stimulation techniques for the development of communications skills are taught by trained personnel. Parents observe, practice and receive instructions for the development of activities to be carried out at home. They are given criteria for communication and language stimulation and are encouraged to promote continuous communication between family and child throughout the day. In this way, daily family activities such as eating, playing, bathing and dressing become more meaningful to the child when the family shares and talks about the activity with him.

Besides the training for the development of language and communication skills that enable the child to participate in large groups, he also receives training in other areas if it is considered necessary. Those children who acquire the above-mentioned skills are gradually integrated in the regular nursery program, maintaining a ratio of one child with communication disorders or hearing impairment for every four to five normally developing children. On the other hand, children with severe problems whose progress is slow continue to receive stimulation and training in individual sessions or are transferred to special schools.

For hearing-impaired children, our goal is the development of oral language by means of the Auditory-Global Method as the initial approach. Great importance is placed on the need for early identification of hearing loss in order that the auditory modality can be stimulated simultaneously with cognitive, social, emotional development, and, importantly, language growth. Our program is designed to provide the child with opportunities for developing speech primarily by use of the auditory channel, the input being fluent connected speech. Prior to entering the center for his education, each child is evaluated by a team of professionals for precise diagnosis in order to develop a well-planned program for the child. Not having our own diagnostic facilities at the center, we work closely with the diagnostic team that is organized for each child's case. For the audiologic evaluation, it is important to establish a threshold and hearing spectrum in order to utilize effectively the residual hearing through the use of amplification. The audiologist uses either evoked response audiometry or impedance testing, depending on the child's age. Adaptation of aids is also done by the audiologist by means of the procedure used at Central Institute for the Deaf, St. Louis. Parents receive instructions for proper use and maintenance of the aid, and its proper functioning is technically checked on a periodic basis.

Activities for the development of oral education take place at home and at the center. We focus on the child's total environment and orient all those persons with whom the child relates to stimulate communication at all times through all sense modalities. Especially important, however, are meaningful auditory experiences with the input being fluent connected speech and other sounds of his immediate environment. Situations are arranged for the child to associate spoken language with observation and action during daily life activities. The child's environment must be positively responsive to the child's utterances and must progressively reinforce those sounds that will lead toward the development of speech sounds. The child is given opportunities to imitate oral patterns varying in length, intonation and rate of utterance.

Parent education at this center is oriented toward illustrating to the parents the importance of early stimulation, and to provide training in language stimulation for use during daily home activities. We meet with parents individually or in groups. Our personnel makes itself available to parents in order to maintain frequent communication with them. In addition, periodic individual meetings with each family are scheduled according to the needs, as follows: quarterly meetings with parents of normally-developing children and those included in the high risk register, and monthly meetings with parents of children with communicative disorders or hearing impairment. Meetings, conferences, and short courses are conducted in groups. All parents are encouraged to attend general meetings in which topics of common interest are discussed. There are also group meetings for parents, according to the child's age, for discussion of topics related to normal child development. Lastly, parents of children with communicative disorders or hearing impairment meet, as professionals of the field discuss with them topics related to the specific problem of the child and family. Short courses are being developed in response to the needs observed during our work with both children and parents.

In the manner described, we hope that the child may acquire effective skills of communication and develop language adequately for a far-reaching participation in his society.

A.M.J. vAN UDEN, pr., Ph.D.

Director
Institute for Deaf Children
St. Michielsgestel
Netherlands

14

Hometraining Service for Deaf Children in the Netherlands

General Survey of Services Available in the Netherlands

There are many aspects to the hometraining service for hearing-impaired children in the Netherlands. By "home-training service," I mean the expert service given to parents (or their substitutes) of hearing-impaired children and to the children themselves from birth to, at the most, six years of age. This service is offered outside the schools by audiological centers, which must be acknowledged as such by the governmental Department of Health. There are two kinds of audiological centers in the Netherlands: one kind is a department in a hospital (mainly a university hospital). A few of these centers are not fully integrated into hospitals, but still work in close cooperation with them. The other kind of audiological center is based in a special school for hearing-impaired children and is responsible only for the children in that particular school.

Questionnaires were sent to all of these audiological

centers in order to gather statistical data about the services offered in the Netherlands. We were fortunate to receive a 100% response to these questionnaires. The results are as follows:

Audiological centers in hospitals. There are sixteen such centers in our country, two of which are not limited to children. The following information applies to the remaining fourteen centers. Three centers have a section in which healthy hearing-impaired children can be accommodated for several days or even weeks for intensive observation; eleven centers have no such service. All fourteen centers offer hometraining service through both home visitation and individual treatment at the center; three add training through correspondence, and four have group instruction for parents. None of the centers has an apartment to accommodate parents and children together. In all fourteen centers, the staff has expertise in the following areas: audiology, otology, psychology, acoupedics (expertise in audiometric testing and treatment of hearing-impaired children), speech therapy, medical social work, and technology. In addition, pediatric expertise is demonstrated in thirteen centers, neurology in nine centers, habilitation in six centers, instructional methods in three centers, elementary education in two centers, early childhood education in two centers, and family therapy in one center. Many of the audiological centers have contacts with other educational centers as well. Thirteen centers are continuously in touch with one or more schools for hard-of-hearing children, ten centers are in contact with schools for normally hearing children, nine centers deal with schools for profoundly deaf children, nine centers have contacts with centers for remedial teaching, eight centers are in touch with nursery units for health-endangered children, six centers communicate with centers for medical and socio-educational counseling, five centers are in contact with observational clinics for children, and four centers keep in touch with institutes for the study of child development.

Guidance for families with a hearing-impaired child is given in thirteen centers by a specialized social worker, in twelve centers by an audiologist specialized in aural rehabilitation of children (an acoupedist), in eight centers by a speech teacher, in five centers by a psychologist, in four centers by an habilitation specialist, in two centers by a nursery school teacher, in two centers by an elementary school teacher, and in two centers by a pedagogue. The main work is usually done by the social worker. Many centers offer more than one specialized service, so there is overlap in the centers enumerated above.

All fourteen centers refer the profoundly deaf child to a hometraining service in a school for the profoundly deaf as soon as the children are judged to be ready and/or the parents are ready to accept it. Nine centers are specialized in both hard-of-hearing and prelingually deaf children; five deal only with hard-of-hearing children and immediately refer the profoundly deaf to hometraining services in schools for the deaf.

Audiological centers in schools. There are twenty-two schools for the hard-of-hearing and five schools for the profoundly deaf in the Netherlands. Three schools for the profoundly deaf have their own audiological center and their own hometraining service; one school does not have either, but is in continuous contact with one or more of the audiological centers in nearby hospitals. One school for the deaf is in the same building as an audiological center, and shares the same director. The audiological centers in schools are staffed by an audiologist, otologist, psychologist, acoupedist, speech teacher, and pedagogue.

Hometraining is carried out mainly by specialized social workers. Three schools for the profoundly deaf have an apartment to take in a profoundly deaf child for diagnosis and treatment; two of them have an apartment to take in the child with his parents as well. The hometraining service of St. Michielsgestel has an itinerant teacher of the deaf who visits the homes of profoundly deaf children, ages two to three, in order to give speech training at home.

Statistical Survey of Programs

During the period 1972-77, there were approximately 1000 profoundly deaf children 4-16 years of age in the Netherlands. All of them were enrolled in the five special schools for the profoundly deaf. Practically no profoundly deaf children in this age range have been mainstreamed. In contrast, very many of the profoundly deaf children 17 years of age or older are integrated into normally hearing schools (primarily vocational schools).

During the same period of time, there were approximately 4000 children in the age range of 4-16 years in special schools for the hard-of-hearing. There are no partially-hearing units and/or itinerant teachers in the Netherlands. Based on statistics, we would expect to find approximately 10,000 hard-of-hearing children in the country, i.e., children with a degree of hearing loss that requires that they receive special treatment. It can be concluded, then, that the majority of hard-of-hearing children are not in special schools, but in schools for the normally hearing (regular schools and/or schools for other handicaps).

Studies have also been made of average age of detection of hearing loss, of referral to experts, and of start of treatment (van Uden, 1963). In cases of profound hearing loss of more than 90 dB, the impairment is detected earlier, the children are referred to an audiological center at a younger age, and the amount of time parents wait in seeking an evaluation after they first suspect a hearing loss is less than in cases of severe hearing loss of 60-90 dB.

Recently (1977-78) we investigated the medical histories of thirty-four deaf children in our preschool, aged 4.1 - 5.8, who had had at least one full year of hometraining before entering our school. (Eight children entered our school between ages four and five without any previous hometraining. These were mostly children of immigrants, foreign workers, and the like). From these cases we obtained the following data:

Average age of detection of hearing loss: 14 ± 3 months

Average age of referral to an audiological center: 22 ± 6 months

Average starting age of participants in our hometraining service at St. Michielsgestel: 27 ± 11 months

Average age of receiving the first hearing aid: 25 ± 7 months

There seems to be much too long a delay between the detection of deafness and the first effective help--an average of 12 months. Sometimes the parents were sent from pillar to post before they finally contacted an audiological center; sometimes audiological centers had too long a waiting list, especially for lengthier observations requiring more than one day; sometimes audiological centers seemed to have hesitated much too long in advising the parents to go with their child to a hometraining service of a school for the deaf; sometimes, unfortunately, parents were opposed to the idea of going to a school for the deaf. Very often a deaf child did not get a hearing aid at all before coming to our Institute. Twenty-five of the thirty-four profoundly deaf children were given their first hearing aid by our own audiological center in spite of the fact that they had been seen at another audiological center prior to coming to us. Usually the best service at the audiological center in St. Michielsgestel is associated with cases of hereditary deafness, that is, deaf children of our own former deaf pupils. We are usually alerted to these children a few months after their birth through our after-care service.

Special note should be made of the use of manualism in our country. The problem of total communication has come up only recently in the Netherlands. There are very few people who know a systematic sign language. Historically, there were two sign languages, one in Groningen and one in St. Michielsgestel, but they have been almost completely forgotten. At the present time, the hometraining services in our country are using neither sign language or fingerspelling.

The Philosophy of the Hometraining Service at St. Michielsgestel

Our institute started its hometraining service in 1955 with qualified home-visitors. Through the past 23 years of experience, we have witnessed a definite improvement in the attitudes of parents and in the effects of education.

One of our objectives is the prevention of "mutism" and "deafism." Mutism is a behavior characterized by silence, a lack of vocalization; deafism is a behavior characterized by an over-adaptation of stillness, to the absence of sound. Because all deaf children (if not multiply-handicapped) babble (Mavilya, 1969), look at people's faces, and can perceive sound through a hearing aid, we believe that lipreading and auditory training should start as soon as possible in order to transfer these natural tendencies and abilities to aural-oral behavior without any discontinuity. Ideally, hometraining should start immediately after birth (van Uden and van Uden, 1957; van Uden 1959; 1963).

We believe that the parents face a special challenge in that they are the backbone of their children's education (van Uden, 1977). This is true for several reasons. First, without acceptance, the child cannot be a happy human being, even as an adult. Lack of love in the first years of life results in a hunger for love that lasts a lifetime (Maslow, quoted by Allport, 1964). Second, without the parents' full cooperation, the educational effort cannot succeed. This is required of parents especially in the area of reading. "True" reading begins at ten years of age in a normally hearing child in a regular school, given that the normal program of education is followed (Smith, 1971; van Uden, 1975). True reading, therefore, is the ability to read at least the reading books written for the average ten-year old. This requires (in the Dutch language) a sight vocabulary of at least 7000 words with a total of about 15,000 meanings. A deaf child would begin to learn how to read at four years of age. With 200 school days in a year, it would add up to 1400 school days by the time the child reaches ten years of age. He would need to learn, then, on the average about <u>ten new word meanings every school day</u>. This is impossible, by far, for most deaf children; the school simply cannot accomplish that. The complete cooperation of the parents is absolutely necessary in conversing frequently with their child, in explaining things to him, and in working on reading and writing with him at least one hour a day. But even then, the collective ability of the parents and school is not enough. A more realistic goal for deaf children who are not multiply-handicapped is true reading by 16 years of age, with an average of three to four new meanings learned each day (including weekends and holidays). Parents must accept their share of the responsibility of educating their child, for only they can guarantee the continuity of education.

Education in general is the activity of guiding children to an adult human existence, i.e., to a meaningful life, by love. It is the activity of guiding them to unhampered self-actualization, relative independence, and social integration (cf. Korherr and Hierzenberger, 1973). This calls for "basic trust" (Erikson, 1963), a reliable survey of situations, feelings of security, and continuous models of human values, from early childhood through about 18 years of age. If the conditions are not fulfilled, education may fail--adult existence is not reached. The individual may be impeded by inner conflicts, lack of social empathy, and lack of realism in life. No school and/or residence can completely provide for these conditions because they lack continuity. Only the parents can and should provide this continuity. Thus, even if a child is in residence at a special school, he should feel the complete support of his parents.

Integration into the hearing society requires first integration into one's own family. The formation of minority groups is undesirable not only for society as a whole, but for the individual who builds up feelings of distrust and resentment. A "minority formation" is a sociological phenomenon such that the members of the group become dependent upon that group for their main social contacts, to the exclusion of other groups. It has been shown that such a dependency <u>can</u> be prevented among the deaf and the deaf multiply-handicapped (van Uden, 1972, V) when social integration within one's own family is first accomplished. This is possible even for families with oral deaf parents. There is strong evidence that a crucial factor in successful integration into the hearing society is the adequate development of acceptance processes by the parents, who promote "basic trust" (see above) in their children. Rodda (1970) has shown that those deaf who enjoy the fullest social integration with the hearing are those who show a "charming character," usually the fruit of these well-developed acceptance processes.

Our Institute endorses separate facilities for deaf children, according to their potential and progress. There are quite a few deaf children who need very specialized care beyond that required by other deaf children. They need not only small classes and small groups in the dormitory, but also more highly qualified personnel in order for their education to be a success. The practice of grouping all deaf children together regardless of differences is harmful to individual growth, and tends to promote the formation of minority groups among the deaf. Early diagnosis of multiple handicaps is necessary to identify both learning disabilities and emotional disturbances. Therefore, each school for the deaf must be selective in order to allow each deaf child to realize his full potential. Our institute is not selective on the campus itself. We are fortunate in that the Ministries of Education and of Health provide facilities for deaf-blind children, for deaf children with subnormal intelligence, and for deaf children with learning disabilities. These different children live in separate facilities each of which is organized, staffed, and equipped according to the special needs of its children. Their common goal is to realize each child's full potential in communication, in school achievement, and in human growth.

When programs are organized to meet the needs of the individual, then his particular abilities and talents come to light. Here are some exemplary cases (van Uden, 1977). The belief that the prelingually profoundly deaf can never accomplish real artistic creativity (Revesz, 1946) has been refuted by the fact that at least one prelingually profoundly deaf woman, Annemarie Leenders-Kusters, has been certified, *cum laude*, as a sculptress by an Academy of Arts. The general opinion that the deaf can never accomplish any significant scientific work is challenged by the fact that several deaf persons (Peter Heezemans; Irma van Gorkum-van Diepen; Toos Verdonschot-Kroef), have done studies of acknowledged scientific value. The fact that many deaf persons participate in sports activities alongside their hearing competitors refutes the belief that the deaf can never excel in physical activities or athletics. (van Uden, 1965) Some of them have achieved the highest award in the country

(Caspar van Beek, ballroom dancing; Hetty v.d. Ven, archery; etc.). How often has it been said by authoritative people that "the deaf" are unable to do this or that. It is mainly because they have never seen highly accomplished deaf children and adults. The selectivity mentioned above is necessary in order to keep the mind of the hearing world open to the real possibilities that exist for deaf children. And this does not apply only to gifted deaf children, but very often to the multiply-handicapped too, if we consider each child within his own setting.

We are fortunate to have our own hometraining service. Until 1955 there was no hometraining service for deaf children and their parents in our country, apart from some exceptional individual treatment. We started this work with our own funds. It was difficult getting our service acknowledged by such official authorities as The Ministry of Education and even now it is not yet fully financed by them. This situation is not traumatic, however, because our hometraining service is just a part of the whole network of services we offer. Because of the follow-up care program we began in 1942, the philosophy of our education can now be applied from the very beginning of a child's life, through his early years.

How Our Hometraining Service Works

Educational methods and didactics will not be explained at this point, rather, the basic procedures involved in our service will be presented through an exemplary case. Let us suppose that some parents write or come to our director, telling him that they supposedly have a deaf child eight months of age. Soon afterwards the principal of our hometraining service visits the parents in their home to observe and collect data for the case history. His report is then discussed by the enrollment team: the director, the otologist (physician-coordinator of the institute's health service), the audiologist, one of the psychologists, and the principal himself. An initial visit to our audiological center is scheduled for the parents and their child.

Presently the hometraining service is comprised of three specialized social worker-instructors, one of whom is assigned to each family. After each visit the instructor makes a note of visual attentiveness, his babbling behavior (intonation and articulation), his reaction to sound from the radio, television, and sound-making toys she brings with her; play behavior; manner of handling, especially by the mother; the nature of the family constellation; etc. In particular, she teaches the child, with the cooperation of the mother, to respond to some simple commands. When the child is thoroughly familiar with the social worker, the parents are invited to come to our audiological center where the instructor arranges a meeting together with the audiologist and psychologist. As soon as possible, the child is fitted with a hearing aid.

The instructor visits the parents frequently, about once a week or once every two weeks, depending on the need. Methods, programs, educational procedures, instruction, future opportunities, and so on, are discussed with the parents. From time to time, the family's progress and problems are discussed with the principal. Sometimes the psychologist is consulted; sometimes medical specialists are also called in, in cooperation with the otologist of the institute. Another visit to the audiological center is scheduled in order to test auditory response, hearing aid performance, etc., and in order to arrive as soon as possible at a fully reliable audiogram.

As soon as the child can walk (on the average at age two) an observational week is scheduled, in a specialized building fully equipped for this purpose. There are observation rooms with one-way windows, playrooms, speech amplifiers, mirrors, videotape recorders, etc. The home-like decor and furnishings of the department are designed to appeal to children. The crucial point about this observational week is that the instructor invites about three of her other case children, and stays with all of them each night of the week. This is to prevent emotional trauma in the child; the experience should be pleasant, and indeed most children are happy and content during their stay. The child becomes familiar with the institute which will be his future home for many years. He meets the housemothers, the teachers, the psychologist, and others on the staff.

The child is evaluated again by the audiologist, psychologist, and otologist; in addition, he is seen by the ophthalmologist, and very often by the neurologist, too. It is important to find out whether the child, apart from his intelligence, has any other handicaps affecting any of the following areas (van Uden, 1974):

- his motoric behavior--seizures, athetosis or athetoid reactions, ability to perform coordinated movements, seen mainly in relation to social maturity (van Uden, 1972).

- his intermodal integration behavior--whether sensory and motor experiences are smoothly becoming integrated (this aspect of behavior is investigated by means of an observational inventory of coherent versus chaotic behavior).

- his personality (van Uden, 1973)--extroversion-introversion; behavior exhibiting creativity, inventiveness, and dominance; behavior resembling hysteria; neuroticism and neurosomatism; anxiety; symptoms of desolation.

Some deaf children are in danger of failing to acquire a purely oral mode of communication if they are not given intensive treatment. These are children with dyspraxia or apraxia of speech, related to a general dys- or a-praxia (van Uden, 1972; 1974). There are other deaf children who are in danger of never acquiring verbal language if they also are not treated intensively. These are the children with disorders of intermodal integration who are impeded by integration-dyslexia and dyssymbolia. Usually the initial observation does not yield a clear diagnosis, but it may indicate a warning. Definite problems become apparent by the time the child is four to six years of age. The treatment of the child is then planned according to these findings.

Unfortunately, there seems to be an increase in the number of multiply-handicapped children, which is perhaps associated with an increase in the incidence of deafness in children. We think that a special department in our institute will be necessary in the future, in order to study some very disturbed deaf children who need longer observation and intensive care.

When the child is about two years of age, an itinerant <u>speech teacher</u>, qualified as a teacher of the deaf, is included in the hometraining service. This aspect of hometraining began in 1976 and we hope to be able to provide it to even younger children in the future. At this time we have one speech teacher who treats five to six children, visiting them twice a week at home until they enroll in the preschool at about four years of age. This teacher has composed a check-list (Wetzels, 1978) of phonemes to be filled in by the parents as the child produces them. He has also made up check-lists for future progress in oral-aural behavior. When the child enters our preschool at four years of age, the speech teacher submits a report of the tangible achievements of the child, so that the preschool teachers have an established basis for their teaching.

The building used for the observational week has a two-fold purpose. Observational weeks are scheduled about nine times a year. During the other 31 weeks there are <u>intensive classes</u>, again comprised of about three to five children, depending on their needs and abilities. When the observational week is over, the work at home continues under the guidance of the instructor. After five to eight weeks, the child is again observed for one week. The same housemothers and teachers are there as during the first observational week (very often they have visited him at home), and, most important of all, his instructor is there again. During intensive class, some aspects of the observational week may be repeated, verified, and completed. The audiogram and hearing aid performance are verified; in addition, the child's behavior is tested, especially his motor development and coordination, and intermodal integration. However, the main reason for having the intensive classes, which we started in 1961, is that, unfortunately, not all parents are doing their job equally well.

During the intensive class, the work of hometraining is carried out more thoroughly: the child is given speech training, auditory training, training in lipreading, drawing, social maturity, etc. The parents are kept informed through telephone calls and letters. Very often they visit the child, work with us, and gain extra training in this way when necessary. There is a small apartment where they can stay if necessary. After about five to eight weeks, depending on the child's needs, the intensive class is repeated. In all, the child will have visited this class six or eight times before he is enrolled permanently in the preschool at four years of age. From that time, most children stay for 200 days a year in the school, going home every weekend; a small number of the children are day-pupils. The majority of children two-and-a-half to four years of age are integrated into so-called creches, or day nurseries for infants, and into nursery schools and kindergartens for normally hearing children.

CONCLUSION

The education of deaf children calls for great devotion on the part of parents, teachers, and houseparents: it is perhaps a greater and more intense devotion than is required for the education of children with any other handicap. It is a strong challenge, but handicaps can be overcome and our dear deaf children are worth this effort. May God bless all involved in this work!

REFERENCES

Allport, G.W. Pattern and Growth in Personality. New York, 1964.

Erikson, E.H. Childhood and Society. New York, 1963.

Korherr, E.J. and Hierzenberger, G. *Praktisches Worterbuch der Religionspadagogik und Katechetik*. Herder Freiburg, 1973.

Mavilya, M.P. Spontaneous vocalizations and babbling in hearing-impaired Infants. Unpubl. doct. diss., Teachers College of Columbia University, 1969.

Revesz, G. *Creatieve Begaafdheid*. The Hague, 1946.

Rodda, M. *The Hearing-Impaired School Leaver*. London, 1970.

Smith, F. *Understanding Reading: A Psycholinguistic Analysis of Reading and Learning to Read*. London, 1971.

Uden, A.M.J. van and Uden, L. van. *Het Behoeden Voor Verstomming: Hometraining*. St. Michielsgestel, 1957.

Uden, A.M.J. van. *Erfahrungsbericht uber drei Jahre Haussprach-Erziehung Tauber Kleinkinder*. Neue Blatter fur Taubstummenbildung, 1959, 76-82.

Uden, A.M.J. van. Leeftijd van Ontdekking van Hoorverlies en Leeftijd van Aanmelding, Vergeleken Met Mate van Hoorverlies. Eeen taak voor Volksgezondheid. *Het Gehoorgestoorde Kind*. April 1963, 67-68.

Uden, A.M.J. van. Das Gegliederte Ziel der Hausspracherziehung. In Bericht Uber die Arbeitstagung *Fruherziehung Horgeschadigter Kinder*, Berlin, Aachen, 1963, 93-119.

Uden, A.M.J. van. The physical education of prelingually deaf children: A summary. *The Teacher of the Deaf*. 1965, 307-314.

Uden, A.M.J. van. Techniques for the hometraining of deaf children as employed in St. Michielsgestel. In Uden, *They Will Grow by Human Speech*. 1972, *I*, 1-22.

Uden, A.M.J. van. A soundperceptive method for severely and completely deaf children. Appendix: A program for rhythmical training in hometraining and nursery-school. In Uden, *They Will Grow By Human Speech*. 1972, *II*, 23-55.

Uden, A.M.J. van. Early diagnosis and therapy of dyspraxia of speech in deaf children. In Uden, *They Will Grow By Human Speech*. 1972, *IV*, 84-93.

Uden, A.M.J. van. About the integration of deaf children and grown-ups into the hearing society: The philosophy of St. Michielsgestel. In Uden, *They Will Grow By Human Speech*. 1972, *V*, 94-108.

Uden, A.M.J. van. *They Will Grow By Human Speech: The Deaf Child and His Family*. Washington, D.C.: The Alexander Graham Bell Association for the Deaf, 1972.

Uden, A.M.J. van. Emotional disturbance in deaf children, lecture in Dublin 1973, St. Michielsgestel, 1973.

Uden, A.M.J. van. *Dove Kinderen Leren Spreken*. Rotterdam, 1974.

Uden, A.M.J. van. Methodische Overweigingen Over Het Leren Lezen Door Prelinguaal Doven. Het Gehoorgestoorde Kind. 1975, 75-91.

Uden, A.M.J. van. Should parents play the principal - or a supporting role in the education of deaf children? St. Michielsgestel, 1977.

Uden, A.M.J. van. Het belang van het exemplarisch geval. Dove elite kinderen. Speciaal Onderwijs, 1977, 354-365.

Wetzels, A.F.H. Hometraining in een nieuw perspectief: Een experiment in de voorzorg. Scriptie Diploma-B, St. Michielsgestel, 1978.

RALPH L. HOAG, Ph.D.

Superintendent
Arizona State School for the
Deaf and the Blind
Tucson, Arizona

with Joan Kiser, M.S.

15

The Role of State Schools for the Deaf in Early Childhood and Infant Education

The title of this chapter may suggest, when you first think about it, that a state school probably should have no role at all to play in early childhood and infant education. Early childhood education is thought by many to be an area better served by others. Accordingly, the study and evaluation of state operated schools is in progress in many states. Those schools that do not clearly identify their role in today's educational setting are destined to closure or phasing out. The mission of state operated schools is changing. The larger group of handicapped children being served have special needs and many require the very special attention our state schools are equipped to give. Our state operated programs are as much needed in almost every state and region of our country as they were when they were originally established.

Several national professional organizations have addressed themselves to the problems of this changing world as well as the changing role in program focus needed for all of our schools. The changing population we serve demands this attention on our part. Dr. Barry Griffing, a former teacher of the deaf, now Deputy Commissioner of Education in the State of California, prepared a paper on the subject, "Reshaping the Role of State Schools for the Deaf in Public Education" (1977). When he presented this paper at a national meeting two years ago we predicted that the role of state operated schools would be changing very rapidly as a result of PL 94-142 and other federal legislation on the rights of handicapped individuals. The influence of increasing public and parent interest in what should be offered by all state operated programs has and will have an impact on what state operated schools are organized to do (Mulholland, 1977). Griffing suggests that state operated schools could move toward serving as:

1. A comprehensive educational center,
2. A child study and assessment center,
3. A learning resources center,
4. A demonstration school, and
5. A community continuing education center.

Within the area of service as a comprehensive educational center, he includes preschool involving parent education and home teaching.

The focus here is on early childhood and infant training. The literature is full of reports of research and demonstration programs dealing with early childhood education. Some of the presenters at this international conference have dealt with this topic in one way or another. The need for early intervention has been made very clear (Ruben, 1978; Shah, et al., 1978). The literature also seems to indicate that a major key to more success in this is in the medical profession. This profession is the major link to early identification of high risk children, yet many of its members appear to be among the least concerned. They seem also to be quite limited in their preparation and training in this area. Although their numbers are increasing, still far too few hearing-impaired children who are at risk are appropriately referred for services early enough.

ABOUT ARIZONA

The State of Arizona is the fifth largest in the United States but sparsely populated in most parts of the state. Major population centers are Phoenix and Tucson, about 100 miles apart in the south-central part of the state. The Phoenix area has a population of about a million and Tucson about 500,000. Both are growing very rapidly. Major interdisciplinary universities are located in both cities. Comprehensive services for the population we are concerned about are available in these two areas. In the rest of the state, a million or more citizens are spread over a vast area in small communities involved in mining, cattle, sheep, or farming activities. Educational programs and services for the hearing-impaired are virtually non-existent in these areas, and the potential for providing services in a coordinated way would be almost nil if left to local communities. The only effective way to develop a program of total service to the rural areas of the state with solid links to urban service centers for the support that they can offer is through some sort of statewide service network (Arizona White House Conference, 1976).

The Arizona State School for the Deaf and Blind was established with statutory authority to serve the sensory-impaired in the state wherever services are unavailable in the local public schools. In most parts of the state, the State School is the only source that parents of hearing-impaired children can turn to for help. We have directed our attention to this need. Over the years the school has developed and maintained working relationships with university programs for teacher preparation, speech and hearing, rehabilitation, and counseling. Access to professionals in these fields are additional resources available to the school, the program, the children, and their parents.

In Arizona we have four separate school programs operating under the administrative umbrella of the Arizona State School for the Deaf and the Blind, and the agency provides other services throughout the state as well. On one campus, in Tucson, is a residential/day school with three programs serving some 275 school-aged hearing-impaired children, about 100 visually handicapped students, and about 35-40 seriously multiply handicapped sensory-impaired children. The program for the multi-handicapped is a part of a special educational diagnostic and treatment center designed to investigate and manage the services required for children in this population. In addition, this agency monitors programs for many other sensory-impaired children located in other educational programs throughout the state. On the other campus, in Phoenix, is a day school for hearing-impaired children serving the general Phoenix and Maricopa County area. Some 125 children are enrolled there.

Preschool programs serving children and parents of children in the age range 0-4 have been sponsored by the Arizona State School for a number of years. Currently in Tucson there are two off-campus programs, one for the visually handicapped and one for the hearing-impaired. Both of these programs maintain cooperating links with the university speech and hearing program, the university medical school, community service organizations and volunteer organizations. In Phoenix, the infant-parent education program is currently located in a house on part of the campus of the day school. As a preschool program for the hearing-impaired, it shares in serving the community and county with a privately supported program known as the Samuel Gompers Clinic. Cooperative working relationships exist between these two programs which complement one another in many ways. In addition to our preschool programs in Tucson and Phoenix, our statewide outreach program consists of three parent educators. Two specialists work in the area of the hearing-impaired and one serves in the area of the visually handicapped. Their areas of service and contacts are in the homes of very young, preschool-aged, sensory-impaired children who live primarily in small towns, rural and tribal areas, and hard-to-reach places. In addition to parent counseling, they coordinate diagnostic, social, medical, and other state services to assist in many of their cases.

Our record has been that a substantial majority of children and families served by preschool and outreach personnel have found their way eventually into public school programs. The success record is unquestionably due to early intervention, amplification, parent education and parent support. The major goal of the entire agency with all of its programs is to provide every child with all of the assistance that can be mustered to help him/her develop the skills needed for full involvement and integration into general society. There are, as we know, many levels of competence that can be demonstrated by children in the area of effective functioning in a hearing world. We are steadily moving in the direction of programming for children in a manner that meets their needs educationally and in such a way as to facilitate the exiting into other educational settings as soon as the potential for success appears to be a possibility.

OUR CENTER FOR HEARING-IMPAIRED CHILDREN - CHIC

One outstanding and effective off-campus parent education and preschool program administered by our agency is the one in Tucson known as the CHIC Program. It is supported by Title I funds through the State School, the Southwestern Region Deaf-Blind Center, and the Easter Seal Society of Arizona - a not too uncommon linkage of financial support services. The Center, in a home demonstration setting, serves primarily as a parent education and counseling resource for parents of hearing-impaired children from birth to age four. The major goal of the program is to assist families in understanding their children and in becoming more proficient and active as participants in planning for their child's education. The parent in our program is considered an active participating member of the multidisciplinary evaluation team for their child. The CHIC Program provides short and/or long term training depending on the needs of the family and child. The class sessions range from 45 minutes to two hours daily depending on the age and the educational needs of the child. Many families and children are exited into community preschools after a short-term speech, language, auditory training program, and hearing aid counseling. Other children require more extensive evaluation, education, and training. In any case, a concerted effort is made to enhance and facilitate effective communication between professionals and the families.

In a cooperative team effort, we have found the parent to be an invaluable contributor and observer to the evaluation team. We have found that although the parent may be unable to label hearing loss, he is accurate in describing the child's functional hearing problem prior to amplification. By sharing our observations and experiences mutually, we are able to tap a concerned and accurate resource and enhance the families' feelings of self-worth and competence. The program is not merely a preschool education activity for children. Rather, it is designed in a way to be totally oriented to the family as a whole. The purpose is to increase parents' understanding and knowledge and improve their own communication skills for dealing with others in educational planning for their child, wherever they might be located.

It is our opinion that too often the professional assumes the condescending attitude of "talking to" the consumer rather than "talking with" them. The "father knows best" attitude is unfair to everyone participating in an educational, medical, audiological team because it places an unbalanced amount of responsibility for decisions on the professional. This eliminates the most concerned and one of the most capable members, the parent. Such an attitude fails to recognize that the parent is the one who must carry through the plan and follow up the decisions. It is obvious that parent participation is more active when he or she, or both, are included in the decision-making process at all levels. All too often, one hears professionals say, "Parents don't care, they won't participate", "Parents refuse to be active." There is a solution, and we think we have found a combination of techniques that seem to work. A parent education program with the goals we have should include the following considerations:

1. Mutual communication between the professionals and the family must be a primary goal.
   The professional must want and encourage the parent to make decisions, whether or not the decision is an agreeable one. Additionally, the parent must want to make decisions. By assuming some of the burden of decision-making, greater self-worth and feelings of competence are gradually developed and achieved by the parents.

2. The parent must be involved in a program of instruction of sufficient length, depth, and substance prior to direct involvement in a decision-making meeting dealing with the education of their child.
   That means written records, evaluations, and professional recommendations must be available to parents and they should understand the general content of these records in order to be an effective participant in staffing and program planning activities for their child.

3. Daily feedback including both positive and negative comments on learning activities should be an important part of the parent's program.
   At the Center, parents are able to have constant contact with professionals in speech and hearing. The families become more familiar with technical jargon that they will hear for years to come. Parents are able to observe their children in class through one-way mirrors. There is always a parent-teacher with the family discussing their observations, concerns, and the child-teacher interaction.

4. <u>Parent group meetings, parent education programs and parent assertiveness training programs should be an integral part of a parent-infant program.</u>
   Parents provide additional support and education to parents of newly identified hearing-impaired children. If parents are to be considered contributing members of the educational-medical evaluation team, it is imperative that they receive training in expressing themselves, requesting information, and implementing change.

5. <u>Parents should be considered and dealt with as one of the specialists involved in programming for their children.</u>
   They have the time, interest, and responsibility for the education of their children. They can be primary participants in their child's education if we include them. We as professionals can benefit greatly from their support, observations, and information. They are a teacher's most important resource for information.

6. <u>Parents should be given an opportunity to learn to evaluate the changing needs of their children as they develop and grow educationally.</u>
   Parents can be evaluators if they have a basic knowledge of child development and language development. A comprehensive preschool/parent education program can provide a developmental base for future parent awareness of educational programming.

LANGUAGES AND CULTURAL BACKGROUNDS

Today in America we are much more sensitive to understanding, appreciating, and preserving the many cultures that have provided us with the roots of our American heritage. The preservation of language and the teaching of cultural differences when dealing with deaf children or severely hearing-impaired children presents some very difficult and complicating problems. In Arizona we have more different languages and cultures to deal with within our border than most other states. In addition to a large Mexican-American population, where Spanish is often the spoken language used in the home, we have over twenty or more tribal groups of native Americans (American Indians) many of whom, in more remote areas, depend very much on their tribal languages in their homes and communities for communication in family living.

Our outreach and preschool program personnel have the added job of being knowledgeable and sensitive to all of this. Yet, they must be persuasive enough to convince families that concentration on one language for the deaf child may have to be accepted, and then all may work together toward achieving that end. With the involvement and co-operation of the parents, they can develop in the child an appreciation and understanding of the family's cultural background. Workshops, managed by our outreach people in cooperation with tribal leaders and Indian Affairs personnel, are held regularly for small groups. The input from parents in these sessions has been amazingly useful and most rewarding. Special workshop activities for Spanish-speaking parents have been equally rewarding.

CONCLUSIONS

State supported school programs throughout the country have a very important and continuing role to play in the education of the hearing-impaired children of our country. In many instances the network of the contacts they have throughout a state help fill the gaps where existing services cannot reach. The story of Arizona is just one example of how the resources of a state supported school can work more effectively to the benefit of a greater number of deaf children and their families than could be properly served without them.

REFERENCES

Arizona White House Conference: Summary Report. December, 1976.

Griffing, Barry. Reshaping the role of the State School for the Deaf in public education: Changing role of school programs for deaf children: Conference of Executives of American Schools for the Deaf, January, 1977.

Mulholland, Ann N. and Hourihan, John P. Parents and due process in education of the handicapped - a case history. Volta Review. 1977, Vol. 79, 303-316.

Ruben, Robert J. Delay in Diagnosis. Volta Review. May 1978, Vol. 80, 201-202.

Shah, C.P., Changler D., and Dale, R. Delay in Referral of Children with Hearing Impairment. Volta Review. May 1978, Vol. 80, 206-215.

Part III

Research and Analysis

Research and analysis are essential tools to evaluating educational effectiveness. More specifically, using a scientific model one can identify the dynamic variables specific to parent-child, teacher-child, teacher-parent interaction that optimize the quality of exchange in order to achieve maximum potential. The chapters of this section emphasize the importance of communication between researchers and teachers being open and constructive. Examples of this data exchange occur in the following chapters. Only through such dialogue can service programs be most effective.

BERNARD Z. FRIEDLANDER, Ph.D.

Director, Infant-Child
Language Research Laboratory
University of Hartford
West Hartford, Connecticut

16

Finding Facts of Value and Value in Facts

Over the last 10 years or so a group of research colleagues and I have carried out a number of investigations of receptive language development and other aspects of listening behavior in normal and hearing-disabled children. We have conducted these studies with a method and from a point of view that are somewhat different from those that generally prevail among language developmentalists, audiologists, speech pathologists, and teachers who work with the hearing handicapped. I think the distinctiveness of our methods will become apparent in the descriptions that follow. Perhaps the point of view deserves a word of explanation.

From the very outset of my professional training in psychology I was profoundly influenced by the then emerging studies of ethology. One of the fundamental doctrines of ethological analyses of behavior is that the organism must be studied in its natural environment or in a very close simulation of its natural environment. A corollary of this principle holds that information about behavior gained in naturalistic settings makes real sense only in the context of those settings and behavioral sequences in which the information is embedded. This principle and its corollary explain my title for this report. In my view, the facts about children's auditory and linguistic behavior that have greatest value--facts to which significant value can be attributed--are those which rise out of children's ongoing adaptive interaction with their environment. This can be stated in another way. Samples of children's behavior that genuinely represent larger sequences of natural behavior, which unfold in the children's extended encounters with their real world of daily experience, are more likely to be genuinely meaningful in understanding children's abilities and disabilities than are samples of behavior derived from brief encounters, which have little relevance to real world experience.

Many of the evaluation techniques that are commonly used in assessment and program planning for normal children, as well as for disabled children, follow the model of using brief behavioral samples that have little relevance to children's actual experience--past, present, or future. Hence the results of this kind of evaluation are frequently very misleading. They often overemphasize aspects of behavior with which the children have at least partly spurious difficulties, and they deprive children of the chance to demonstrate some useful adaptive competencies which they actually do possess. Because the technologies associated with these testing methods are so elaborate and seemingly so self-confirmatory, it is often difficult to recognize the shortcomings, the errors, and the injustices these methods drag along in their heavy wake. There is a growing awareness that something is basically wrong, perhaps tragically wrong, with the way we measure and categorize children with respect to IQ. The whole concept of intelligence and its assessment is now being subjected to rigorous re-examination. Perhaps it is time we also begin to re-examine some of our fixed assumptions about the assessment of children's sensory acuity, perceptual functions, and information processing operations. When we do, it may prove to be true that coming to understand the synthesizing ways in which children utilize sensory-perceptual-cognitive experience in their ongoing environmental adaptation is really more significant for their lives than the exact measurement of sensory thresholds, no matter how highly refined that measurement might be.

I think this is a point of view that is especially significant for teachers to think about, to discuss, and to evaluate. After all, teachers are a part of the ongoing environment with which their pupils must maintain ongoing interactions, just as pupils are a part of the ongoing environment with which teachers must maintain ongoing interactions. Considering the nature of this reciprocal relationship, it is logical that teachers should seek out the best, the most meaningful, the most useful--not simply the most available or the most traditional--evaluative information about the children with whom they work and in whom they invest their personal hopes and their professional aspirations. It seems to me that this search is especially important for teachers of children with disabilities--children who require special planning, special preparation, and special devotion. In this chapter I will discuss what I consider to be the principal distinctive features that characterize the methods we have devised to pursue our work, illustrating the discussion with representative data from some of the more significant studies in which these methods have been employed.

BACKGROUND

Just to establish my own identity--and biases--I would like to explain at the outset of this review something about my own research training and orientation, and how I became involved in the field of child disability in general, and language disability in particular. With a few facts about my own background and experience, I think it will become evident that there is a fundamental logic to the goals and methods I will describe--a logic that may not be apparent immediately to professional people whose training has followed different lines of development. When I began my graduate study in psychology in the late 1950s a chain of accidental encounters led me as an inexperienced research assistant to the Behavior Genetics Laboratory in the Psychology Department at Case Western Reserve University. Professor Jan Bruell was then developing a wholly new approach to the study of genetic aspects of behavior organization in purebred strains of mice. People who are not familiar with the scientific rationale for using mice in behavioral research often think of them as a rather ludicrous species for this sort of work. In fact, the exceptionally high degree of genetic identification and control that has been established in many genetically pure mouse strains makes them a superior species for conducting extremely precise studies to distinguish between genetic factors and environmental influences in the shaping of behavior.

In addition to making a number of valuable contributions to the conceptual developments of this field, Professor Bruell and his students have made some outstanding methodological innovations in the work with mice--innovations that led directly to the work my associates and I have devised in our studies with normal and disabled infants and young children. The Bruell laboratory's main methodological innovation was to create numerous toy-like electronic measuring devices which could be inserted into the mouse's "play space" in its ordinary environment as a means for testing its behavior under specific conditions. The tests had to be conducted:

1. over extended periods of time,

2. in numerous repeated episodes or sessions,

3. with forms of behavior that were self-rewarding, not requiring an extrinsic reinforcer, and

4. with precise numerical measurement of critical behaviors.

With these devices it was possible for investigators in the behavior genetics laboratory to make very large numbers of repeated measurements, with large numbers of subjects engaged in purely voluntary behavior that was measured at high levels of numerical accuracy.

It is difficult to imagine how these scientific advances could have been made if Professor Bruell and his associates had not generated their remarkably imaginative techniques for deriving highly stable, highly replicable, and highly statisticizable measurement data from what was fundamentally just the spontaneous, seemingly random adaptive play behavior of ordinary laboratory mice. Visitors to the laboratory were often surprised at the apparent simplicity of the behaviors in which they saw the mice engaged--especially in the light of the very sophisticated concepts of genetics, psychological organization, and behavioral adaptation which the data illustrated. Some mice would be running in wheels, some would be climbing up or down ladders, some would be wandering around in darkened mazes that had neither a startbox nor a goalbox, some would be crawling through small darkened tunnels, and some would be jumping back and forth from one side of an enclosure to another over a low divider fence, like self-activated tennis balls--all forms of behavior that were perfectly natural to the mice in the environmental circumstances in which they found themselves.

New tests for new behavioral effects were continuously under development, but the best tests were generally the simplest ones, and they all had at least these same four characteristics:

1. extended testing sessions, so the subjects would encounter the same circumstances over and over again under conditions that were or would become thoroughly familiar;

2. numerous repeat test episodes, to provide multiple measurements of the behavioral effects and stimulus variables under examination;

3. purely self-activated performance with self-rewarding outcomes, to avoid food or comparable positive incentives and electric shock or comparable punishments, and

4. precise, continuing enumeration of the critical, voluntary test behaviors, to provide clear numerical data for statistical analysis.

I worked in this laboratory for the first two years of my graduate studies, before I switched over to a program in Professor Jane Kessler's Mental Development Center, that involved research with babies and young children. Those two years were not long enough for me to make any substantial contribution to the behavior genetics field, but they were long enough for me to finish a half-dozen or so minor studies--and gain a thorough understanding of the tremendous power of Bruell's methods for studying behavior in virtually <u>any</u> context in which organisms adapt behaviorally in a voluntary, self-activating fashion to the realities of the environment in which they are embedded. In the course of conducting those minor studies and mastering the techniques they involved, I learned that the four principles of extended test episodes, repeated testing, voluntary behavior, and continuous numerical measurement could be reduced to a number of extremely practical rules.

TRANSITION TO CHILDREN

When I sought to apply those research principles to studies of auditory-visual perceptual development, and adaptive behavior in babies and young children, the practical rules of the mouse laboratory proved to be just as practical in the baby nursery and the preschool. It made no difference whether we were studying infants' responses to self-initiated sights and sounds, infants' differential recognition of familiar and unfamiliar voices, infants' discrimination of high and low levels of verbal redundancy, young children's selection among different combinations of signal/

noise ratios, young children's differentiation of appropriate and inappropriate soundtracks accompanying self-activated video programs, hearing-disabled children's selection of preferred levels of amplification, normal and emotionally disturbed children's selection between correct and garbled speech, or children's differentiation of normal and distorted speech sounds. In whatever situations and with whatever sound and language variables we conducted our studies, these rules seemed to apply with equal force.

1. The test setting had to fit the children; the children could not be forced to fit the tests.

2. The tests had to be appealing to the children so the children would perform them voluntarily on the basis of intrinsic motivation, without involving extrinsic rewards or threats.

3. The tests had to be simple and standardized in terms of performance requirements, but highly versatile and variable in terms of individual performance styles and auditory/visual perceptual interests.

4. The tests had to be close approximations or extensions of the children's ordinary environments, and they had to be convenient, acceptable, and appealing to the parents in the home and teachers in the school.

5. The tests had to operate almost totally automatically, by themselves, day after day, at a high level of reliability in the home or in the school, with a minimum of attention and intrusion in the child's environment in the home or school by an investigator or technician.

6. The tests had to operate economically once they were set up. Even though they might be expensive to devise, the tests could not consume large budgets for labor or materials while they were in operation.

7. The tests had to generate stable, significant data on babies and children's development and performance that would justify the effort and cost of creating them, and they had to provide insights into the children's adaptation to their sensory-perceptual environments that were not obtainable by simpler, more economical means.

Two other equally practical rules became important when it proved desirable to apply these same measurement methods to evaluations of babies and children with various sensory and performance disabilities:

8. The tests had to be adaptable to children with the widest possible range of unique individual combinations of sensory and motor dysfunctions, while requiring the least necessary modification of the devices to suit the limits of individual handicapping conditions.

9. The tests had to be conducted in a way that allowed for rigorous control over the stimulus properties of the auditory-linguistic "messages" that were the consequence of the self-initiated activity of the children being tested. Another way to state this rule is to say that it was necessary to regulate and specify the loudness, the filtered frequencies, the signal/noise ratios, the word counts, or other critical properties of the sound sources on which the children were being tested.

UNDERLYING CONCEPT

One basic concept lay at the foundation of the whole research effort that was guided by these rules. This was a concept of great power that was just emerging in many aspects of psychology and child development research in the early 1960s when our work was gathering strength. This was the idea that most vertebrates in general, and children in particular, are stimulus-seeking, arousal-seeking, experience-seeking organisms. They are not simply passive, experience-accepting recipients of stimulation acting upon them in one-way traffic from the outer environment. Rather, they are active and highly interactive with the environment in a two-way fashion, with inherent needs and motivations to pursue forms of activity that provide optimal levels of environmental stimulation they can instigate and regulate by their own behavior. It was becoming established across a broad front in psychology--and some of our work contributed to this recognition--that babies and children who were placed in a low stimulation environment with means available to them by which they might increase their environmental sights and sounds could be counted on to do so at a very high level of probability. In other words, it was not necessary to give babies and children extrinsic rewards for learning to activate various sound-producing and light-producing effects. When these effects had certain properties that were inherently interesting and attractive, and available to the babies and children in ways they could operate, the only problems for research were to devise effective ways to measure the children's stimulus-producing activity and regulate the stimuli it was arranged for them to produce.

Furthermore, as later research would subsequently establish, motivations to generate varieties of sound and light stimuli were just as general and reliable in children with mild, moderate, and severe sensory-perceptual deficits as they were in babies and children who were entirely normal. This discovery meant that it was possible to identify sensitivity to various levels and properties of sound stimuli in children with sensory disabilities, in terms of the internally directed organization of their own behavior and modes of interacting with the environment. In other words, assessment of stimulus processing competencies and disabilities with handicapped children did not have to be an arbitrary process concerned only with abstract properties of the isolated sensory systems involved. Whatever advantages that kind of assessment might have in terms of absolute rigor, it says little or nothing about the way in which the children actually employ their residual competencies in ongoing encounters with their experiential world. These new findings meant that the evaluation of children with sensory disorders could be conducted in terms of their ordinary, ongoing interaction with the dynamic environment that surrounded them and which they could regulate themselves. And in addition, these evaluations could be conducted with the same properties of highly rigorous basic science research which Professor Bruell and his students had developed in the Behavior Genetics Laboratory in Cleveland: repeated measurements of voluntary behavior, over extended time periods, with numerical precision.

THE TESTING SYSTEM

Having sketched in a brief overview of the sources and practicalities that guided the development of this approach to assessing children's listening behavior, let me now give a short description of how the system operates. We can then go on to review some of the evaluation problems to which it has been applied, and the distinctive data on children's performance it can provide.

The generic name PLAYTEST is applied to any of several different forms of what is basically a two-channel audio-visual playback system. The child being tested operates one of two separate response devices (Fig. 16-1) or a single two-directional switch (Fig. 16-2) in order to turn on one channel or the other of a prerecorded audio or video tape program. A central electronic control unit (Fig. 16-3, tabletop) counts and measures the frequency and duration of each response the child makes on either of the two response channels, and the audio or video program plays so that the child can hear it or see it only as a function of the play responses. If the child makes no responses, he/she hears or sees no program. The internal circuits of the control unit are designed so that the child can secure only one of the two audio or video programs at a time.

FIG. 16-1
Hearing-impaired toddler with hearing aid in PLAYTEST-equipped crib at home for long-term assessment of selective listening. The child's play responses on either of the two lighted knobs activate different audio playback programs from loudspeaker mounted between the knobs. Audio tape players, control circuitry, and response registers are out of sight under the crib. Response record indicates child's listening preferences for either of two listening options. Various audio tapes offer a very wide array of acoustic or linguistic assessment variables, such as loudness, frequency composition, verbal content, voice familiarity, etc. Response data usually indicate very high performance output for audible playback programs--even among children with severe hearing impairment.

FIG. 16-2
Hearing-impaired preschool child with two-choice switch that activates an audio-video PLAYTEST system. The child's responses to either side of the switch produce different audio soundtracks that accompany the video program. Response data indicate the child's selective listening for the regulated audio stimulus properties under evaluation.

As shown in these photos, the testing units can be set up in a baby's crib, in an open playspace, or in multiple units in ordinary playpens. Various response devices have been devised so that children with very severe motor disabilities can operate the units successfully with only minimal force. In the standard units shown in these pictures, the switches operate with approximately two to eight ounces of force. The systems are highly modular in nature and any kind of audio or video stimulus that can be recorded on audio or video tape can be used with any of the various response devices. Also, the audio or video programs can be processed by synthesizer, filter, mixer, attenuator, or any other means to regulate any desired stimulus effects at any points in the system between the tape source and the end-point display of the loudspeaker or video tube.

In any of these various applications the investigator's task is to offer any two possible stimulus effects on the two channels, and the child's only task is to indicate by his/her preferential play performance which of the two programs he/

FIG. 16-3
Multiple PLAYTEST playpen units in an institutional setting indicate potential for large-scale data gathering in settings where it is desirable to evaluate large numbers of children in regularly scheduled multiple testing sessions. A playpen unit of the type shown here first demonstrated the effectiveness of this technique for demonstrating auditory sensitivity and complex audio information processing in profoundly retarded "deaf" infants (Friedlander, McCarthy, & Soforenko, 1967).

she prefers to listen to or watch. As noted above, the frequency and duration of all the children's responses on both channels are registered separately on the response registers. Standard research procedures are employed to establish the reliability of the response record and to protect the data from artifacts such as position preference or wild scores. When both channels are provided with the same

FIG. 16-4
Illustrates the diversity of different types of PLAYTEST systems. Numerous types of PLAYTEST instruments show diverse options for evaluating selective auditory/visual performance among children of various ages with various disabilities.

stimulus programs, or if the child cannot or does not detect a difference between two stimulus programs, the response data on the two channels--compared over multiple test sessions--accumulate approximately equal values. When the two programs are different and the child detects that difference in a preferential way, the performance data reflect his/her differential preferences over multiple testing sessions. Ordinary arithmetic and simple statistical procedures provide standardized ways for determining when such differences occur. They provide clear indicators of children's capacity to detect differences and show preferences in such auditory-linguistic values as loudness, filtered frequencies, signal/noise ratios, normal vs. garbled word order, or such visual values as brightness and sharpness of focus.

When the PLAYTEST units are set up in babies' cribs at home they operate and are responsive to the children's play whenever the children are in the cribs. The audio tape players operate either with continuously running loops or with quick-start cassette players whenever the children make a response. In these situations the data for an entire day may be considered as the data for a single session, and data may be collected day after day for as long as weeks at a time. The stimulus values of the tapes are changed from one program to another whenever the investigator judges it appropriate to make the change. Some studies of individual children have run as long as two or three months, with as many as 20 different successive pairs of stimuli. The investigator goes to the home or calls in by telephone once a day to record the data.

When the PLAYTEST units are used in schools the testing is generally conducted in sessions of predetermined length. The length of the sessions may vary from as little as a minute up to 10 minutes or more, depending upon the competence level of the children and the objectives of the evaluation series. The data for individual sessions are recorded independently for each channel and are then examined for similarities or differences in the response pattern on each channel. In these kinds of sessions, the investigator uses his/her judgment and is guided by the evaluation objectives in deciding when to change from one set of stimulus programs to the next. In all cases, pre-established criteria are decided upon as to what constitutes preferential selection between the two channels (usually a minimum of 65% total response duration for one channel or the other) and over how many sessions the child must display this preference in order to have the record considered a conclusive indicator of differential selection. (Friedlander, McCarthy & Soforenko, 1967)

REPRESENTATIVE STUDIES

Auditory Sensitivity

A very detailed study of auditory sensitivity in a group of profoundly retarded multi-handicapped deaf-blind children is a good example of how the PLAYTEST procedures operate in practice, and how they can help gain information about children's listening that may be unattainable by other means (Silva, Friedlander, and Knight, 1978; Friedlander, Silva, and Knight, 1973). The objective in this study was to secure data on auditory thresholds for selective listening to pure tones and speech among a group of children whose disabilities were so great they had been found to be untestable by other means of assessment. The basic structure of the other testing methods calls for a degree of cooperation from the child in a person-to-person setting in which the child is required to make some kind of meaningful responses to a procedure administered by an examiner. These procedures demand some combination of attention, cooperation, motivation, purposeful behavior, motor coordination, and conditionability to extrinsic reinforcers which the examiner regulates.

Subjects--The children in the study I am describing here were so profoundly impaired they could not meet these criteria. All other efforts to assess their auditory capabilities had been inconclusive and disappointing. Nevertheless, despite the children's profound multiple disabilities, it was considered desirable and important to assess their hearing in order to determine if there were any unrecognized ways in which auditory experience could play a significant role in their institutional management and efforts at self-care training. It was acknowledged from the very beginning of the efforts to assess the children's hearing that the evaluations were not an exercise in abstract research. Rather, they were an attempt to learn facts about the children's residual competencies and prospective competencies that could feed directly into training and program planning. Hence, the focus was not upon a laboratory procedure in determining the purest threshold stimulus that might elicit some flicker of a fragmentary behavioral or neural reaction. The goal was to find out what hearing levels, if any, might prove significant in the children's ongoing encounters with their environment on a daily basis. The nine children in this study ranged in age from 7.8 years to 13.4 years. The mean age was 9.1 years. One child had a chromosomal defect and the others manifested the prenatal rubella syndrome, in very extreme form. All the children were legally blind, but a few seemed to be able to make some use of visual cues for mobility.

In the auditory domain, one child showed an irregular capacity for imitating a few sounds, but the others showed no reliable responses to sound whatsoever. All the children had been examined with orthodox audiological procedures by certified university-level audiologists with experience in evaluating persons deemed difficult to test. Most of the children had been examined repeatedly, and six of them had experienced at least four examinations. None of these assessments produced meaningful information on the children's hearing competence.

All the children were also regarded as untestable by all standard indicators of IQ. As for their adaptive behavior in terms of such ordinary functions as walking, running, holding utensils, and opening doors, fewer than half the children were even remotely as competent as the bottom of the range for blind children of their age. Most had only just learned to walk, only a few could or would feed themselves, and only a few could be considered as being partially toilet-trained. In their gross behavior they all displayed some degree of such neurological indices as seizures, finger-waving, light-gazing, tooth-grinding, rocking, eye-poking, and head-banging. With a few minor exceptions they had no reliable response repertoire in any domain, and they could not be counted on to eat without constant assistance and urging.

In short, these pathetic children were a scant notch or two above the level of being chronic crib cases. In fact, some of them had been long-term crib cases prior to the outreach program that brought them into the institution where efforts were just beginning to train them for some measure of self-care. It is a credit to the dedicated work of the teachers and other staff who guided these children to develop every trace of adaptive skills they possessed that the children were not allowed to slide back into the status of helpless, hopeless dependency.

My reason for taking the space here to portray their severe and profound disabilities is to demonstrate the power of a testing technique that could develop reliable, authoritative assessment information about children who had so many handicaps working against them in their interactions with their environment.

Procedure--Each child was tested individually without hearing aids in daily four-minute sessions on the simplest of all the PLAYTEST tasks. The task in these evaluations was like the one shown in Fig. 16-2, except that the response box and the switch handle rising up out of it were smaller and easier to operate. (Also, in these evaluations there was no television screen.) The only consequence of operating the switch in one direction or the other from the neutral center position was the possibility of producing regulated pure tones or speech sounds through the earphones the children had been taught to wear in a preliminary phase of the study.

The children had learned to operate the switch box successfully in what was for some of them a rather protracted program of behavior shaping that involved various combinations of light, sound, and vibratory reinforcement. Considering the extremely disorganized state of their adaptive behavior in most situations, it is remarkable that they learned this task so well, and that they pursued it so attentively. Some of the children learned not only to work the PLAYTEST switch, but also to get to the testing room on their own. This was especially remarkable, since these same children had virtually no other adaptive capability in any other domain of experience. It was a pathetic sight, and a great confirmation of the behavior-organizing power of self-instigated stimulus experience, to see these woefully disabled children gradually learning to navigate the corridors of the building, and even the pathways of the multi-building campus, simply to spend four minutes in a little room operating a switch handle to turn on a sound in their earphones.

The two-direction switch was connected to the PLAYTEST control unit in such a way that moving it from neutral in one direction operated the reinforcing sound stimulus, while moving from neutral in the other direction produced no reinforcement. As noted above, the response registers recorded the frequency and duration of each response. The switch circuitry was not as simple as it may appear. Special electronic elements introduced two important control factors. First, one automatic timer changed the effective position of the switch every 60 seconds. Thus, if a <u>push</u> response generated the audio feedback for the first and third minutes of the session, the child had to <u>pull</u> the switch in the opposite direction in order to secure the sound feedback in the second and fourth minutes. The sound-reinforced positions for each minute were alternated each day. This arrangement protected the response data from reporting simply a position preference. It gave assurance that data on selective responding actually did indicate selection based on the auditory stimulus and the auditory stimulus <u>only</u>--not some spurious situational artifact. It is worth noting that the children's ability to master this pattern of 60-second alternation of the reinforced switch position was in itself a considerable accomplishment for children as disabled as these--an accomplishment that could not have been predicted to be within their capability, judging solely by clinical observation.

The second factor of procedural control involved protecting the response record from perseverative responses--a situation in which the child might just make one accidental response and hold the switch in that position, without regard to the presence or absence of the sound reinforcer. As a control for perseveration, a second timing circuit in the PLAYTEST control limited the duration of sound reinforcement to 10 seconds for any single response. After the 10-second limit, the sound automatically turned off even if the child continued to hold the switch in the response position. In order to regain the sound reinforcer, the child had to release the switch to the neutral position and make a new response. Their learning to "obey" this time limit was another indicator that successful selection between the reinforced and non-reinforced switch movements required the children to be alert to the stimulus consequences of their own behavior.

Test stimuli--One phase of each evaluation was conducted with amplified pure tones of 500 Hz, 1000 Hz, and 2000 Hz. The other phase of each evaluation was conducted with speech samples of the actress Claire Bloom reading children's stories. Her voice was processed with a bandpass filter so as to pass a 100 Hz wide band centered at 500, 1000, and 2000 Hz. The rigorous means for providing acoustical control over these stimuli are described at length elsewhere (Silva, Friedlander, and Knight, 1978). The pure tones and the speech stimuli were presented in order from the lowest to the highest frequency. At each frequency level the stimuli were presented at up to five different loudness intensities, ranging from 120 dB to 60 dB SPL, in 15 dB steps, starting from the top.

Testing began for each child at a level of intensity the evaluator believed the child could hear, based on observation and performance in the preliminary procedure. The children progressed downward to the next lower level of intensity after meeting a criterion of attaining 65% selectivity for the sound reinforcement on two consecutive days. If a child did not attain this criterion in five sessions on any given set of frequency/intensity conditions, the child was deemed not to have passed that frequency test and he/she was advanced to the next frequency. The children started the evaluations at different intensity levels and finished at different levels, depending upon their performance. The children's selective listening threshold for each condition was the lowest level of intensity at which they were able to attain the selectivity criterion.

Results--These test sessions produced three different measures of the children's performance: a) selectivity, the percentage of a child's total response time spent selecting the sound reinforcer; b) time on task, the percentage of the total session length spent responding, regardless of selectivity; and c) mean duration per response, the average length of time the child held the switch in either position for each response. Each of these three forms of the data tell something different about the nature of the children's responses in the test situation. The full report of the evaluations (Silva, 1974) explains these forms of the data, so it is not necessary to restate them here. However, it is important to point out a very important aspect of this kind of multiple data record. It greatly enhances the authoritativeness of the numerical indicators of selective auditory performance when the record can be examined and interpreted from several different points of view. The voluminous record of repeated testing sessions for each child is not simply a mind-numbing accumulation of senseless statistics. When the numerical data are examined by simple arithmetic they offer several different pathways of mutually confirmatory evidence showing how and when a child gains control over the distinctive properties of sound and language stimuli he/she may be learning to recognize for the very first time. Thus, the PLAYTEST record shows not only the child's sensitivity to the stimuli at a single point in time, but also the evolution of his/her adaptation to various sound properties as a function of personal progress in learning.

A glance through some of the PLAYTEST reports shows that there are several ways for reporting PLAYTEST DATA. Different methods suit different purposes. Dennis Silva, the principal investigator in these evaluations, devised an especially versatile way of reporting these data on children's selective thresholds of sound sensitivity. The representative data in Figs. 16-5, 16-6, and 16-7 show different patterns of selection for the different auditory properties of loudness intensity, frequency, and pure tones and speech. It is much easier to understand the information presented for each child if one takes a moment to figure out how these charts are laid out.

The intensity levels are indicated on the upper baselines and the frequency ranges are noted on the lower baselines. In each figure, the child's response to tones is shown on the graph at left and response to speech is shown at the right. The different patterns of the vertical bars are used to simplify distinguishing the performance data at the various intensity levels. The vertical height of each bar denotes the mean (average) percent response selectivity for the sound reinforcement in the multiple test sessions in which the child did attain or did not attain the 65% selection criterion. The critical information on each graph is whether the vertical bar at a given intensity level for that frequency does or does not reach the 65% criterion. That level is indicated by a horizontal line on each graph. Performance above 65% denotes selective listening. Performance under 65% denotes non-selectivity and, by inference, non-hearing. The position of the asterisk between the Intensity and Frequency baselines at the bottom of each cluster of vertical bars shows the Selective Listening Threshold for that set of stimulus conditions.

The interesting point to note is that most of the vertical bars that do attain the 65% criterion are well above the criterion line. This indicates that in most cases the ability to meet the criterion was associated with a preponderance of responses on the sound reinforced side of the switchbox. Conversely, most of the vertical bars that do not attain the

65% criterion hover in the range of 50%. That pattern suggests just the kind of 50-50 response activity one would

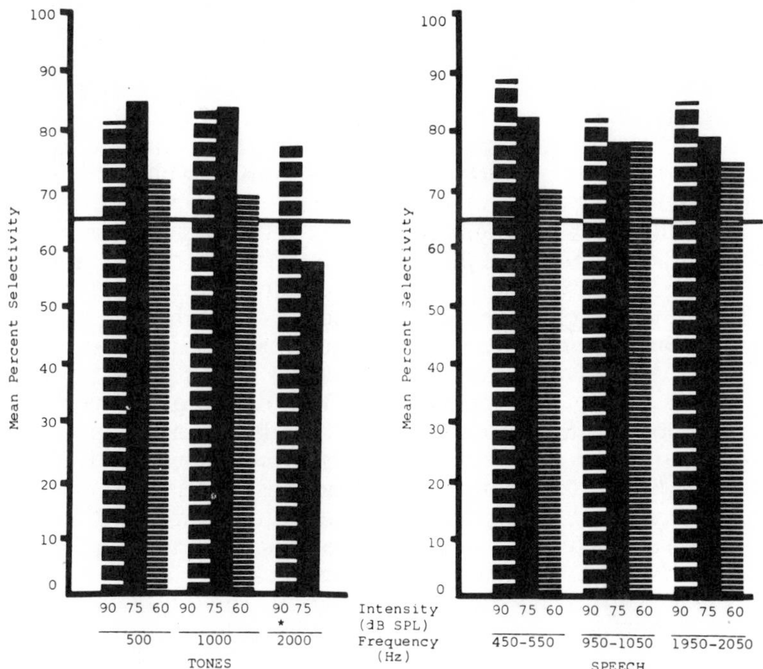

FIG. 16-5

Concise record of selective listening thresholds for pure tones and speech in a profoundly impaired, "untestable" post-rubella child at three different frequencies. Each column represents the average of pooled data for multiple testing sessions. Columns projecting above line marking 65% criterion indicate selective listening for that loudness/ frequency condition as shown at baseline. This "deaf" child could hear all tones above 60 dB, except at 2000 Hz, where threshold was at 90 dB, and all speech samples above 69 dB. See text.

expect of a child who did not hear the sound that his/her responses actually produced on the reinforced side of the switch.

Each child in the group showed a pattern of selective listening that was unique. No two children were entirely alike. Selective Listening Thresholds ranged from below the 60 dB lower limit for the child with the most sensitive auditory acuity (Fig. 16-5) to 120 dB (Fig. 16-6) on some of the tests in the evaluation sequence. No child was without at least some responsiveness to sound at the 120 dB level. As might be expected, Selective Listening Thresholds varied with the different frequencies, but not always in the expected direction. It was not always true that higher frequencies were associated with higher thresholds. Several children revealed lower thresholds at higher frequencies (Fig. 16-7).

Also, there was no consistent pattern in the relationship between thresholds for pure tones and for speech, though where there were differences they tended to favor the stimulus effectiveness of speech over pure tones. For some children the thresholds were identical or nearly identical for both categories of sound stimulation (Figs. 16-5 and 16-7). Several children showed lower thresholds for speech than for pure tones at some frequencies (Fig. 16-6). Only one child at one frequency showed a lower threshold for a pure tone than for speech. This finding bore out the general observation that the irregularly and intermittent energy bursts of the speech stimuli were more effective in mobilizing selective listening responses than the more predictable invariant properties of the pure tones. That point, though provocative, must remain speculative for children such as these, pending further research.

The irregularity and diversity of the children's unique patterns of Selective Listening Thresholds suggest at least two major inferences. First, on the basis of these data, no single clear pattern of hearing loss can be associated with the post-rubella syndrome that characterized all but one of these children. In that respect these data confirm the findings of traditional audiometry carried out with less severely afflicted children. Second, and probably far more important, these data demonstrate very clearly that not even the most "untestable" apparently non-hearing children should be considered to be without capacity for auditory sensitivity--and that hearing capability in such children can have extremely important potential in such children for organizing significant adaptive behavior.

The procedures described here demonstrated in an incontrovertible way that, when given opportunities to reveal their latent abilities, these children could hear, and that their hearing could have major significance in their behavioral training, and in the conduct of their lives. These data confirm the need to take a broader, more inclusive view of the assessment of hearing capability in severely impaired children. As important as it is to strive for rigorous control over the acoustical properties of sound and language stimuli, over modes of presentation, and over elements of central nervous system response, technological elegance in these domains is not the true center of gravity when evaluating sensory capacities in children with grave adaptive disabilities. The real weight of attention should be devoted to exploring every means at hand with which to circumvent the disabilities, structure the assessment technique so as to uncover responsive capability wherever it may lie, and install utilization of that capability in the children's daily lives.

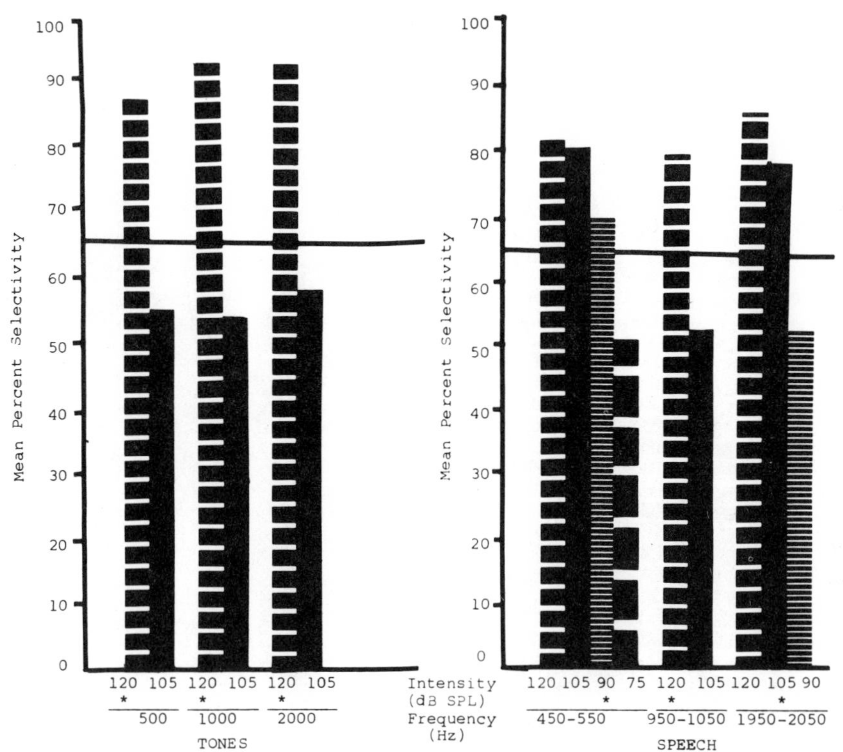

FIG. 16-6

For this "untestable", "deaf" child, selective listening performance for pure tones at 120 dB was very decisive--near or above 90%. Nearly random responding at 105 dB suggests auditory sensitivity at that level was highly improbable. Selective listening for speech stimuli indicates a mixed threshold pattern at 90 dB, 120 dB, and 105 dB in the three different frequency ranges.

OTHER STUDIES

While I have alluded to the versatility of the work that has been carried out with the PLAYTEST system, the amount of detail devoted to this study of auditory sensitivity with profoundly disabled children might convey the impression that this is the sort of work to which these techniques are best suited and that other applications are only secondary. If I have created this impression I would like to correct that

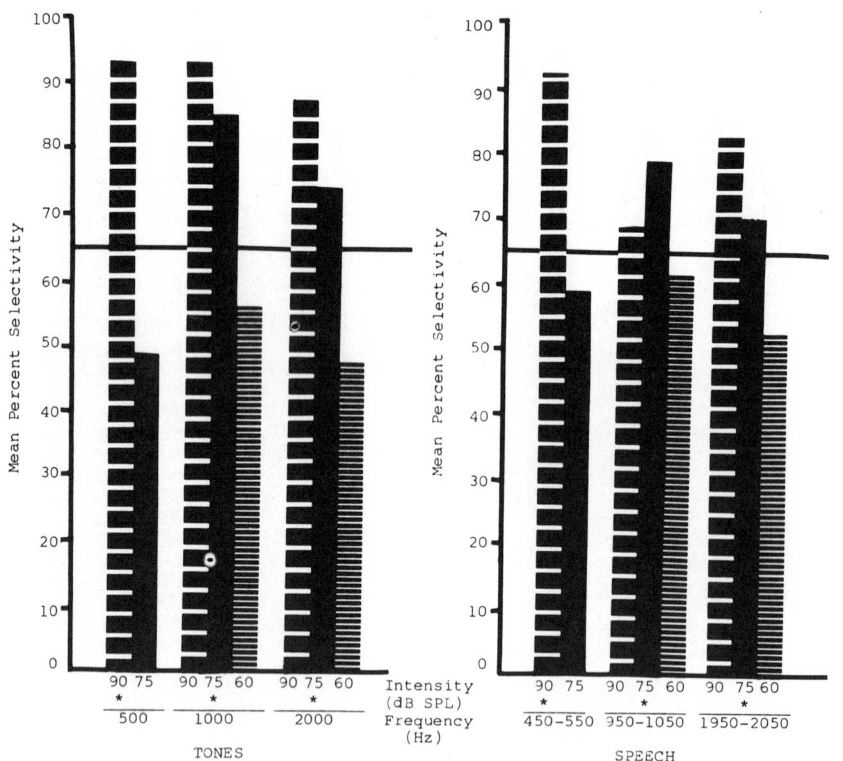

FIG. 16-7
This post-rubella child's selective listening performance was the same for pure tones and for speech at the different frequency levels. These findings show the specificity of the PLAYTEST data for each child's unique pattern of auditory sensitivity.

notion by describing, more briefly, a few other studies that indicate the breadth of possibilities inherent in the basic technique--possibilities that are by no means fully exploited. I gave as much emphasis as I did to the auditory sensitivity report simply because it is the one most recently published, it dealt with simple acoustical variables that are readily understood by workers in all the professions that are concerned with hearing and language deficits in children, and because the topic of listening thresholds is a fundamental issue in any approach to auditory phenomena. Also, the extremely disabled status of the children involved in that study rather dramatically underscores the system's capacity to gain information that is generally not available with other assessment techniques.

The best way to appreciate the versatility of this mode of evaluation is to point out the fact that PLAYTEST evaluations can be carried out with <u>any</u> pairs of auditory or visual stimuli that can be recorded on audio or video tape. We usually confine our research and evaluation efforts to specific auditory or visual stimulus variables that can be identified rigorously and related to existing sensory, perceptual, or cognitive values such as loudness, frequency composition, signal/noise ratios, vocabulary, verbal redundancy, intonation, brightness, visual clarity, and the like. Sometimes we've gotten a bit frivolous in our pairing of test variables, just out of curiosity, for fun, or to indicate the untapped potentials of basic science.

In one infant listening study about ten years ago my friend and former colleague at Wisconsin, Alan Moffitt, concluded a lengthy series of investigations with his baby daughter by giving her a listening choice between "Bach" and "Rock." He paired a recording of Bach organ music with a tape of some selections by the rock group, Led Zeppelin. I can't recall now which music the baby preferred, but the data were consistent, impressive, and genuinely worthwhile from a methodological point of view. In one of my own flights of fancy we used the PLAYTEST to measure several young children's preferential listening choices between Louis Armstrong's classic jazz rendition of "Mac the Knife" and a tape of the three barons' pretentious apologia for killing Becket in the last act of T.S. Eliot's <u>Murder in the Cathedral</u>. The children clearly preferred jazz to poetry. The University of Wisconsin press office considered that item newsworthy, and it went out to all the wire services and was printed in newspapers around the country with clever headlines and a photo generally comparable to Fig. 16-1.

Receptive Language Anomaly and Reading

A report published in 1973 (Friedlander and Cohen de Lara, 1973) used the same basic procedures described above to try to identify language listening problems among primary level children associated with problems the children might be having in learning to read. This study was carried out in a public school setting in an affluent Connecticut community with excellent diagnostic services and special education facilities. All 44 of the five-to-eight-year-old children in this study were in regular ungraded classes. None was regarded as having any degree of learning disability or other educational handicaps that might justify special placement. However, the children were recognized to be distributed across a spectrum from high to low achievement. The task called for the children to move the lever on the PLAYTEST switch to one side to turn on a prerecorded program of television cartoons of the Muppets with a clear, upgraded audio soundtrack. If they moved the switch to the other side they turned on the same video program, but with a soundtrack that was mildly, moderately, or severely degraded with voice interference. The soundtrack was degraded by imposing systematically regulated signal/noise ratios in which the noise consisted of an incomprehensible babble of voices, like cocktail party chatter.

The expectation in this study was that "good" listeners would reject the response option that produced the degraded soundtracks, after a bit of sample listening just to hear what it was like. We suspected that "poor" listeners would be less decisive in rejecting the degraded soundtracks, and that listening responses among the "poorest" listeners would hover in that 50-50 range. This would indicate that the children were not demonstrating any clear preference between the comprehensible and the incomprehensible dialogue accompanying the Muppets cartoons. We also hypothesized some degree of association between selective listening acuity at this level of meaning orientation and progress in reading skills. (The estimates of the children's reading progress were made by the classroom teachers and the school principal on the basis of standard test scores and their knowledge of the children's classroom performance. These estimates were made and recorded before the teachers and the principal had any knowledge of the PLAYTEST numerical scores.) Following familiarization trials, each child was allowed up to three six-minute sessions at each level of soundtrack degradation to try to attain the 65% criterion of selective listening.

The unambiguous clarity of the findings was as astonishing to the school principal and the teachers as they were to me and to my collaborator in the PLAYTEST part of the study, Hans Cohen de Lara. Of the 44 children who took the listening test, 33 consistently attained or surpassed the 65% selective listening criterion in favor of the upgraded soundtrack, thus decisively rejecting the less comprehensible dialogue. Meanwhile, 11 children consistently failed to attain the 65% selective listening criterion and remained at or near the 50-50 range of random, non-selective listening responses. In other words, the non-selective listeners each spent nearly half of at least nine six-minute sessions (54 minutes!) watching highly verbal cartoons in which the soundtracks were partially or entirely incomprehensible--sessions in which the perfectly clear soundtrack was freely available simply by moving the switch to the opposite position on the switch box. It was apparent that the 11 non-selective listeners were very different from the 33 selective listeners in their demand for comprehensible, meaningful discourse! Another datum accentuated the difference between the selective and the non-selective listeners in their different levels of demand for comprehensible speech: the time on task for both groups was almost identical at the very high level of 92%. That means both groups showed approximately the same strong appetites to watch and listen to the cartoons. Yet the selective listeners had a very low tolerance and the non-selective listeners had a very high tolerance for "linguistic garbage" (Friedlander, 1971).

The stunning facts on the connection between language listening and reading progress in these 44 children, <u>all of whom were considered normal in a sophisticated school system</u>, emerged when the independently arrived at PLAYTEST scores and the reading progress reports were brought together. The two groups matched perfectly with no overlaps. All 33 selective listeners were competent readers, at or exceeding expectations, while all 11 non-selective listeners were independently rated as being problem readers. These findings seemed so remarkable and improbable, we replicated the study with 66 other children and got almost identical results (Rileigh, 1973; Bohannan and Friedlander, 1973).

It seemed astonishing to us then, and it still seems astonishing to me now, that the relationship between language listening acuity and reading progress could have worked out with such an extraordinarily close fit between two entirely different modes of measurement. I thought it would turn out with tendencies in this direction, but I had no idea the relationship between language listening and reading would prove to be so strong. It seems to me that there are many implications for the education of hearing-handicapped children in this demonstration that critical listening is associated with good progress in reading, and uncritical listening is associated with poor progress in reading. I don't know whether to be surprised or not that the educational community seems to make little use of findings of this nature. I should think that teachers, educational planners, and curriculum developers should take some interest in the finding that approximately 25% of a representative sample of an affluent community's primary school children had a language listening deficit closely associated with reading difficulty, and that educators of the hearing-handicapped should be even more strongly tuned to results such as these. Although the report was published in a respectable journal and picked up and widely printed in national media, I'm not aware that anything was or is being done about this provocative PLAYTEST research finding.

Listening Deficit and Emotional Disturbance in Preschool Children

The procedure described above in the study of language listening and reading progress was originally devised to try to answer a question about differences in language listening between emotionally disturbed children and normal children in the preschool years. Donna McPeek conducted this study with me when my laboratory was located at the University of Wisconsin, Madison; then Harriet Wetstone helped recalculate the statistics and write the report after I moved to the University of Hartford (Friedlander, Wetstone and McPeek, 1974). The question has some elements of the chicken-egg question: can we use listening data to examine the well recognized link between language deficit and emotional disturbance? It is broadly known that language difficulties and emotional disturbance go hand in hand. What remains unclear is which, if either, of these conditions is primary and which is secondary. It is most commonly supposed that the language problem follows as a consequence of the emotional disturbance. But is it necessarily so that the language disorder is a consequence of the turbulent emotions? Is there a chance that there might be cause-effect linkages working in the other direction--the children being emotionally disturbed as a secondary consequence of a primary communication problem? Or could it be that both emotional disturbance and language dysfunction rise from some common, more fundamental information processing disorder that disrupts both communication and emotional adaptation? We did not expect any final answers to such weighty questions, but it seemed likely that solid data on language listening might at least clear up some of the uncertainties in this cloudy picture.

The study was conducted with fifteen normal preschoolers in the four to six year age range in a community day care center, and seven moderately disturbed and six severely disturbed children of the same age in a special program under the jurisdiction of the Madison Children's Treatment Center. The procedure was almost identical to that followed in the public school listening-reading study. The children had multiple six-minute PLAYTEST sessions that offered a choice between the upgraded and degraded soundtracks accompanying highly verbal segments of the Muppets cartoons.

All the critical information for this study is shown in Fig. 16-8. The acoustical properties of the signal/noise ratios of the language interference are shown on the baseline; the percent of selective listening to reject the degraded soundtrack is shown on the vertical axis, and the status of the children is shown in the descriptions of the three curves. The numerals by each data point apply to the mean (average) of the selective listening responses for all the multiple test sessions for all children in the several groups at each condition of the signal/noise ratios.

The data tell their story very succinctly. With all responses hovering about the 50% mark in Condition 1, in which both audio channels were fully upgraded, the children did not make any selective differences in their responses to listen to the two identical audio channels. They responded approximately the same on each side of the switch for exactly the same audio feedback. As the degraded audio channel became progressively more incomprehensible in Conditions 2, 3, and 4, the normal children rejected the babble with increasing decisiveness in order to listen to the upgraded soundtrack. The moderately disturbed children rejected the less comprehensible soundtracks to a moderate degree. The severely disturbed children did not reject it at all: they listened to the incomprehensible dialogue and the comprehensible dialogue with just about equal acceptance. As in the listening-reading study, the time on task, showing the overall listening times, averaged above 75% for all groups in all conditions and they were very close to being identical. The published report cites the detailed statistics with great specificity.

These data did not give any final answer to the big diagnostic question of which came first, the disturbed children's emotional difficulties or their manifest language problems. However, they did answer one extremely important set of questions with information that had not previously been known: whatever problems the children had with expressive

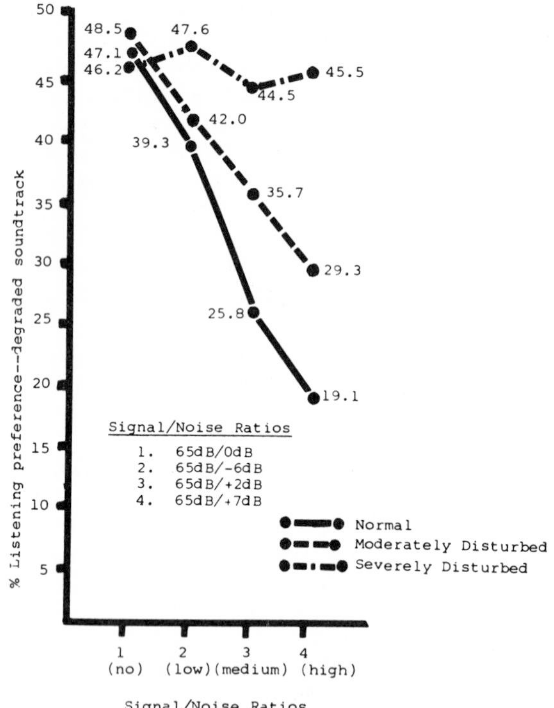

FIG. 16-8
In this summary of selective listening preference, normal and moderately disturbed children showed decisive and intermediate rejection of degraded television soundtracks, while severely disturbed children showed no rejection at all of the unintelligible dialogue.

language, they also had serious problems in the domain of receptive language. If they would listen so eagerly and acceptingly to meaningless babble, there was no basis on which to assume that ordinary, sequential meaningful speech would have any special meaning for them. They could not be expected to understand speech directed toward them any more than they could be expected to speak clearly to others.

This set of facts was of great importance in their daily treatment and training because it alerted therapists and teachers to the children's problems in language comprehension, difficulties which had not been fully appreciated because receptive language problems are covert while expressive language problems are overt. Consequently, this study demonstrated that with these children (and presumably with others like them) all efforts at communication between the teachers and the children had to be structured against the constraint that sequential speech directed toward these children might be an empty communications channel, like trying to carry water in a bottomless bucket.

The next and final study I will review here takes this important finding one small but important step further.

Language Listening in Psychotic Children

Each of the PLAYTEST reports I have described thus far, and most of the others noted in the References, have been published in juried journals or been presented at scientific meetings after their methods, statistics, and results were subjected to the normal practices of peer review by other competent investigators and editors. They have passed muster in the research community as having been conducted in accordance with high standards of design and procedure. The study I will describe next has not been published and will not be published because of a minor procedural irregularity. I have as much confidence in the integrity of the data from this study as for any of the others despite this minor flaw, and the findings are so important I think they deserve to be noted here. This work was carried out at Oak Hill School in Hartford by Richard Wallstein and Gary Hesse before they left my laboratory to continue their work respectively at the University of Chicago and at Harvard (Wallstein and Hesse, 1975).

Wallstein and Hesse used the two-choice selective listening paradigm to test the listening preferences of three different groups of low-vision children in the six to nine year age range. In the first group there were six congenital rubella children specifically diagnosed as psychotic by the school's consulting psychiatrists. The second group included six non-psychotic, brain-injured children regarded as having language handicaps generally comparable to the language problems of the psychotic children. In the third group there were five "normal blind" children whose language status was considered near normal. All clinical testing and classifying was carried out as part of the ordinary routines of the school.

In the PLAYTEST listening evaluations all the children were tested repeatedly with voice recordings only, without video. The upgraded audio channel in each session consisted of a woman's voice telling stories. The degraded audio channel was distorted in three different ways in the three phases of the study. Wallstein and Hesse did not use three different degrees of a single mode of voice degradation. The first condition involved the same kind of signal/

noise multivoice babble that was used in the studies described above. In the second condition, an electronic chopper was used to delete approximately 50% of the message stream, rendering the speech unintelligible, but not altering its gross acoustical properties. The voice in the third condition was presented in a dull, flat, intelligible, but uninteresting monotone.

With one conspicuously outstanding exception, the grouped data were a mixed bag of selective and non-selective listening responses, not very different from the data in prior studies. The conspicuous exception, which I think deserves very serious thought, was that in Condition 1 and Condition 3 the psychotic children showed strong aversion to the normal, upgraded voice and surpassed the selective listening criterion to hear the degraded voice. In all the many other PLAYTEST studies conducted in my laboratory and elsewhere I have never encountered this finding of active preference for the degraded, unintelligible or less intelligible voice, except in a precursor study at Oak Hill in the previous year, for which the Wallstein and Hesse work was a replication. In all the other studies with other normal and clinical populations, the listeners either attained the selection criterion for the upgraded normal voice or they showed no preference at all between the two channels. In this case, the psychotic children showed a positive rejection of the normal speech and a positive preference for the unintelligible babble and the unattractive, very abnormal flat monotone.

Here is why I think this finding is so important: it raises serious questions about one of the most sacred, fundamental assumptions in virtually all treatment and training efforts with language handicapped children and adults. This assumption is that the teachers' and therapists' natural voices are one of the most potent resources available for dealing with their clients. This assumption works out in practice as an almost constant stream of verbalization by the teachers and therapists to fill in the empty moments of interpersonal association. We operate with our clients on the unexamined assumption that if we cannot do anything else with or for them, it is always good to talk at them. The Wallstein and Hesse findings challenge that assumption. This group of children, at least, did not want to hear normal speech, and they demonstrated their negative desire in a highly operational fashion. Given a chance to choose, they made their choice for listening to speech we would ordinarily regard as distinctly non-normal, non-supportive, non-intelligible or unattractively barely intelligible, and perhaps even anti-social.

That finding raises the provocative question: if these

children did not want to hear normal speech, how many other clinically aberrant groups are there that do not want to hear normal speech either? To what extent are we neglecting their real needs and increasing instead of decreasing the distance between them and ourselves when we operate on the assumption that talking to them is among the best of available ways to "reach" them? These are disturbing questions to ask ourselves when we think hard about our usual ways of conducting treatment and teaching with language-handicapped people. The questions are disturbing because they carry the possibility of eliciting answers we do not want to hear. One answer is that there may be more that we do not know about language listening than what we do know. As long as that remains true, then the burden is on us to expand our knowledge and learn far more than we presently understand about the role of receptive language functions in children's adaptation to their larger world. I hope the PLAYTEST procedures described here will continue to contribute to the expansion of this knowledge.

NOTE

I am aware that this chapter has not given any information on application of the PLAYTEST procedures to studies of receptive language performance among normal and hearing and language-disabled babies. These procedures are very much like the ones described above except that they are conducted on a continuing basis in the natural environment of the infants' cribs at home, as is illustrated here in Fig. 16-1. Readers wishing more information about PLAYTEST studies with babies are directed to articles by Cyrulik-Jacobs, Shapira and Jones (1975) and Friedlander (1968, 1970, 1975).

I am especially grateful to Shirley Siegel and Michael Levinson for their help in preparing this chapter.

REFERENCES

Bohannon, J.N., and Friedlander, B.Z. The effect of intonation on syntax recognition in elementary school children. Child Development. 1973, 44, 675-677.

Cyrulik-Jacobs, A., Shapira, Y., and Jones, M. H. Automatic operant response procedure ('Playtest') for the study of auditory perception of neurologically impaired infants. Developmental Medicine and Child Neurology. 1975, 17, 186-197.

Friedlander, B.Z . The effect of speaker identity, voice inflection, vocabulary, and message redundancy on infants' selection of vocal reinforcement. Journal of Experimental Child Psychology. 1968, 6, 443-459.

Friedlander, B.Z. Receptive language development in infancy: Issues and problems. Merrill-Palmer Quarterly of Behavior and Development. 1970, 16, 7-51.

Friedlander, B.Z. Listening, language, and the auditory environment: Automated evaluation and intervention. In J. Hellmuth, (ed.), Exceptional Infant. Vol. 2, NY: Brunner/Mazel, 1971.

Friedlander, B.Z. Notes on language: Screening and assessment of young children. In B.Z. Friedlander, G.M. Sterritt, and G.E. Kirk (eds.), Exceptional Infant. Vol. 3, Assessment and Intervention. NY: Brunner/Mazel, 1975.

Friedlander, B.Z. Automated evaluation of selective listening in language-impaired and normal infants and young children. In B.Z. Friedlander, G.M. Sterritt, and G.E. Kirk (eds.), Exceptional Infant. Vol. 3, Assessment and Intervention. NY: Brunner/Mazel, 1975.

Friedlander, B.Z., and Cohen de Lara, H. Receptive language anomaly and language/reading dysfunction in "normal" primary grade school children. Psychology in the Schools. 1973, 10, 12-18.

Friedlander, B.Z., McCarthy, J.J., and Soforenko, A.Z. Automated psychological evaluation with severely retarded institutionalized infants. American Journal of Mental Deficiency. 1967, 71, 909-919.

Friedlander, B.Z., Silva, D.A., and Knight, M.S. Selective responses to auditory and auditory-vibratory stimuli by severely retarded deaf-blind children. Journal of Auditory Research. 1973, 13, 105-112.

Friedlander, B.Z., Wetstone, H.S., and McPeek, D.L. Systematic assessment of selective language listening deficit in emotionally disturbed pre-school children. Journal of Child Psychology and Psychiatry. 1974, 15, 1-12.

Rileigh, K. K. Children's selective listening to stories: familiarity effects involving vocabulary, syntax, and intonation. Psychological Reports. 1973, 33, 255-266.

Silva, D.A. Evaluation of residual auditory capabilities in severely impaired multi-handicapped deaf-blind children. Unpublished thesis, University of Hartford, 1974.

Silva, D.A., Friedlander, B.Z., and Knight, M.S. Multi-handicapped children's preferences for pure tones and speech stimuli as a method of assessing auditory capabilities. American Journal of Mental Deficiency. 1978, 85, 29-36.

Wallstein, R. and Hesse, G. Free choice selection of natural and distorted speech by psychotic congenital rubella children. Unpublished report, Infant/Child Language Research Laboratory, University of Hartford, 1975.

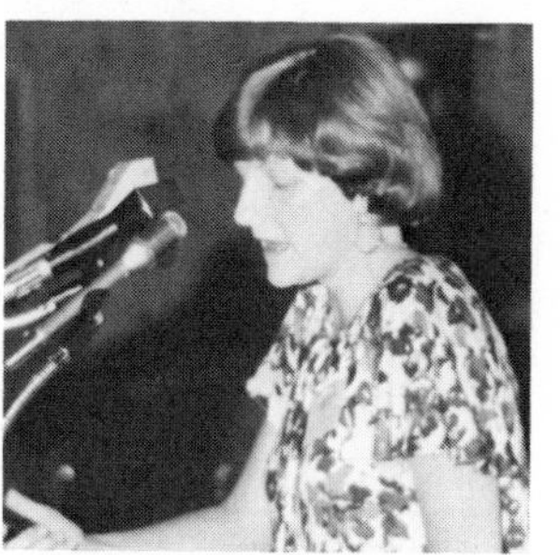

BARBARA J. ANDERSON, Ph.D.

Department of Psychiatry
and Pediatrics
Washington University School
of Medicine
St. Louis, Missouri

17

Parents' Strategies for Achieving Conversational Interactions with Their Young Hearing-Impaired Children

Linguist Catherine Snow (1977b) has recently suggested that "Children learn to talk by conversing with adults (p. 39)." How do adults manage conversations with these young partners who are only learning the rules of language and of verbal exchange? The focus of the present research was the speech that parents direct to very young children who are hearing-impaired. The intent of this study was a descriptive, in-depth analysis of the speech patterns of three mothers with their severely hearing-impaired infants in order to identify conversational turn-taking features in the speech of the mothers.

It is important to point out that almost no research exists describing in detail the interactions, including verbal interactions, of mothers and their young deaf infants (Greenstein et al., 1976). We do know, however, from extensive, carefully researched literature on parents and hearing infants, that a turn-taking system is evident in a variety of early reciprocal interactions. In visual interactions, parent and infant alternate regularly between eye-to-eye contact and gaze aversion (Stern, 1974). A back-and-forth pattern has been reported during early feedings, in which babies display bouts of bursts and pauses while sucking, and mothers alternate with physical stimulation (Kaye, 1977). Turn-taking is a prominent mode of vocal communication between mothers and hearing infants in the first six months of life (Anderson et al., 1977; Bateson, 1975; Stern et al., 1975). Also turn-taking is demonstrated in interactions with objects during which infants "point," at first with their eyes, and parents follow by visually co-orienting to the object and by verbally acknowledging that the infant has taken a turn (Bruner, 1977). In all of these modes of turn-taking, though the infant actively participates, the responsibility for maintaining the exchange falls on the parent (Bruner, 1977).

The turn-taking model evident in early visual, feeding, vocal, and object-centered interactions has an adaptive function for early development by creating the foundations of reciprocity upon which more complex interactional games, sequences of imitation, and eventually verbal conversations are built (Anderson, 1977). As Kaye (1977) has concluded, turn-taking is "... a necessary context for language acquisition as well as other kinds of learning (p. 94)." Based on these premises, the present study was undertaken to describe the turn-taking features in the speech of mothers to their severely hearing-impaired infants in the first three years of life.

A Structural Model of Conversation

From the outset we must have a common idea of what is meant by a "conversation", so I will briefly discuss a structural model of conversational behavior generated from research on adult speakers. Sacks and his colleagues (Sacks et al., 1974) have presented a carefully researched structural model of conversation. Their model is not dependent on the content or context of the talk, but rather on the organizational rules that speakers in a conversation exhibit. This conversational model, therefore, can be applied to all speakers, regardless of age.

The basic structural feature of conversation is a system for alternating turns. In a conversation the order of turns is negotiated by the participants in one of two ways: 1. the next turn may be determined by self-selection, or 2. the next turn may be determined by the current speaker's selecting the next speaker (Sacks et al., 1974, p. 703). This second strategy is called turn-passing. The current speaker can pass the turn by asking a question, making a request, or directing a greeting, a challenge, or a compliment to the partner. Each of these utterances constrains another speaker to take his turn: a question demands an answer; a greeting deserves a return; a request may be carried out or rejected, a compliment or challenge is accepted or denied (Sacks et al., 1974). The use of a turn-passing utterance insures that the speakers stay in contact and maintain their partnership, at least momentarily. In addition to techniques for passing the turn, there are strategies by which a speaker may "repair" a conversation when the turn-alternating system breaks down (Sacks et al., 1974, pp. 723-24). For example, simultaneous talk between two speakers is rare in adult conversations because one speaker will usually stop talking to restore the one-at-a-time rule (Sacks et al., 1974). In addition, one speaker may repeat or reformulate his request or even answer his own question to repair the turn-taking sequence when his partner fails to respond (Snow, 1977a).

The third and perhaps most prominent feature of conversation is "recipient design". According to Sacks et al. (1974), recipient design refers to "... a multitude of respects in which the talk by a party in a conversation is constructed or designed in ways which display an orientation or sensitivity to the particular other(s) who are the co-participants (p. 727)." Therefore, recipient design refers to the adjustments made in the content, form, or tempo of speech to fit the particular needs of the listener.

In summary, the model of conversation adopted here involves three major components: 1. strategies for passing turns, 2. strategies for repairing the back-and-forth sequence when it breaks down, and 3. evidence of speaker sensitivity to the partner in the choice of vocabulary, utterance forms, topics, and expectations for turn-taking. The present research was designed to investigate the presence and extent of these features in the speech of mothers with their hearing-impaired infants.

It is important to describe the broader context in which these observations of mothers' speech to hearing-impaired children were made. There are special constraints on turn-taking in a verbal-auditory mode imposed on the mother by the hearing impairment of her young child. These mothers were obliged to secure their infants' visual attention in order to enable their words to be effective stimulation. Therefore, they constantly had to be attuned to the optimal interpersonal distance for the child to see them speaking -- which meant a face-to-face orientation at the child's eye level. As the children moved about, attracted to a cupboard in one part of the room or drawn to a toy in a far corner, these mothers had the extra responsibility, compared to mothers of hearing infants, of speaking so that the child could catch their words visually and auditorily. These mothers managed this with remarkable ease and spontaneity that makes it valid to discuss their verbalizations as being child-directed turns in an interactive context.

METHOD

Subjects

For the present study three families were selected from those currently participating in the Parent-Infant Program at the Central Institute for the Deaf, St. Louis, Missouri. These three families were chosen because each had sought out hearing assessment and intervention services from Central Institute immediately following a suspected hearing loss, and videotape recordings of parent-infant interaction were available for analysis on each family from their early months in the program. Each child had received appropriate amplification by the first videotaped session. In this paper the names of parents and children have been changed. The parents are between thirty-three and forty-three years of age, and family incomes range from lower-middle to upper-middle levels. Each family is a two-parent family, and in each home the mother is the primary caregiver. The parents in all three families have normal hearing.

Setting

At the Parent-Infant Program each of the three families is seen weekly for one hour by the same teacher-counselor. The program is housed in a medium-sized, comfortable home which has been equipped throughout for unobtrusive videotaping with remotely-monitored cameras. Families are aware of and accustomed to being videotaped, a procedure which is done regularly for teaching purposes.

Procedure

Five videotape sequences were selected for each family spanning the time from their early months in the program to the present. As tapings are done for teaching purposes, intervals between videotapes varied across families. For the purposes of this study, it was necessary to have on each videotape five minutes of time when mother and child were free to interact in an unstructured activity without the interventions of the teacher-counselor. For the first three tapes analyzed for the Adams family, the first four for the Brown family, and the first two for the Cain family, five minutes of uninterrupted mother-child interaction interspersed throughout each thirty-minute tape were selected for analysis. For all subsequent tapes, a five-minute segment of unstructured mother-child interaction was videotaped for analysis before the teacher-counselor entered to begin instruction.

Transcription and Coding

From each five-minute segment, all maternal utterances directed to the child and all child vocalizations were transcribed in sequence. An utterance or turn was defined as those words or sounds, regardless of length, spoken together without a noticeable pause. For those sessions in which the father participated along with the mother (session one for the Browns and sessions one, three and four for the Cains), utterances of each parent were identified in the transcription but were combined for the purposes of data analysis. Each utterance was coded as to its form, content, and function. A manual (Anderson, 1978) explaining the transcription process and the coding of categories is available from the author.

Inter-Coder Reliability

Two trained observers independently coded four five-minute videotaped segments. A percentage agreement score was calculated for Form, Content, and Function categories based on the number of disagreements - omissions and commissions - for each category relative to the total number of maternal utterances for that tape. Table 17-1 lists the categories and inter-coder reliabilities.

RESULTS

In presenting the data, I will first discuss each of the three longitudinal records of maternal speech and then point out some general patterns that emerge from these individual histories. In describing each family I will focus on data which has specific reference to three components of the general conversational model discussed earlier (Sacks et al., 1974): 1. the mother's strategies for passing the turn to her infant, 2. maternal techniques for repairing the turn-alternation sequence when it breaks down, and 3. the mother's demonstration of recipient design or sensitivity to her partner in the speech she directs to her developing child.

TABLE 17-1

List of Categories and Inter-Coder Reliabilities

Maternal Language Codes	Mean Percentage Agreement	Range
Form of Utterance	98%	95% - 99%
1. Question		
2. Imperative		
3. Declarative		
4. Exclamatory		
Content of Utterance	93%	91% - 99%
1. Interpretation of child's state		
2. Object references		
3. Interpersonal references		
Content Repetition	96%	94% - 98%
Function of Utterance	84%	74% - 88%
1. Attempt to elicit turn/ response		
2. Acknowledge turn by child		
3. Narrate		
4. Take child's turn		

Mrs. Adams and Billy

Billy is the third child of well-educated, professional parents who have one older child with a profound hearing loss. Billy had a moderate-to-severe hearing loss at birth. His loss is progressive, and the most recent assessment at 18 months of age indicates a profound loss. His motor and cognitive development has been consistently age-appropriate, and at 18 months, Billy is described by his teacher-counselor as delightfully social, gregarious, and persistent in his activities with objects. He maintains good eye contact with his mother and other social partners. At 18 months his vocalizations have a purposeful quality and while Billy does not yet imitate specific sounds, he imitates mouth formations and mouths sounds silently. The five videotaped sessions for the Adams were made at 4.5 months, 6.5 months, 8.5 months, 12.5 months, and 17.5 months.

Form

Figure 17-1 presents Mrs. Adams' utterances categorized as to form. Each utterance was coded as one of four possible forms: 1. question, 2. imperative or command, 3. declarative, or 4. exclamation. Each point on the graph represents the percentage of the total number of maternal utterances for that tape that were coded as questions, exclamations, etc. There are no clear developmental trends in the mother's use of form categories. Among all categories, questions consistently made up the lowest proportion, between 15% and 20%, across the 4.5 month to 17.5 month-age period studied. Mrs. Adams' use of commands was higher and more varied across this period. Questions and commands, however, were frequently used interchangeably. The mother shifted between the two form types as she repeated or reformulated her utterances. Sequences of questions and commands such as the following were common: "Billy, can you make the frog jump? Make it jump over here. Can you do that? Can the frog jump here? Move the frog to Mommy..." When the percentages for questions and imperatives are combined within each session, these utterances for passing the turn to the infant generally made up the majority of the mother's utterance forms until Billy was 17.5 months, when declaratives accounted for over 50% of Mrs. Adams' utterances. This was the highest use of declaratives revealed for any of the mothers.

Content

Figure 17-2 represents the content of Mrs. Adams' speech. Each maternal turn was coded as referring to one of three content themes: 1. references to the mother-child interpersonal relationship which did not include references to the child's feelings or objects, for example, "Ok, I won't stop.", 2. references to objects in the immediate environment, and 3. references to the child's state or feelings, such as "You're a happy baby." There are consistent developmental changes in Mrs. Adams' use of content themes. Her references to Billy's feelings declined steadily, so that by 17.5 months they accounted for only 5% of her utterances. Her references to the mother-child relationship which initially accounted for more than 50% of her utterances also consistently decreased to 10%. References to the baby's interactions with objects, however, steadily increased from 24% at 4.5 months to 84% at 17.5 months. Content repetition was fairly consistent, with between 20% and 30% of her turns a repetition of the immediately preceding utterance.

Function

As shown in Figure 17-3, each maternal turn was coded as one of four possible functions with respect to initiating and maintaining a conversation: 1. attempting to elicit a turn or specific response from the child, 2. acknowledging a turn by the child, 3. narrating in a manner which does not serve to elicit or acknowledge a turn, or 4. taking the child's turn by speaking for the child. We see a developmental trend only for the category of acknowledges a turn by the child which declined from 39% at 4.5 months to 8% by 17.5 months. This may be due to the fact that at the youngest ages, Mrs. Adams responded to every coo and fuss as if it conveyed specific information. As the frequency of spontaneous babbling by her profoundly deaf infant decreased, there was a corresponding decrease in Mrs. Adams' attributing intention to her son's behavior. Ranking the other categories in terms of frequency of occurrence across sessions, the majority of Mrs. Adams' utterances were attempts

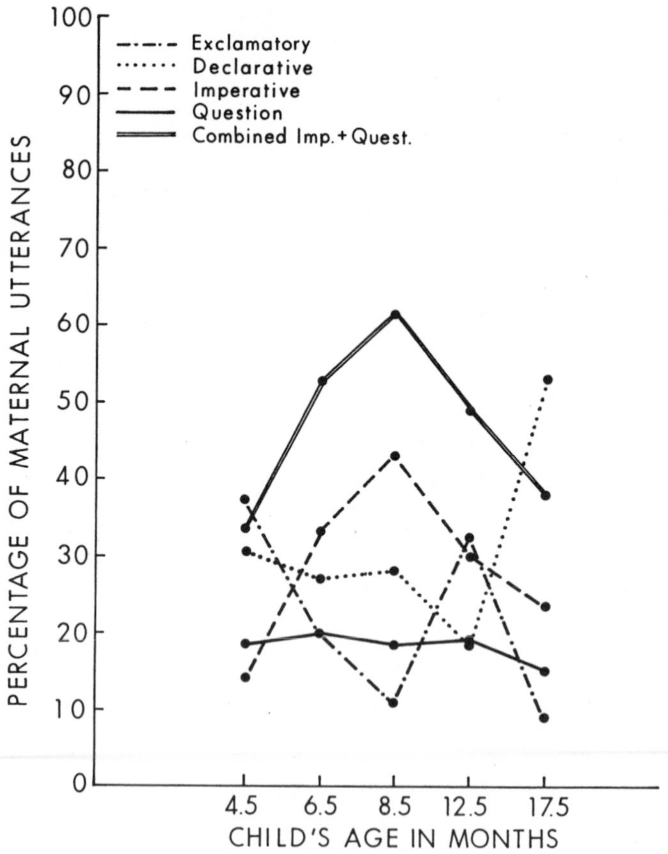

FIG. 17-1
Form categories as percentages of all utterances of Mrs. Adams.

to elicit a response from Billy, between 50% and 83%. Narrations accounted for between 8% and 21%. Utterances in which the mother took the child's turn in the exchange never accounted for more than 5% of all maternal turns.

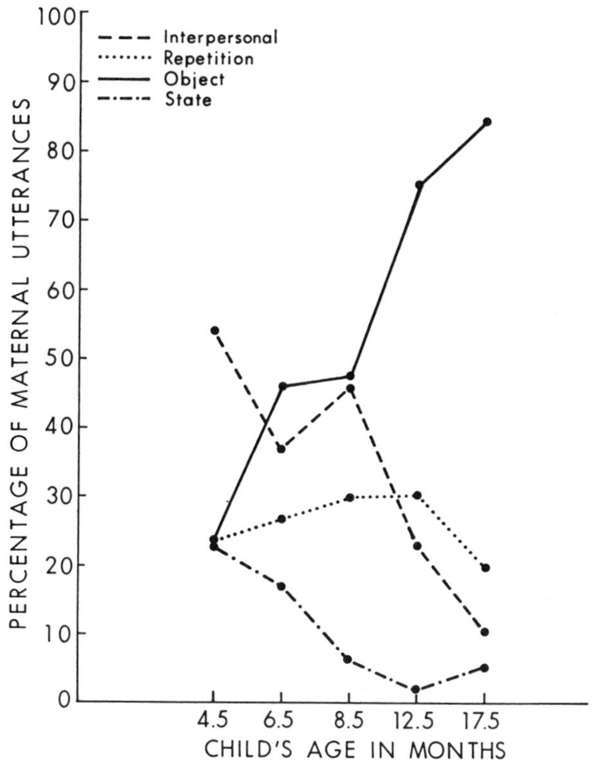

FIG. 17-2
Content categories as percentages of all utterances of Mrs. Adams.

In summary, the primary form of Mrs. Adams' utterances was a combination of imperatives and questions. In terms of function, she consistently tried to achieve the goal of eliciting a turn from Billy. As for conversational repair techniques, Mrs. Adams would repeat a request or question rather than answer for Billy. Finally, recipient design was clearly demonstrated in the shifts in her speech content as Billy developed. Mrs. Adams' references to objects increased as Billy became more visually attracted to objects and skillful in manipulating toys with a corresponding decrease in talk about herself or her child alone.

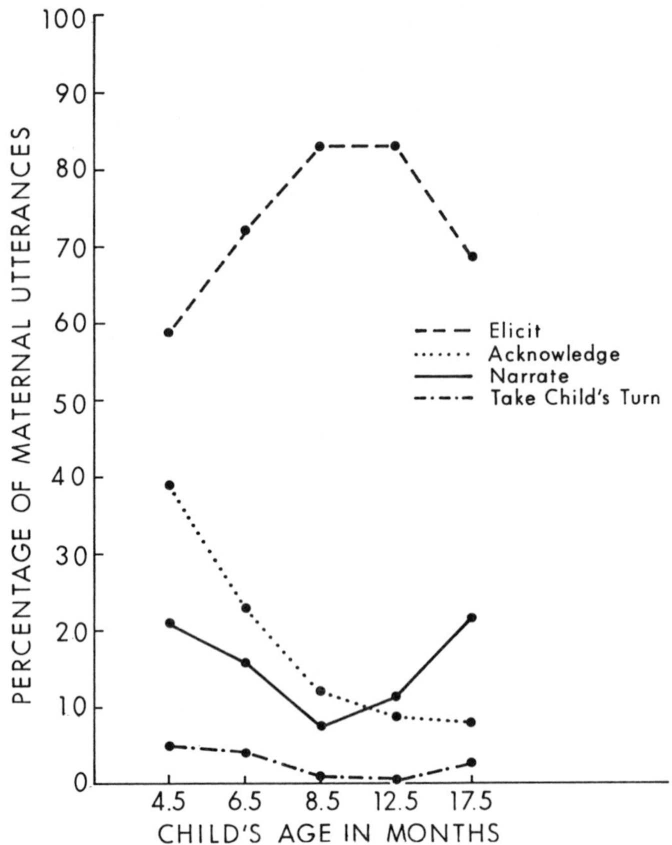

FIG. 17-3
Function categories as percentages of all utterances of Mrs. Adams.

Mrs. Brown and Jimmy

Jimmy developed normally until eight months of age when he contracted meningitis. With the meningitis he suffered a moderately-severe hearing loss. Jimmy is otherwise physically healthy, a robust, energetic, and active child. His motor and cognitive development has been age-appropriate. At 19.5 months the teacher-counselor describes Jimmy as bright, alert, and aggressively social. He uses very refined, specific gestures to communicate and watches his mother's face constantly. He imitates specific sounds and communicates vocally. The five videotaped sessions for the Browns were made at 9 months, 12.5 months, 14 months, 16.5 months, and 19.5 months.

Form

Figure 17-4 presents Mrs. Brown's utterances categorized as to form. Developmental trends are evident for the category Exclamations and for the category combining Questions and Imperatives. Exclamations made up over 50% of maternal utterances at 9 months and 12.5 months. Recall that these three months followed Jimmy's sudden hearing loss. It is quite likely that exclamations were an initial strategy used by the mother to attract Jimmy's attention. Exclamations soon dropped, however, to 16% for the final three sessions. The combined question and command category also showed a developmental trend. The initial percentages more than doubled for the final three sessions accounting for between 56% and 66% of maternal utterances.

Content

Figure 17-5 describes the content of Mrs. Brown's speech. The changes across time are striking. At 9 months almost 100% of the mother's utterances were references to the mother-child relationship. This emphasis on interpersonal themes may be an index of the mother's strong efforts to re-establish contact with her now severely hearing-impaired baby. This use of interpersonal references, however, decreased rapidly. References to objects, on the other hand, increased steadily from 5% at 9 months to 74% at 19.5 months. Content repetition decreased steadily, and utterances referring to the child's feelings were consistently low across the eleven-month period.

Function

Figure 17-6 presents the distribution of Mrs. Brown's utterances as to function. Utterances which acknowledged that the child acted intentionally decreased across time. There were no other developmental changes in maternal speech functions. Across the eleven-month period, attempts to elicit a specific response or turn from Jimmy were prominent, accounting for between 75% and 90% of maternal turns. Mrs. Brown's use of narrations was consistently low, as was the frequency with which she took Jimmy's part verbally in the exchange.

In summary, after an initial period of adaptation to Jimmy's hearing loss, Mrs. Brown used both questions and imperatives to pass the turn to Jimmy. In terms of function, utterances oriented to eliciting a response from Jimmy were extremely prominent. As for conversation repair techniques, Mrs. Brown's profile is very similar to that of Mrs. Adams' in that she used repetition to maintain the conversation and

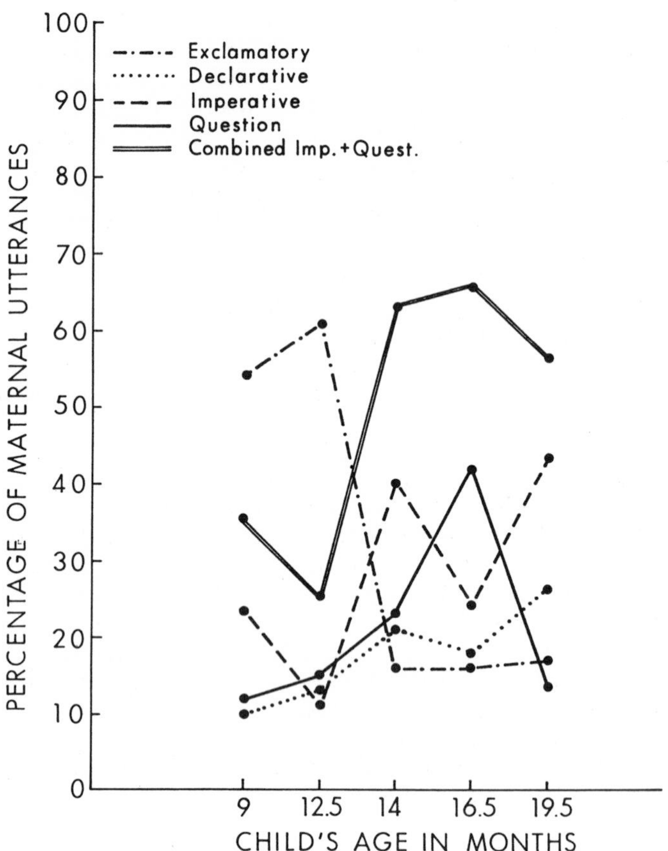

FIG. 17-4
Form categories as percentages of all utterances of Mrs. Brown.

very infrequently took Jimmy's turn in the interaction. Mrs. Brown's sensitivity to Jimmy's developmental changes is clearly documented in what she talked about. After an initial intense verbal focus on their interpersonal relationship following Jimmy's sudden hearing loss, Mrs. Brown modified the topics of her conversation in accordance with Jimmy's increased interest in the inanimate environment.

Mrs. Cain and Mary

Mary, the only child of professional parents, was adopted at two months of age. Her hearing loss was suspected at ten months and confirmed at twelve months. Mary has a severe loss of unknown etiology. She was born pre-

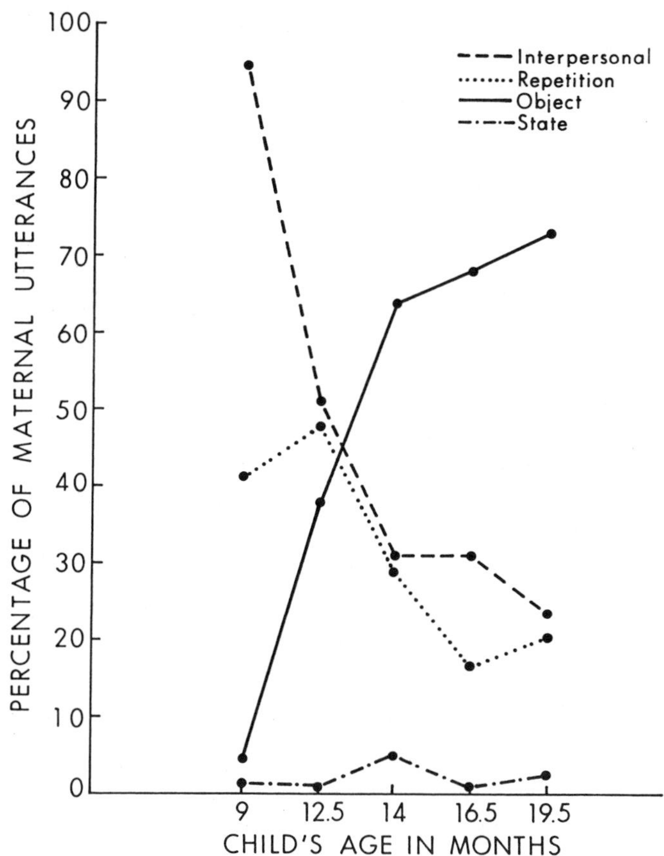

FIG. 17-5
Content categories as percentages of all utterances of Mrs. Brown.

maturely but has been in good subsequent health. Mary showed some delay in fine motor skills and is described by her teacher as extremely vocal and somewhat socially immature. At 32 months she can communicate with vocalizations and words, imitates extensively, and constructs her own sentences. She maintains irregular eye contact with her mother and other social partners. Mary is the oldest child in this study. The five videotapes for the Cains were made at 16.5 months, 20 months, 25 months, 26 months, and 32 months.

Form

Figure 17-7 represents the distribution of Mrs. Cain's utterances as to form. Her use of questions increased stead-

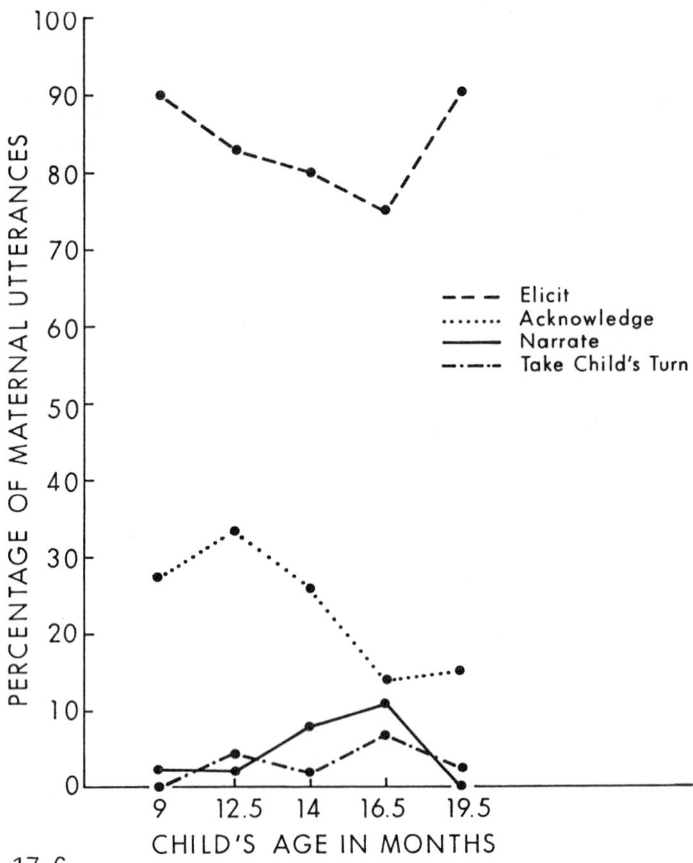

FIG. 17-6
Function categories as percentages of all utterances of Mrs. Brown.

ily from 20 months, and accounted for 61% of the maternal turns at 32 months. This was the highest percentage of questions revealed by any of the three mothers. There was a corresponding steady decline in imperatives from 31% at 16.5 months to 4% at 32 months. This was the lowest percentage for use of imperatives demonstrated by any of the mothers. This pattern is most likely due to the fact that at 32 months Mary is more than a year older than Billy or Jimmy, and is much more competent in answering questions. This verbal competency is clearly reflected in her mother's turn-passing strategy of asking questions.

Content

Figure 17-8 indicates that Mrs. Cain's use of content

categories changes consistently with Mary's age, though not as dramatically as for the other two mothers whose children are younger. Her use of object-oriented statements was initially very high, 66% at 16.5 months, and increased to 82% by 32 months. Mrs. Cain's prominent focus on the inanimate environment reflects her two-year-old child's attraction to the world around her. Utterances which refer to the parent-child relationship declined to 17% by 32 months. References to Mary's feelings were consistently infrequent across the 16-month period. Content repetition was fairly stable, with between 15% and 30% of her turns a repetition of the content theme of her preceding turn.

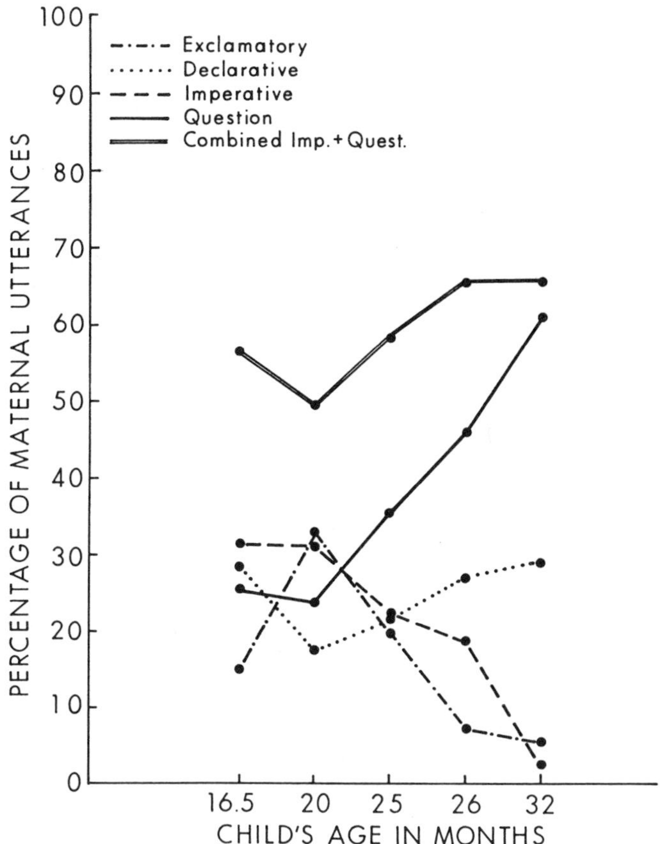

FIG. 17-7

Form categories as percentages of all utterances of Mrs. Cain.

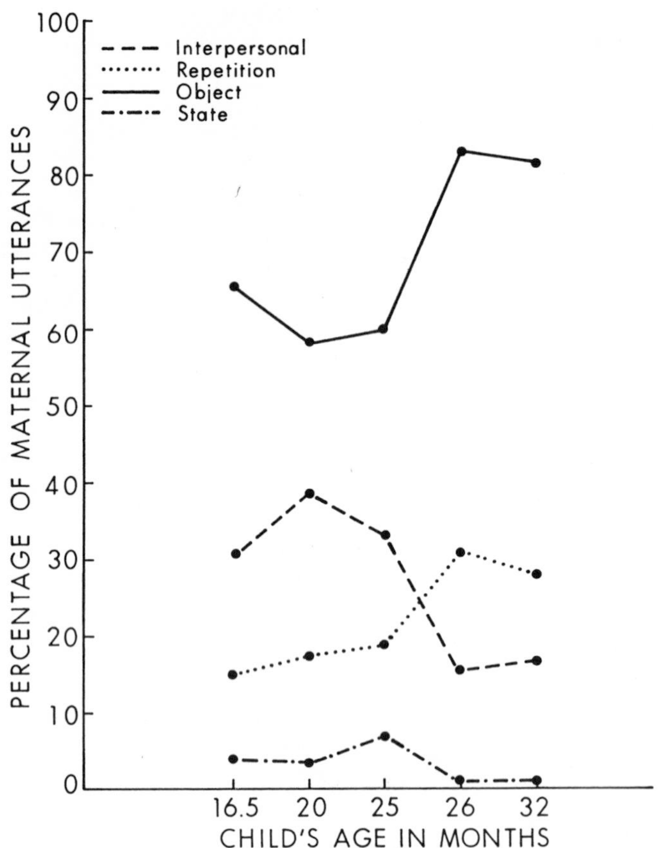

FIG. 17-8
Content categories as percentages of all utterances of Mrs. Cain.

Function

Figure 17-9 shows the categorization of maternal turns as to function. Only verbalizations which acknowledged that the child had acted intentionally showed a developmental trend as the child grew older. These acknowledgements initially were quite low, 2% at 16.5 months, but increased to between 16% and 24%. Mrs. Cain consistently attempted to elicit specific responses from Mary, accounting for between 75% and 82% of all maternal utterances. Narrations were low, ranging between 6% and 20%. Similar to the other mothers studied, Mrs. Cain very infrequently took Mary's part in the conversation.

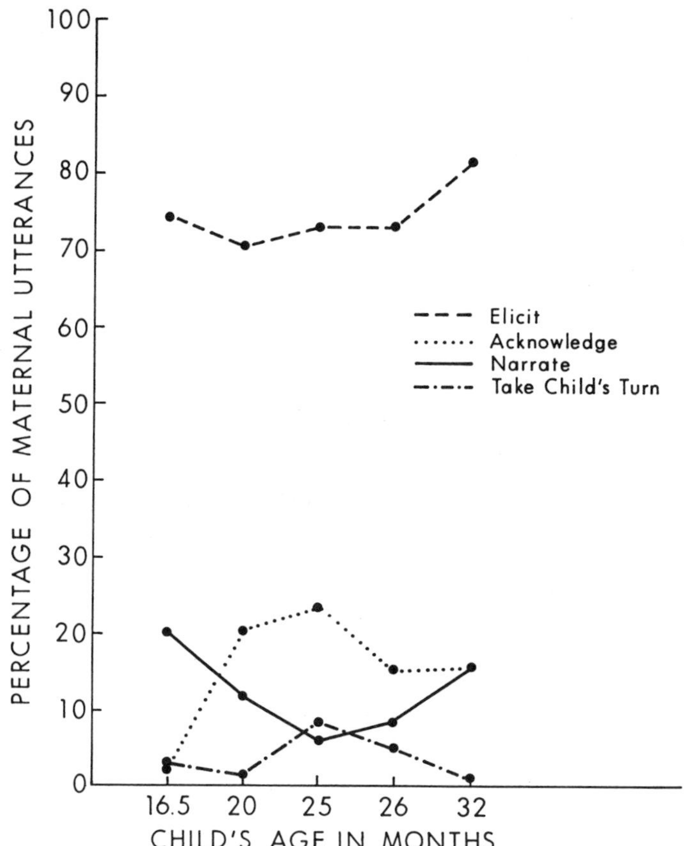

FIG. 17-9
Function categories as percentages of all utterances of Mrs. Cain.

In summary, as a strategy for passing the turn to her child, Mrs. Cain clearly relied on questions, not on commands. In terms of function, her utterances consistently attempted to elicit a response from Mary. Similar to the other mothers, Mrs. Cain frequently repeated her turn as a conversational repair strategy but did not take the child's turn.

The quality of recipient design is shown in the initial prominence of her talk about objects which also increased as the child grew older. In addition, of the three parents, Mrs. Cain showed a more defined rule for what constituted a child's turn, that being primarily verbal answers to questions. This was facilitated, of course, by her daughter's language competence. Thus, the initially low percentage of maternal utterances acknowledging the child as taking an intentional turn and the corresponding increase as Mary's verbalizations expanded most likely reflected the child's change in language skills.

DISCUSSION

Some interesting general characteristics emerge from these individual histories. Table 17-2 presents these in summary form. First, these mothers were very goal-oriented as they talked to their hearing-impaired infants. They consistently encouraged the child to take a turn through the use of question and imperative forms and a wide variety of utterances which functioned as attempts to elicit a specific response from the child. Secondly, as efforts to repair the conversation when the turn-taking system broke down, mothers repeated and reformulated their utterances but rarely answered their own questions or spoke for the baby. Finally, each of the parents showed an increase in talk about the inanimate environment which was attuned to the infants' developing interest in and skill with objects.

TABLE 17-2

General Patterns in Mother's Speech to Hearing - Impaired Children:

1. Speech was oriented to the goal of child's taking a turn in the conversation.

2. Mothers repeated and reformulated utterances to repair breakdowns in conversational turn-taking.

3. Maternal speech content reflected developmental changes in infants' cognitive and motor skills.

The data reported here are restricted as to generalizability. The sample size was small; each mother was participating in a parent-oriented intervention program; and no comparison families were studied. Given these limitations, however, the data do provide some tentative answers to the question of what verbal strategies mothers use to converse with young children who have a significant hearing loss and delayed speech production.

How do the findings compare with what is known about mothers' conversations with young children of normal hearing? Recognizing that such comparisons can only be speculative without appropriately controlled studies, it is constructive to note areas of similarity and divergence between the results of this exploratory study and the literature on maternal speech to hearing children.

First, the percentages of questions and commands shown by the mothers in the present study are very similar to those reported for mothers of hearing children by Snow (1977a) in a summary of six major studies of maternal language. Secondly, research on the content of maternal speech to hearing infants has shown that mothers increase their object-oriented statements and decrease baby-centered references as the infant develops (Sherrod et al., 1978; Snow, 1977a). This developmental pattern was also shown by the mothers with hearing-impaired children. In addition, the extent of content repetition revealed by the mothers in the present study is similar to that reported for mothers of hearing children of the same age (Snow 1977b). Finally it has been noted that during the first year of life mothers of hearing babies direct much more of their speech to eliciting responses from the baby than to responding to the baby's behavior as if it constituted a turn (Snow, 1977a). There was a similar tendency in the speech of the two mothers studied here with deaf infants under twelve months of age. The present findings, therefore, are strikingly similar to research reports of maternal language to hearing children.

There is one area of the present results, however, which requires additional explanation. The frequency with which the mothers of the two youngest infants acknowledged that responses of their hearing-impaired infants were intentional turns declined during the second year of life. In a longitudinal study of the speech of two mothers to their hearing infants, Snow (1977a) reported an increase for this age period in the mothers' acknowledging that the child had taken an intentional turn. However, Snow also found that after twelve months, these hearing infants reliably responded to maternal utterances. Similarly, it has been shown that as young hearing children begin to talk, they also begin to ask quite frequently that their mothers repeat an utterance (Baldwin and Baldwin, 1973). Hearing-impaired infants provide this element of feedback specific to maternal speech much less predictably than their hearing peers. Data on maternal responses to the infants' vocalizations, collected in the present research but not reported here, indicated that mothers consistently responded to infant vocalizations as if the baby had communicated to them about a topic under mutual discussion. The infants in our study, however, were increasing their vocalizations at a slower rate than is generally true for hearing children between 12 and 36 months. It is probable, therefore, that the low percentage of maternal utterances which acknowledged the child as taking a turn was a direct, reciprocal effect of the delayed speech production of these hearing-impaired children in the second year of life. This idea is supported by observations of the third mother whose child, at 32 months, is beginning to provide verbal feedback specific to maternal questions. In this dyad there is also a corresponding increase in the mother's verbalizing that her child is taking intentional turns.

What are the implications of this study for further research? First, these findings point out the importance of carrying out research and evaluations of interaction between the hearing-impaired child and his parent for an extended period of the child's early development. Secondly, the child must be brought into the research focus. We need to understand how young deaf children employ a range of behaviors to take their turn, and to bid a partner to take a turn, in social interactions. Finally, studies such as the present one need to be done in collaboration with child language assessments to contribute to the broader research goal of understanding the relationship between the young hearing-impaired child's interactions with his parents and his progress in language acquisition.

What does this study have to say to teachers in early intervention programs? I make three suggestions. First, as turn-taking is so central to the development of a range of early skills, we ought to foster it in nonverbal and verbal modes simultaneously, for example, by verbalizing while engaging in give-and-take with objects, back-and-forth physical games, and motor imitation sequence. Second, we need to encourage parents of hearing-impaired children to define a broad range of early responses as intentional child turns and to see a variety of early behaviors as strengthening the child's conversational participation. A third implication may be diagnostic. Is there a clue as to the parent's perceptions and expectations of the infant in the structure of her speech? Perhaps the young, linguistically handicapped child can tolerate differences in the quantity and even quality of parental speech as long as the underlying structural model is one which enhances the child's role as a co-participant. Finally, as teachers of young children and often language models for their parents, we should attend to the conversational features in our own speech as we intervene with the parent-child partnership.

Increasingly, research into those early interactional experiences which are precursors for optimal social and cognitive development (see Schaffer, 1977) is supporting the idea that "turn-taking is more than just a characteristic of language... it is a necessity for the acquisition of language (Kaye, 1977, p. 93)." In the present study a conversational turn-taking model is clearly provided in the speech mothers directed to their hearing-impaired infants. Their infants, therefore, are being actively recruited into this important partnership shown to be adaptive for the emergence of a range of early skills, including language competence.

[1]The cooperation and support of Dr. Audrey Simmons-Martin, Director of the Parent-Infant Program, Central Institute for the Deaf and the willingness of the families in the Parent-Infant Program to be videotaped were essential for this research. Ken Nicolai skillfully prepared the videotapes, and June Chan diligently worked with me in establishing inter-coder reliabilities. Finally, I am sincerely grateful to Rose-Marie Smith, teacher-counselor for the families in this study, for her many helpful and insightful suggestions and for her commitment to integrating research and service in her work with families.

REFERENCES

Anderson, B. J. The emergence of conversational behavior. Journal of Communication. 1977, 27, 85-91.

Anderson, B. J. Manual for coding parental utterances to young children: Form, content, function, and responsiveness. Unpublished manuscript, Washington University School of Medicine, St. Louis, 1978.

Anderson, B. J., Vietze, P., and Dokecki, P. R. Reciprocity in vocal interactions of mothers and infants. Child Development. 1977, 48, 1676-1681.

Baldwin, A. L., and Baldwin, C. P. The study of mother-child interaction. American Scientist. 1973, 61, 714-721.

Bateson, M. C. Mother-infant exchanges: The epigenesis of conversational interaction. Annals of the New York Academy of Sciences. 1975, 263, 101-113.

Bruner, J. S. Early social interaction and language acquisition. In H. R. Schaffer (ed.), Studies in Mother-Infant Interaction. NY: Academic Press, 1977.

Greenstein, J.M., Greenstein, B.B., McConville, K., and Stellini, L., Mother-Infant Communication and Language Acquisition in Deaf Infants, NY: Lexington School for the Deaf, 1976.

Kaye, K. Toward the origin of dialogue. In H. R. Schaffer (ed.), Studies in Mother-Infant Interaction. NY: Academic Press, 1977.

Sacks, H., Schegloff, E. A., and Jefferson, B. A simplest systematics for the organization of turn taking for conversation. Language. 1974, 50, 696-735.

Schaffer, H. Mothering. Cambridge, MA: Harvard University Press, 1977.

Sherrod, K., Vietze, P., and Friedman, S. Infancy. Belmont, CA: Wadsworth Publishing Company, 1978.

Snow, C. The development of conversation between mothers and babies. Journal of Child Language. 1977, 4, 1-22. (a)

Snow, C. Mothers' speech research: From input to interaction. In C. Snow and C. Ferguson (eds.), Talking to children: Language Input and Acquisition. Cambridge: Cambridge University Press, 1977. (b)

Stern, D. N. Mother and infant at play: The dyadic interaction involving facial, vocal, and gaze behaviors. In M. Lewis and L. A. Rosenblum (eds.), The Effect of the Infant on its Caregiver. New York: Wiley, 1974.

Stern, D. N., Jaffe, J., Beebe, B., and Bennett, S.L. Vocalizing in unison and in alternation: Two modes of communication within the mother-infant dyad. Annals of the New York Academy of Sciences. 1975, 263, 89-100.

PHYLLIS LEVENSTEIN, Ed.D.

Director
Verbal Interaction Project
Freeport, New York

18

The Parent-Child Network

That parents influence the behavior of their children for good or for ill has become a truism. Surprisingly, we know more about the ways parents can be a destructive influence than about their favorable influence on children's social-emotional competence in dealing with the world of persons and tasks around them, and with their own inner emotional states. As recently as 1977, Kohn completed an important book describing a very large, painstaking study of the longitudinal persistence of social-emotional strengths and problems in 1200 children in day care centers, followed from preschool into fourth grade. In conclusion the author (Kohn, 1977) asked, "Is the home life of children who recover more supportive and growth promoting than that of children who remain disturbed?...We know relatively little of the antecedents of emotional health" (pages 265-266). It is not quite enough to hold simply to a belief that good parenting is an antecedent of children's good social-emotional functioning. What specific behaviors go into good parenting? And is such parenting in early childhood indeed a source of social-emotional strength in later childhood?

A number of investigators of parent-child interaction

have made a good start in trying to answer these questions (Clarke-Stewart, 1973; Radin, 1971; Seitz and Stewart, 1975; White and Watts, 1973). Over the last ten years, the Verbal Interaction Project has had a rare opportunity to gather empirical data on parent-child interaction. The information was obtained through direct observations of mothers and their preschool children together in their homes, and of the same children later in elementary school. We had two primary interests: to measure the effects of our Mother-Child Home Program on parents' parenting and on children's social-emotional competence; and to explore the more basic question of whether, and how, parents (particularly mothers) influence their children toward social-emotional competence. We hoped to find answers useful to parents and teachers as well as to ourselves and science. The population for which we intended our program was low-income mothers and their preschool children who were considered vulnerable, because of low-income status, to later academic and behavior problems in school. Your interest is focused on children with communication disorders. The two sources of vulnerability are far apart, but perhaps the results of our study can be useful to both of us.

The Verbal Interaction Project's observations were of 45 mothers and their four-year-old children in their homes. Direct observations are methodologically troublesome but are much more reliable than the self-reports given in interviews with parents (McCord and McCord, 1961). We rated the mothers on observable, concretely defined, desirable parenting behaviors, and we rated the children on observable, concretely defined, desirable social-emotional behaviors. Our criteria for "desirable" was based on a reasonable distillation of goals for mothers and children expressed by human relations experts, and found in the professional literature over the last 50 years. We wondered if we would see, at the child's age of four years, positive relationships between what parents did and how their children acted. Even more, we wondered if any relationships we found would endure into the child's school years. Specifically, we wanted to know if the ratings of children's competence by their teachers in the classroom two years later would correlate with mothers' parenting behavior when the child was four years old.

The 45 mothers and children were participants in the Mother-Child Home Program, which had been developed and was being tested by the Verbal Interaction Project. They had entered the program in October, 1972, and completed it in May, 1974. They were known as the 1972 Cohort. The 1972 Cohort was similar in background to the 600 other low-income families which have entered the Verbal Interaction

Project in yearly cohorts: the families were eligible for low-income housing; most of the fathers had occupations which were no higher than semi-skilled; the average education for both parents was about tenth grade; 35% of the fathers were absent from the home, with about the same proportion of mothers receiving welfare aid; and two thirds of the families were socially defined as Black.

To answer the questions about mother-child relationships, we began ten years ago to develop two new instruments, (no suitable ones were then available), one to measure children's social-emotional coping skills, and one to measure parenting skills. The first we eventually called "Child's Behavior Traits", or CBT. The second became "Parent And Child Together", or PACT. Both were composed of Likert-type scales yielding item and summative scores, all going in a positive, mental-health oriented direction. Both have demonstrated reliability and validity. (Samples of both instruments can be obtained from the Verbal Interaction Project, 5 Broadway, Freeport, New York 11520).

"Child's Behavior Traits" was created on the basis of staff experience, as psychologists, social workers, and teachers. We supplemented this with professional literature (e.g., Murphy, 1962; Baumrind and Black, 1967) and advice from other teachers and outside clinicians. In the CBT's development we tried to satisfy several criteria besides generally accepted standards for social-emotional competence. Since it would be used in our home program as well as later in school, it had to be applicable to children from ages two to twelve in home or school settings. The instrument had to be easily understood and non-abstract wherever possible, and it had to be brief, no more than a page long. We ended up with a 20-item measure, well-tested for reliability and validity (Levenstein, 1976), and anticipating in content many of the 29 social competencies later suggested by a national task force (Anderson and Messick, 1974). All 20 items appear in abbreviated form on Tables 18-1 through 18-4, grouped for convenience in rows at the left side under the categories of Task Orientation, Cognitive Orientation, Responsible Independence, Social Cooperation, and Emotional Stability.

"Parent and Child Together" was a 20-item instrument based on Diana Baumrind's distinguished work at Berkeley, one of the few successful attempts to tease out the parental correlates of outstanding social competence. She used four-year-olds in a Berkeley nursery school (Baumrind, 1967). The parents in her study were described as "middle class, well educated". While they were quite different from Verbal Interaction Project parents, nevertheless we decided to adapt many of her findings into scales for our own observations. We retained in large part her categories and specifics of parental behavior. Like the CBT, the PACT was planned for maximum usefulness, with attention to its practical aspects as well as to test construction considerations. Mainly it had to be easily understood, and short. Its final 20-item form has internal reliability and correlates well enough with other logically related measures to indicate its validity. The 1972 Cohort was the first cohort to be measured on the final form of the PACT and its explanatory "Item Guide."

The 20 PACT items are categorized under:

1. Verbal Interaction (column headings in Tables 18-1 to 18-4)
   - Responds verbally to child's request.
   - Verbalizes expectations of child.
   - Verbalizes approval of child.
   - Tries to converse with child.
   - Verbalizes reasons for obedience.

2. Nurturance
   - Shows warmth toward child.
   - Verbalizes affection toward child.
   - Satisfies child's needs, signalled verbally or non-verbally.
   - Seems comforting to child.
   - Uses positive reinforcement.

3. Encouragement of Autonomy
   - Discourages child's over-dependence.
   - Encourages child's understanding reasons for directives.
   - Actively encourages child's independence.
   - Trains child for self-direction.
   - Seems prepared to respect child's negative reactions to directive.

4. Parental Controls
   - Tries to enforce directives.
   - Refrains from scolding.
   - Directive gains child's attention.
   - Persists in enforcing directions.
   - Is firm with child.

The children and their parents were rated globally on the Child's Behavior Traits (CBT) and Parent and Child Together (PACT) on the basis of observations of their first six Home Sessions in the program and at the end, based on their next-to-last six Home Sessions. They were rated by their "Toy Demonstrators," whose function as home visitors in the program can best be understood by a brief description of the program itself. (More details are in Levenstein, 1977).

THE PROGRAM

The Mother-Child Home Program is a voluntary, "no strings attached", home-based early education program for low-income two-to four-year-olds and their mothers or mother surrogates. The aim is to promote later social-emotional development by enhancing the mother's interactive behavior, especially verbal interaction, as suggested by many studies (e.g. Bee, 1969; Bruner, 1964; Datta and Parloff, 1967; Hunt, 1961; 1969; John and Goldstein, 1964; Phenix, 1964) and supported later by Elardo et al. (1975). The Toy Demonstrator is a home visitor who models interactive skills in home play sessions around gifts of toys and books. Like the CBT and the PACT, the program's model is health, not deficit. Central to the method is complete avoidance of teaching or counseling. Our basic assumption about the mothers is that they are competent enough to run their own lives. Supervisors stand by to offer help only if it is requested by the mother.

The mother and child are in the program for two school years, starting when the child is about two. The half-hour home sessions take place twice a week for seven months within each of the two years, for a total of 46 play sessions a year. Each week a new, carefully selected toy or book is presented to the child. These are the "curriculum materials" around which a fun-oriented cognitive curriculum is built. A developmentally appropriate Guide Sheet is written for each new toy or book, around a list of concepts for the child to learn. The use of the Guide Sheets is demonstrated (modeled) for the mother by the "Toy Demonstrators". These demonstrators are minimally screened, paid or volunteer women with a wide range of education and background. Some are former mother participants, some are former teachers. Almost all make good Toy Demonstrators, as long as they do not try to teach, give advise, or become a close friend of the mother. It is our belief, supported by the program's popularity and by our results, that in a home-based program, "less is more". The Toy Demonstrators are taught not only program techniques and rules of confidentiality, but also techniques to protect the family against any unintended but possible coerciveness or intrusiveness on the part of the program. These Toy Demonstrators, trained to be sensitive and observant, record the PACT and CBT data on the mothers and children at the beginning and end of the program. They are familiar with both instruments, because the PACT and CBT are used in supervision to teach the program's affective curriculum.

Observations in First Grade School Classroom

Two years after they graduated from the Mother-Child Home Program, and after they had entered elementary school, the children, now six years old, were again rated on the CBT. This time the observers were the first-grade classroom teachers. They rated the 39 children, of the original 45, on the basis of their social-emotional classroom competence during the school year from September, 1976 to March, 1977.

Data Management and Analysis

The item and summative (total) scores for the CBT (Child's Behavior Traits) and PACT (Parent and Child Together) ratings of the 1972 Cohort from both time points (at age four and at age six) were entered into a computer. The mean total CBT scores and all CBT items were correlated with all mean PACT items and PACT total scores (along with other variables), using Pearson's product moment correlations. Only coefficients significant below the .05, .01, and .005 levels of probability in the correlation matrices are reported.

Scope of this Report

I will confine myself to a discussion of the relation of maternal verbal interaction to the child's social-emotional behavior. This is the kind of parental behavior we have tried most systematically to foster through the Mother-Child Home Program. It was also found to yield the most correlations of all PACT items. We examined in some detail the links between the five PACT items comprising parental verbal interaction and all 20 of the child's social-emotional coping skills. We looked at these associations as they became manifest when the children were four years old and just finishing the program. Finally, we searched to see if any links still remained in relation to the children's social-emotional behavior when they were six years old and almost past the middle of first grade. The summary of what we found is in Tables 18-1, 18-2, 18-3, and 18-4.

THE PARENT-CHILD NETWORK MADE VISIBLE

Children at Age Four

When the 1972 program children were four years old, they had been in the program for two school years with their mothers, and were just coming to the end of their program experience. At that time the associations between their social-emotional competence and their mothers' verbal interaction with them were very pronounced. Almost every one of the 20 items on the Child's Behavior Traits correlated significantly with at least two aspects (and usually even more) of the mothers' verbal interactions with the children. There was a large number of significant relationships between the 20 social-emotional competencies and the five varieties of mothers' verbal interaction as seen in the PACT item scores.

The relation was especially striking in regard to the Task Orientation and Cognitive Orientation categories of child's social-emotional skills. The correlations of the eight coping skills grouped under these headings, with the mothers' verbal interaction, are recorded in Table 18-1. Almost every one of these eight intellectual competencies of the four-year-olds was linked to every one of the mothers' five verbal interaction behaviors, thus:

Mothers' Verbal Interactions

- Responds verbally to child's request.
- Verbalizes expectations of child.
- Verbalizes approval of child.
- Tries to converse with child.
- Verbalizes reasons to obey.

↓ CORRELATED WITH CHILDREN'S ↓

Task orientation:

- Initiates goal directed activities.
- Completes tasks.
- Enjoy mastering new tasks.
- Is attentive and concentrates.

Cognitive orientation:

- Is well organized.
- Expresses ideas in language.
- Knows difference, facts/make-believe.
- Is creative, inventive.

TABLE 18-1

Correlations of Mothers' Home Verbal Interaction with Children's Task & Cognitive Orientation at Child's Age 4 (Pearson's r, N=45)

Child Task and Cognitive Orientation at Age 4 (home observations)	Mothers' Verbal Interaction at Child's Age 4	
	Responds Verbally to Child's request	Verbalizes expectations of child
	Task Orientation	
Initiates goal directed activities	.37*	.31*
Completes tasks	.33*	
Enjoys mastering new tasks	.38**	.37*
Attentive & concentrates		.33*
	Cognitive Orientation	
Well organized	.43***	.38*
Expresses ideas in language	.57***	.30*
Difference, facts & Make believe	.37*	.37*
Creative, inventive	.32*	.33*

*p $\leq$ .05

**p $\leq$ .01

***p $\leq$ .005

TABLE 18-1

Correlations of Mothers' Home Verbal Interaction
with Children's Task & Cognitive Orientation at Child's Age 4
(Pearson's r, N=45)

Mothers' Verbal Interaction at Child's Age 4		
Verbalizes approval of child	Tries to converse with child	Verbalizes reasons for obedience
Task Orientation		
.35*	.50***	.48***
.52***	.41***	.47***
.49***	.43***	.36*
.48***	.43***	.50***
Cognitive Orientation		
.45***	.54***	.52***
	.52***	.42***
.39**	.34*	.43***
.41**	.49***	.48***

*p ≤ .05

**p ≤ .01

***p ≤ .005

TABLE 18-2
Correlations of Mothers' Home Verbal Interaction with Children's Independence, Cooperation, Emotional Stability, at Child's Age 4
(Pearson's *r*, N = 45)

Child Independence, Cooperation, and Emotional Stability At Age 4 (home observations)	Mothers' Home Verbal Interaction at Child's Age 4: Responds verbally to child's request	Mothers' Home Verbal Interaction at Child's Age 4: Verbalizes expectations of child
	Responsible Independence	
Accepts, asks for help		.31*
Protects own rights		
Self-confident	.42***	.47***
Refrains: physical risks	.38***	.40**
	Social Cooperation	
Refrains: physical aggression	.33*	.40**
Cooperates with adults	.31*	.58***
Follows rules	.32*	.65***
Puts own needs second		.34*
	Emotional Stablility	
Cheerful and content	.38**	.32*
Spontaneous, not explosive	.32*	.30*
Tolerates frustration		.44***
No sudden mood changes	.37**	.48***

*p ≤ .05
**p ≤ .01
***p ≤ .005

TABLE 18-2

Correlations of Mothers' Home Verbal Interaction with Children's Independence, Cooperation, Emotional Stability, at Child's Age 4 (Pearson's *r*, N = 45)

Mothers' Home Verbal Interaction at Child's Age 4		
Verbalizes approval of child	Tries to converse with child	Verbalizes reasons for obedience
Responsible Independence		
.38**		
	.39**	
	.30*	
		.37*
Social Cooperation		
		.32*
.37**		.45***
.38**		.41**
.44***		.40**
Emotional Stability		
.50***	.34*	.41***
.34*		.41**

*p ≤ .05
**p ≤ .01
***p ≤ .005

The children's coping with social responsibilities and inner emotional demands was not as frequently correlated with mothers' verbal interaction as was their competence with intellectual tasks and ideas. Table 18-2 contains the correlation of mothers' verbal interaction with three categories of such coping: Responsible Independence, Social Cooperation, and Emotional Stability. Table 18-2 shows that every one of the twelve coping skills grouped under these headings correlated with at least two of the five maternal verbal interaction behaviors. The major maternal verbal interactions and associated child coping skills are:

<u>Mothers' Verbal Interactions</u>
- Responds verbally to child's request.
- Verbalizes expectations of child.
- Verbalizes approval of child.
- Tries to converse with child.
- Verbalizes reasons for obedience.

CORRELATED WITH CHILDREN'S

<u>Responsible Independence</u>
- Accepts, asks for help.
- Protects own rights.
- Is self-confident.
- Refrains: physical risks.

<u>Social Cooperation</u>
- Refrains: physical aggression.
- Cooperates with adults.
- Follows rules.
- Puts own needs second.

<u>Emotional Stability</u>
- Is cheerful and content.
- Is spontaneous, not explosive.
- Tolerates frustration.
- Has no sudden mood changes.

The Verbal Interaction Project correlations at four years were similar to those found at the same age by Baumrind with more advantaged families. However, it is well to be reminded that part of this wealth of correlations at age four in our own research may have resulted from "halo" effects because the same Toy Demonstrator rated both mother and child. It should certainly be emphasized that it is not possible to establish a clear cause and effect relationship among these correlations existing concurrently, at the same point in time.

No more -- but also no less -- has been demonstrated than the possible existence of a network of concurrent parent-child behaviors, each probably influencing the other. The children were four years old, and both mothers and children were just completing their two school years in the Mother-Child Home Program. Thus made visible in these low-income, low-schooled families were threads of a parent-child network which might prove genuine enough and strong enough to form a lasting social-emotional support system for the child. For if the mother's verbal communication truly interacted so functionally with the child's social-emotional competence at age four, perhaps it could continue to do so into the child's school years. Perhaps the parent-child network found in earlier years could be the underpinnings for the child's constructing in first grade the foundations for his later school learning. For this the mothers' verbal interaction contributions to the network when the children were four would have to relate significantly to the children's social-emotional competence two years later, when the children were six-years-old, in the first grade classroom, and rated by an independent observer.

The Parent-Child Network at Children's Age of Six Years (First Grade)

The same PACT scores reflecting mothers' parenting, which formed part of the network when the children were four, were used for the correlations with the 1972 Cohort's social-emotional behavior at age six. But the children's age six CBT social-emotional scores came out of quite different circumstances than their age four ratings:

1. The children were, of course, at a much later stage of social-emotional, cognitive, and physical development.

2. The same social-emotional skills observed (at age four) in the home were rated (at age six) in the school classroom.

3. For the first-grade ratings, the child was observed among classmates, not alone with the mother or other family members, as he or she was at age four.

TABLE 18-3

Correlations of Mothers' Home Verbal Interaction
at Child's Age 4
with
Child Task & Cognitive Orientation in First Grade at Age 6
(Pearson's r, N = 39)

Child Task and Cognitive Orientation in First Grade at Age 6 (school classroom observations)	Mothers' Home Verbal Interaction at Child's Age 4	
	Responds verbally to child's request	Verbalizes expectations of child
	Task Orientation	
Initiates goal directed activities		
Completes tasks		
Enjoys mastering new tasks	.48***	
Attentive & concentrates		
	Cognitive Orientation	
Well organized	.39*	
Expresses ideas in language	.48***	
Difference, facts and make believe	.61***	.34*
Creative, inventive	.40*	

*$p \leq .05$

**$p \leq .01$

***$p \leq .005$

TABLE 18-3

Correlations of Mothers' Home Verbal Interaction at Child's Age 4 with Child Task & Cognitive Orientation in First Grade at Age 6 (Pearson's *r*, N = 39)

Mothers' Home Verbal Interaction at Child's Age 4		
Verbalizes approval of child	Tries to converse with child	Verbalizes reasons for obedience
Task Orientation		
	.35*	
	.54***	.36*
Cognitive Orientation		
	.41**	.35*
	.48***	
	.61***	.52***
	.52***	.44***

*p ≤ .05

**p ≤ .01

***p ≤ .005

4. The CBT ratings were by the children's school teachers, not by the program's Toy Demonstrators. The teachers had a page of written information about the Verbal Interaction Project and a written guide to scoring the CBT. They had limited acquaintance with the project staff member who distributed the CBT, and no association with the Verbal Interaction Project nor knowledge of whether the child had been a Program or no-Program subject in the Project.

Thus the children's social-emotional skills at age six were judged in a different setting, within a group, by an observer almost completely independent of the Verbal Interaction Project, and at a different stage of development from the ratings at age four. Under such widely differing circumstances, it seemed unlikely that the mothers' verbal interaction observed at the child's age of four would still be visible in association with the child's social-emotional competence at the age of six. Yet the influence of the mothers' earlier verbal interaction did become visible in 27 correlations with the children's social-emotional competence at the later age, in the first grade classroom.

The enduring strands of the mothers' part of the parent-child network can be clearly seen in Tables 18-3 and 18-4. These tables follow exactly the same format of Tables 18-1 and 18-2, which were filled in with mother-child correlations from two years before. But the CBT categories and items on the left hand rows of Tables 18-3 and 18-4 came out of the classroom, not out of the home, and were scored by teachers, not by Toy Demonstrators. The PACT scores for the mothers' Verbal Interaction used for the correlations with the children's classroom social-emotional scores, in the right hand columns, were, of course, exactly the same as two years earlier. Instead of these indicating that there were no significant correlations with classroom CBT scores, with columns being totally blank, as one might reasonably expect, 27 significant correlations are to be found on Tables 18-3 and 18-4. Mothers' verbal interaction at the child's age four can be said to <u>predict</u>, probably to <u>influence</u>, and possibly to <u>cause</u> the children's first grade social-emotional competence in 27 visible ways.

The word "cause" must still be used cautiously. It is incontrovertible that the mothers' verbal interaction behavior with the children at age four preceded the children's classroom behavior at age six. But it is not impossible that the six-year-old behavior resulted not alone from the mothers' prior behavior, but from a continuing network of interacting parent-child behaviors, or other unknown factors. [For instance, in a recent <u>Science</u> article the lead and cadmium content in hair samples reliably discriminated between learning-disabled and normal children (Pihl, 1977).] However, it is more parsimonious to accept, from the evidence presented here, the strong influence on the graduates' competence in first grade of the mothers' verbal interaction with them at age four and to consider those verbal interactions as precursors of the children's first grade social-emotional competence. Closer examination of Tables 18-3 and 18-4 reveals that in the main only three kinds of antecedent verbal interaction had this continuing influence: responds verbally to child's request, tries to converse with child, and verbalizes reasons for obedience. Their influence is visible and pervasive on four out of five categories of the children's social-emotional skills listed on Tables 18-3 and 18-4: Task Orientation, Cognitive Orientation, Responsible Independence, and Emotional Stability. The fifth CBT category is "Social Co-operation"; the four skills listed under this heading (refrains from physical aggression; cooperates with adults; follows rules; puts own needs second) show no relationships with the mothers' prior verbal interaction.

Two of the three maternal verbal interactions that predict the child's later competence involve the give-and-take that Ira Gordon has felicitiously called the "ping-pong" interaction between parent and child (Gordon, 1977). The details of the mother's contributions to this exchange are described in the PACT Item Guide as follows:

1. Mother tries to converse with the child.

"Tries to conduct conversation. Responds to child's utterance (whether or not it is a question) with a comment, question, or an association to what the child has said. The conversation may be long or short, and it may or may not contain information for the child. The 'conversation' may be more of an accompaniment to the child's activity than an actual verbal give-and-take."

One example is the following dialogue:

Child: "Green."
Parent: "Yes, it's a green block. And something you're wearing is green too."
Child: "Green."
Parent: "Well, look at your shirt. What color is that?"

Here is another example:

Child: "I'm building (tower of blocks) up, up, up!"
Parent: "Yes, up it goes, up, up, up!"
Child: "Gonna crash!"
Parent: "Bang!"

2. Mother responds verbally to the child's verbal or non-verbal request for attention.

"Uses words to show that she is aware of what the child wants, and that she will either grant his request or will not do so. Doesn't ignore the child's bid for attention." An example is that the mother says, "Yes, I see the dog," when child points or exclaims, "Dog!" while looking at a book illustration.

The last of the three predictive verbal interactions gives the child a reality base for his compliance with the mystifying laws that rule his world. We quote again from the PACT Item Guide.

3. Mother verbalizes the reasons for the child's obedience.

"Explains why it is necessary for child to perform, or desist from, a particular action."

An example is that:

When she suggests that the child put the blocks into the block can, she adds that in that way, the pieces won't get lost.

One common theme of these three maternal verbal interaction components of the enduring network is the mother's response to the child's reality with words, with language which symbolizes and enlarges the child's inter-changes with the world around him. Another theme is her implicit recognition of the child as a unique individual, a person-orientation more functional for social-emotional growth than the status-orientation often characteristic of low-income families (Hess and Shipman, 1965). The effect of her contributions is lasting, and their power is still visible at age six in relation to competencies which will especially help him to develop further in his coping skills. The mother has contributed to the child being, at age six, cheerful, spontaneous, self-confident, ready to protect his own rights appropriately, yet willing to seek help when necessary. She has contributed to the child's being solidly based in reality, yet creative and inventive. He also has the maturity to be well organized and able to express ideas in language and yet also shows joy in mastering tasks. It seems clear that the mother has made a contribution not only to the child's social-emotional competence in school but to the chances for his or her maximum development as a human being.

REFLECTIONS ON THE PARENT-CHILD NETWORK

In sum, we have found considerable empirical support in one group of mothers and children for the existence of a parent-child network. We have demonstrated first the mutual influence of child and parent upon each other at the same point in time, and second, the parent's influence on her child's later social-emotional coping skills in school. We have found the verbal interaction behaviors of mothers to be significantly linked to the competencies of their children at age four at home and having an influence enduring to the child's age of six. The 1972 Cohort may be idiosyncratic as a group in some unknown way but is large enough to suggest that the results are generalizable. The network can be strengthened by parents and by special programs for parents and for children. This inevitably means very hard work on the part of parents and teachers of children with communication disorders, but at least our demonstration of the network's existence promises rewards for both adults and children.

The promise must be tempered by a reminder that we don't know much about the children's individual contributions to the network. We can't know in what ways and to what degree the children themselves stimulated their parents' behavior almost from the moment of birth. Certainly, as previously indicated, we can't be certain which came first in the parent-child behaviors when the child was four years old, in spite of the mother's existence prior to the child's. Babies come into the world well-equipped with life savers to get positive responses from parents: cries and coos, smiles and wriggles, gazes and giggles -- a tremendous repertoire to feed into the reciprocal relationship. We can say for sure that the network is the result of dynamic interaction from birth between parent and child behaviors.

In the data we have reviewed here, there is a very strong probability that the mothers' good parenting at the children's age four was a source of the children's social-emotional competence in the first grade of school when they were six. It should also be remembered that these data are from a group of mother-child dyads who, though of low income, lived in homes well supplied by our intervention home program with toys and books rich in verbal interaction possibilities and with a joyous curriculum for using them.

Perhaps these representatives of one educationally vulnerable population (the low-income group) bear a message

TABLE 18-4

Correlations of Mothers' Home Verbal Interaction
at Child's Age 4 with
Child Independence, Cooperation,
Emotional Stability in First Grade at Age 6
(Pearson's *r*, N = 39)

Child Independence, Cooperation, and Emotional Stability in First Grade At Age 6 (school classroom observations)	Mothers' Verbal Interaction at Child's Age 4: Responds verbally to child's request	Mothers' Verbal Interaction at Child's Age 4: Verbalizes expectations of child
	Responsible Independence	
Accepts, asks for help	.38*	
Protects own rights	.33*	
Self-confident	.47***	
Refrains: physical risks		
	Social Cooperation	
Refrains: physical aggression		
Cooperates with adults		
Follows rules		
Puts own needs second		
	Emotional Stablility	
Cheerful and content	.33*	
Spontaneous, not explosive	.42**	
Tolerates frustration		
No sudden mood changes		

*p ≤ .05
**p ≤ .01
***p ≤ .005

TABLE 18-4

Correlations of Mothers' Home Verbal Interaction at Child's Age 4 with Child Independence, Cooperation, Emotional Stability in First Grade at Age 6 (Pearson's r, N = 39)

Mothers' Verbal Interaction at Child's Age 4		
Verbalizes approval of child	Tries to converse with child	Verbalizes reasons for obedience
Responsible Independence		
	.38**	
	.49***	
Social Cooperation		
Emotional Stability		
	.39*	.33*
	.47***	.34*

*p ≤ .05
**p ≤ .01
***p ≤ .005

which will be helpful to another, the special group of children with communication problems which is your interest and is the focus of this conference.

Research supported by Marion R. Ascoli Fund; Carnegie Corporation of New York; Foundation for Child Development; General Mills Foundation; William T. Grant Foundation; Rockefeller Brothers Fund; Surdna Foundation; and U.S. Department of HEW (Children's Bureau; National Institute of Mental Health; Office of Education).

REFERENCES

Anderson, Scarvia and Messick, Samuel. Social competency in young children. Developmental Psychology. 1974, 10, 282-293.

Baumrind, Diana. Child care practices anteceding three patterns of preschool behavior. Genetic Psychology Monographs. 1976, 75, 43-88.

Baumrind, Diana, and Black, Allen E. Socialization practices associated with dimensions of competence in preschool boys and girls. Child Development. 1967, 38.

Bee, L., van Egeren, F., Streissguth, A. P., Nyman, B. A. and Leckie, S. Social class differences in maternal teaching strategies and speech patterns. Developmental Psychology. 1968, 1, 726-734.

Bruner, J. S. The course of cognitive growth. American Psychologist. Jan. 1964, XIX, 1-15.

Clarke-Stewart, K. A. Interactions between mothers and their young children: Characteristics and consequences. Monographs of the Society for Research in Child Development. 1973, 12 (6 and 7, Serial No. 153).

Datta, Lois-Ellin and Parloff, Morris B. On the relevance of autonomy: Parent-child relationships and early scientific creativity. Proceedings, 75th annual convention, APA, 1967.

Elardo, R., Bradley, R. and Caldwell, B. M. Relations of infants' home environments to mental test performance from six to thirty-six months. Child Development. 1975, 46, 71-76.

Gordon, I.J. Baby to Parent, Parent to Baby. New York: St. Martin's Press, 1977.

Hess, R.D. and Shipman, V.C. Early experience and the socialization of cognitive modes in children. Child Development. 1965, 36, 869-886.

Hunt, J. McVicker. The Challenge of Incompetence and Poverty. Urbana: University of Illinois Press, 1969, 109.

Hunt, J. McVicker. Intelligence and Experience. New York: Ronald Press, 1961.

John, Vera P. and Goldstein, Leo S. The social context of language acquisition. Merrill-Palmer Quarterly. 1964, X, 265-275.

Kohn, Martin. Social Competence, Symptoms and Underachievement in Childhood: A Longitudinal Perspective. Washington, D.C.: V.H. Winston and Sons, 1977.

Levenstein, P. The mother-child home program. In M.C. Day and R.K. Parker (eds.) The Preschool in Action (2nd ed.) Boston: Allyn and Bacon, 1977.

Levenstein, Phyllis and Staff, Verbal interaction project. Child's behavior traits. In Johnson, O.G. (ed.) Tests and Measurements in Child Development, Handbook II. San Francisco: Jossey-Bass, 1976, 415-416.

McCord, Joan and McCord, Willian. Cultural stereotypes and the validity of interview for research in child development. Child Development. 1961, 32, 171-185.

Murphy, Lois Barclay. The Widening World of Childhood. New York: Basic Books Inc., 1962.

Phenix, Philip H. Man and His Becoming. New Brunswick, New Jersey: Rutgers University Press, 1964.

Pihl, R. O. and Parkes, M. Hair element content in learning disabled children. Science. 1977, Vol. 198, 198-206.

Radin, Norma. Maternal warmth, achievement motivation, and cognitive functioning in lower-class preschool children. Child Development. 1971, 42, 1560-1565.

Seitz, Sue and Stewart, Catherine. Imitations and expansions: some developmental aspects of mother-child communications. Developmental Psychology. 1975, 11, 763-768.

White, B. L. and Watts, J. C. Experience and Environment. Englewood Cliffs, N.J.: Prentice-Hall, 1973.

ANN E. GEERS, Ph.D.

Assistant Professor of
Psychology
Washington University
Central Institute for the Deaf
St. Louis, Missouri

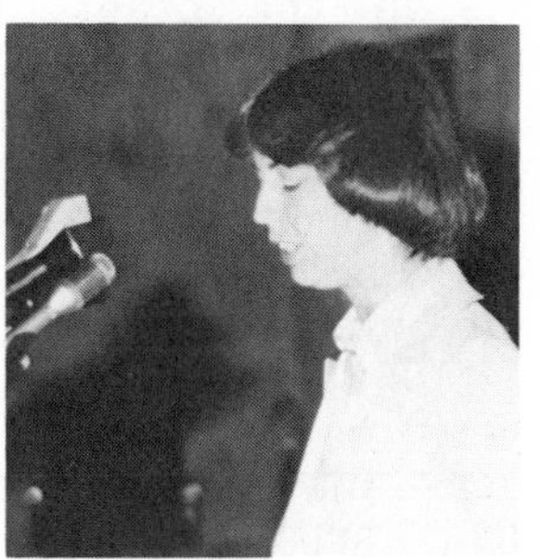

19

Evaluating Educational Effectiveness at the Pre-school Level—Is It Possible?

Teachers have always been concerned with the problem of evaluating whether pupils benefited from their instruction. The ability of school-age children to read, spell, calculate, and so on has been tested with an incredible variety of instruments -- ranging from the teacher-constructed quiz, to complex batteries costing thousands of dollars to develop and standardize. Until quite recently, however, little effort has been made to evaluate the child's acquisition of those skills taught in preschool -- and with good reason. Many of these skills are acquired simply through the process of maturation. The child learns better motor control, becomes more socialized, develops cognitively, and improves his language capabilities simply by growing up in his society. While the stimulation provided by a preschool experience may, no doubt, accelerate the acquisition of these skills -- particularly in culturally deprived youngsters, this progress is generally not the result of specific teaching.

The severely or profoundly hearing-impaired preschool child, on the other hand, requires specific teaching to acquire many of those skills which the normal preschooler seems to acquire as a result of simply growing older. The hearing-impaired child is not able to take advantage of much of the stimulation which the hearing child could hardly avoid. For this reason, preschool education is more crucial to the ultimate development of the hearing-impaired child than it is to the normal-hearing child. Because it is crucial, teachers of the young deaf child share the obligation of teachers of school-aged children to demonstrate that the children are, in fact, benefiting from the instruction or special stimulation provided.

By and large, those responsible for educating the young deaf child have not put the same effort into evaluation of progress that they have put into developing teaching techniques. The primary impetus for evaluation has come from the federal government, which began requiring evidence of effectiveness in order for programs to obtain funding. The practically unanimous outcry from federally funded early intervention programs was; -- "How can you? We have no standard tools to measure progress at this level. Besides, the real benefits of our program probably don't show up until much later," etc. The resounding answer of the Bureau of Education for the Handicapped (BEH) appeared to be -- if you are having an impact on these children it should result in some change in their behavior. If this change exists, it exists in some amount and can be measured, however crudely. It is your responsibility to develop such measures. Technical assistance was provided, such as Technical Assistance Development Systems (TADS), and preschool programs for the handicapped across the country set out to meet the challenge.

The first question these programs were required to ask themselves as a result of this decision was, what behaviors are we attempting to develop or modify? What constitutes progress in these areas? Many early intervention programs, particularly those concerned primarily with the child under three, focus their efforts more on the modification of parent behavior than on that of the child. Therefore the question arises not only <u>what</u> should be evaluated, but <u>who</u> should be evaluated. Since, however, the rationale for teaching the parent is that he or she is the best vehicle for producing change in the child's behavior, evaluation of parent progress does not seem as crucial as the evaluation of immediate and ultimate changes in the child.

At Central Institute for the Deaf (CID) we have been evolving methods of evaluating the young hearing-impaired child for a number of years. The stages we have passed through in this evolution reflect, I think, parallel evolution in similar programs. While this evolution is by no means complete, a review of the process involved may be instructive. A crucial decision involved establishing the behaviors to which the program is directed. At CID the primary goal is to move the child toward acquiring the ability to speak the language of his society and to understand this language when it is spoken. The means by which this goal is achieved are varied and, as I see it, largely irrelevant to the point at hand. The primary issue is whether, after all, the efforts pay off in producing the desired change in the child's ability to communicate.

A logical first step seemed to be to try and use developmental schedules which had been devised for normal-hearing children. It was expected that language acquisition in these hearing-impaired children would be reflected in the developmental stages of normal-hearing infants. Scales selected included the Kirk Scale of Typical Behavior Patterns (Kirk, 1955) and the Vineland Social Maturity Scale (Doll, 1965), among others. These scales, however, evaluate language development in the context of physical development, social development, self-help skills, etc. We found ourselves, for example, comparing the three-year-old deaf child who is beginning to imitate speech sounds with the nine-month-old infant who is just beginning to get around by crawling and whose self-help skills include the ability to hold his own bottle. Although it may be said that these children are at the same "language age", the level of cognitive functioning exhibited by the deaf child who is beginning to learn to imitate his first speech sounds and the nine-month-old hearing infant who is spontaneously exhibiting this behavior is quite different. The language behaviors named on these scales do not have the same meaning when used to describe the deaf child that they do for the normal-hearing infant. One would not teach a two-year-old deaf child to communicate by moving him through all of the language-like behaviors exhibited by the hearing infant (e.g., the ability to make cooing and throaty noises followed by listening to his own voice). Likewise, one should not evaluate his progress using this yardstick.

Similar problems were confronted as we attempted to use standard measures which concentrated exclusively on the development of language skills -- for example, the Receptive-Expressive Emergent Language Scale (Bozoch and League, 1971) -- more commonly known as REEL. Many of the early items on this and similar scales evalute the child's response to sound. Sample items include:

> Often quieted by a familiar, friendly voice.(1 mo.)
>
> Turns head deliberately toward the source of the voice.(3-4 mo.)
>
> Usually stops crying when someone talks to him. (4-5 mo.)
>
> Appears to be able to distinguish general meanings of warning, anger, and/or friendly voice patterns. (5-6 mo.)
>
> Gives some attention to music or singing. (6-7 mo.)
>
> Frequently appears to listen to whole conversations between others. (7-8 mo.)
>
> Responds to rhythmic music by bodily or hand movements in approximate time to music. (10-11 mo.) (Bozoch and League, 1971)

A profoundly hearing-impaired two-year-old who fails to exhibit behaviors like these may obtain a language score which is artifically depressed relative to his real language ability. At higher language levels, test results are confounded by the fact that hearing-impaired children learn the language they have been taught. Therefore the progression may or may not occur in the sequence spontaneously exhibited by normal-hearing children. For example, somewhere between 24 and 27 months, according to the REEL, the normal-hearing child begins routinely combining words into two- and three-word phrases and uses personal pronouns correctly. Later developing behaviors include naming at least one color correctly and repeating two or more numbers correctly at 27 to 30 months; still later the hearing child is able to give both his first and last name when asked and can tell gender when asked "Are you a boy or a girl?" (30-33 months). It is quite likely that a deaf child could be taught the single word responses necessary for satisfying the later developing items long before he is routinely able to produce two- and three-word phrases or use pronouns correctly, -- skills which develop much earlier in normally hearing children.

Because no better measures were available, we adapted the REEL for use with hearing-impaired children and used it as our own primary measure of language development in evaluating the effectiveness of our early intervention program in producing language growth in deaf children. The results of this evaluation were to be provided to our funding agency, The Bureau of Education for the Handicapped. Twenty-seven severely and profoundly hearing-impaired children were tested three times at approximately six-month intervals. The rather discouraging results appear in Figure 19-1.

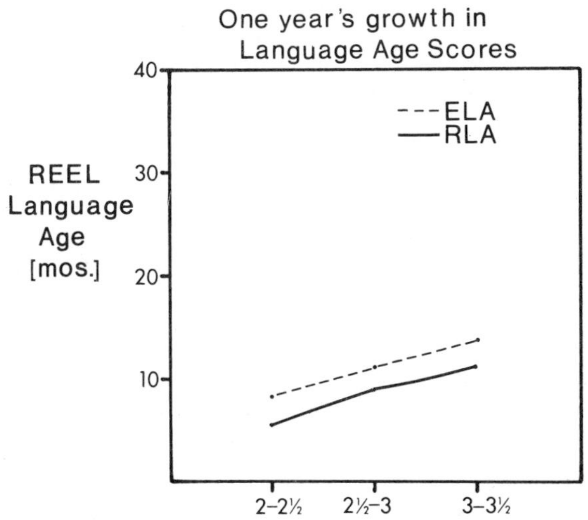

FIG. 19-1

Receptive and expressive language age scores of 27 hearing-impaired children tested at 6-month intervals on the Receptive Expressive Emergent Language Scale (REEL).

As the children increased in age from about two years old to about three years old, their receptive language age scores increased from almost six months to somewhat over eleven months and their expressive language age scores from eight-and-a-half to fourteen months. These test score changes were neither statistically nor practically significant. It was obvious as we looked back on these results that many of the gains made by the children were not reflected in the items of this test. Furthermore, test results on individual children did not provide information that was particularly useful for teaching. It became apparent that a criterion-referenced instrument had to be developed which would both reflect progress in the deaf child's ability to communicate and provide the teacher with some immediate teaching goals.

We began developing such an instrument by analyzing the stages of development characteristic of the hearing-impaired child who is just beginning to learn to communicate. Several years of effort in describing these stages in detail resulted in our publishing the Scales of Early Communication Skills in 1975 (Moog and Geers, 1975). The measure is a teacher-rating device with receptive and expressive skills arranged in the appropriate order of development for the hearing-impaired child. The Receptive Language Scales are designed to provide a device for observing and recording in a consistent manner a behavioral description of the level at which the child is comprehending speech. Receptive skills are evaluated separately in a relatively structured teaching situation (A Scale) and in a more natural situation (B Scale). The Expressive Language Scales describe the level at which the child imitates speech (A Scale) and spontaneously uses speech for communicating (B Scale). Unlike the normal-hearing child who acquires language by mere exposure, it is often necessary for the hearing-impaired child to develop language skills in a structured context. Hence our need for the "A Scales." However, we consider the skill to be fully developed only when the child is capable of demonstrating the skill in unstructured, novel situations as well. This is evaluated by the "B Scales."

The scales were standardized on 372 hearing-impaired children from two to eight years of age across the country. The normative data collected on these scales provided us with evidence of the rate of language acquisition by children enrolled in oral programs for the deaf. Furthermore, the Scales provide a rationale for setting language objectives for an individual child and evaluating the child's success in reaching these objectives.

The normative data were submitted to scaling analysis to determine an appropriate scale value for each developmental item. When this was accomplished, we had a useful tool not only for examining individual pupil progress but for evaluating growth in language ability in groups of children using traditional statistical methods.

Then we were ready to initiate a reasonable evaluation of the effectiveness of our preschool program. We had accumulated scale ratings longitudinally at the rate of two or three per year for four years on all hearing-impaired children in our program between the ages of two and seven years. A repeated measures analysis of variance of the change in these scores over time revealed significant linear improvement in all age groups. When all data were included in a combination cross-sectional and longitudinal design, it was possible to chart improvement in ten consecutive six-month age groups.

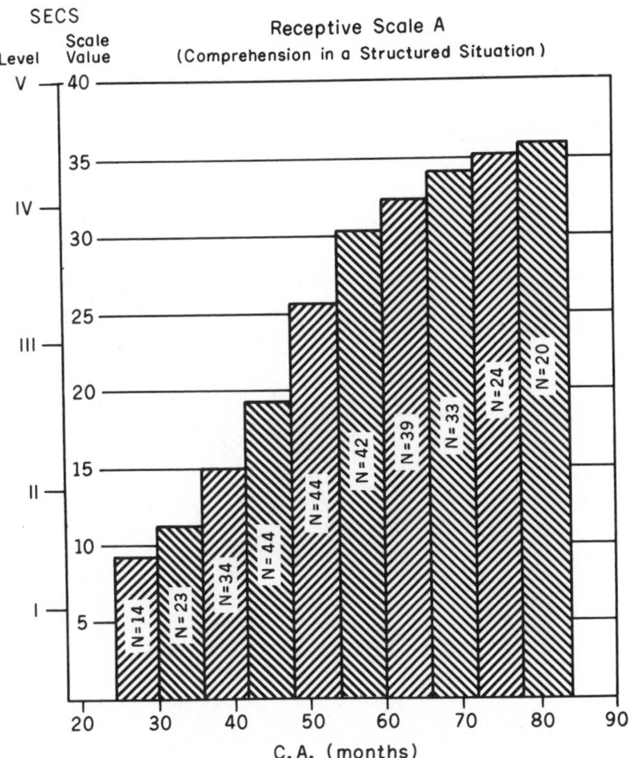

FIG. 19-2
Scores of hearing-impaired children on the Receptive A scale of the Scales of Early Communication Skills.

Figure 19-2 represents the growth of comprehension in a structured situation between 24 and 84 months of age. Both the rated level (Roman numerals I through V) and the corresponding scale values actually used in calculation are presented on the ordinate. The histogram indicates the average scale value of each consecutive age group. Figure 19-3 represents the growth of comprehension in a natural situation. Figure 19-4 represents growth in the ability to imitate language and Figure 19-5 depicts increasing facility with expressive language in natural situations.

In addition to numerical significance, the verbal description of language progress which could be obtained from the test manual provides evidence of practical significance in the behavior acquired.

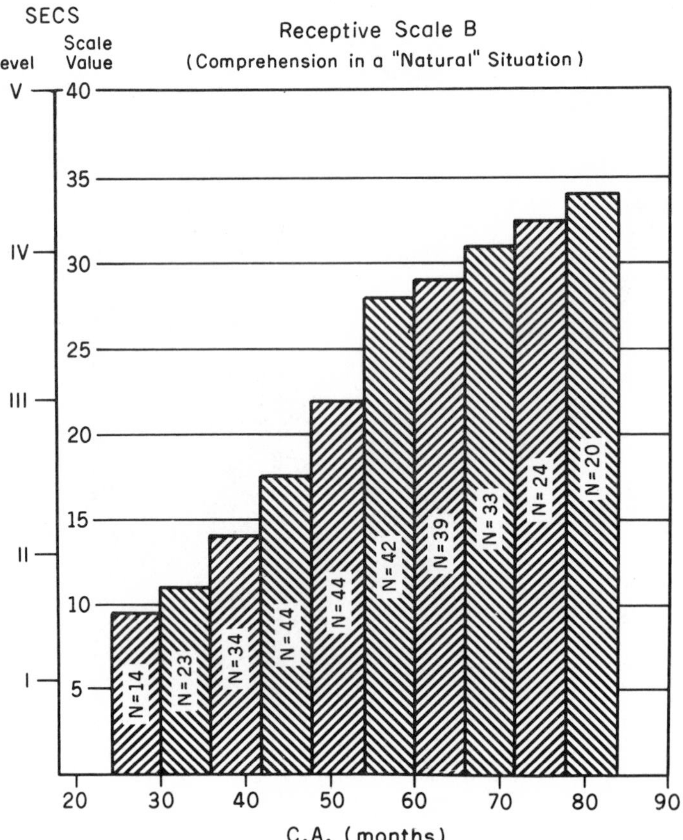

FIG. 19-3
Scores of hearing-impaired children on the Receptive B scale of the Scales of Early Communication Skills.

1. The average two-year-old in this program demonstrates his awareness that the mouth and voice convey information, although he cannot understand or produce spontaneously any real words. He is, however, beginning to imitate a few syllables or words with considerable effort.

2. At three the child understands and uses a few words or expressions (e.g., "bye-bye" or "mama") in natural situations. He is able to imitate a variety of words in isolation.

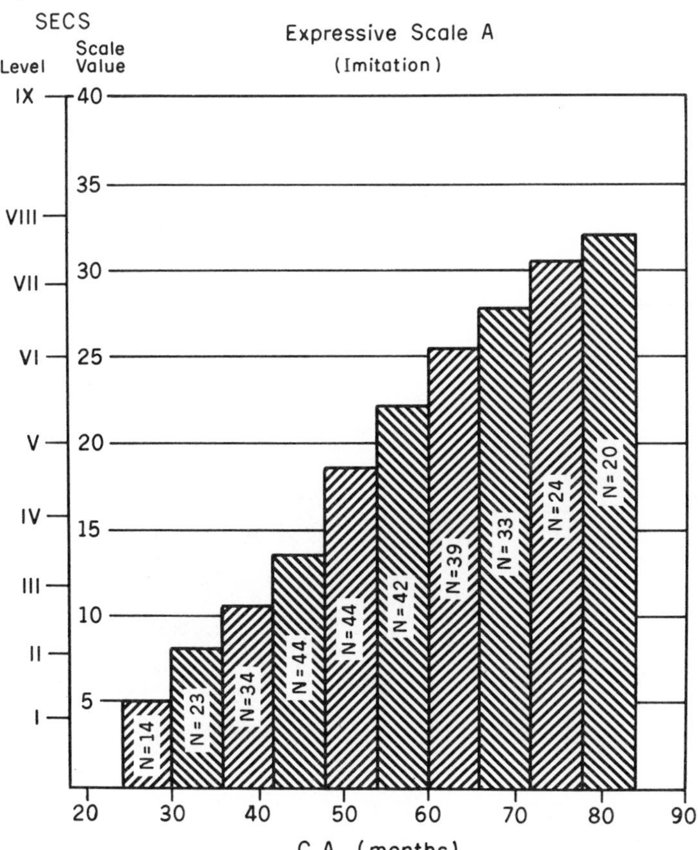

FIG. 19-4
Scores of hearing-impaired children on the Expressive A scale of the Scales of Early Communication Skills.

3. By the time he is four, the average child in this sample is rated as having "caught on" to learning new words. However, the acquisition of new words is still rather slow and labored. He is beginning to express his ideas verbally in one-word utterances, mostly nouns. He is able to imitate two- to three-word phrases, although he does not yet use them in his spontaneous speech.

4. The five-year-old is able to acquire new comprehension vocabulary in the context of phrases and sentences. At this point he begins learning new words after only a few presentations. He understands more than 20 different words in almost any

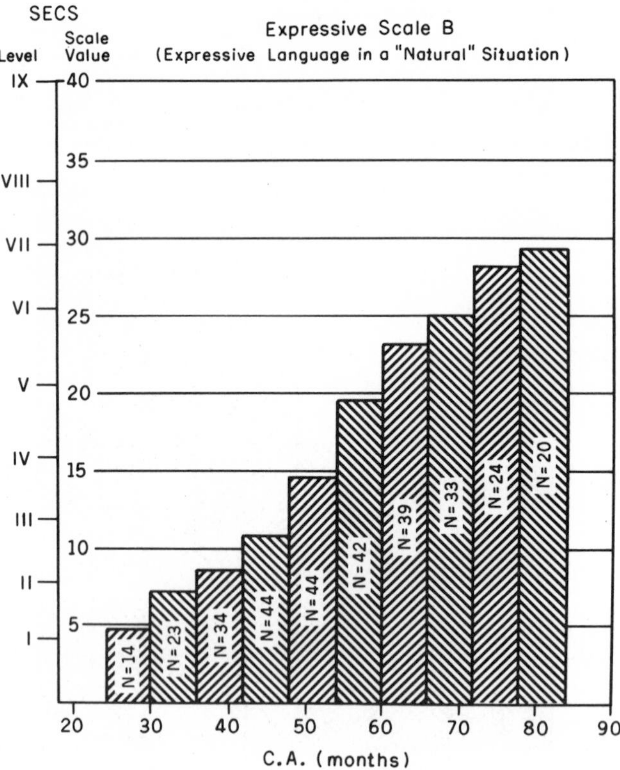

FIG. 19-5
Scores of hearing-impaired children on the Expressive B scale of the Scales of Early Communication Skills.

context. He is now combining words into two-three word phrases to express his ideas and is able to imitate both the noun and the verb in a short simple sentence.

5. The six-year-old can put words together in a sentence-like manner in his spontaneous speech. He is beginning to use a variety of verbs, either preceding (verb-object) or following (subject-verb), a variety of nouns. He is able to imitate at least four words of a sentence, including a noun, the verb, and a modifying word or phrase.

6. Further development of oral language beyond this level involves increasing the length and complexity

of sentences and acquiring facility with connected discourse. The steady linear increase in the scores of this group of children leads one to extrapolate that the average child in this sample will reach this level of fluency before he is nine years old.

Thus it is apparent that communication skills are being acquired by these hearing-impaired children and that these skills can be evaluated meaningfully. We are currently engaged in developing a test procedure which will describe in considerably more detail the specific language structures used by children who are putting words together in phrases and sentences. We hope that these procedures will encourage teachers to analyze their children's language and shape their teaching goals to the specific needs of each individual child. The evolution of our most recent language evaluation technique has required about eight years of trial and error experimentation. This evolution can be characterized as moving from more general to more detailed specification of the child's language and from unstructured subjective observations to a highly structured and objective test situation.

The answer to my question, then, is "yes" -- evaluating educational effectiveness at the preschool level is possible. However, such evaluation requires that we develop instruments which are sensitive to the changes we are trying to make.

REFERENCES

Bozoch, Kenneth and League, Richard. Assessing Language in Infancy. Gainesille, Fl., A Tree of Life Press, 1971.

Doll, E.A. Vineland Social Maturity Scale. Circle Pines, Minn.: American Guidance Service, Inc., 1965.

Kirk, S. A., Karnes, M. B., and Kirk, W. D. You and Your Retarded Child; a manual for parents of retarded children. NY: MacMillan, 1955.

Moog, J. S. and Geers, A. E. Scales of Early Communication Skills for Hearing-Impaired Children. CID Publication No. 103, 1975.

VIRGINIA SHIPMAN, Ph.D.

Educational Testing Service
Princeton University
Princeton, New Jersey

20

Maintaining and Enhancing Early Intervention Gains

The ETS Longitudinal Study of Young Children and Their First School Experiences focuses on two basic questions: What are the components of early education that facilitate or interfere with the cognitive, personal, and social development of disadvantaged children? What are the environmental and background variables that moderate these effects, and how do these moderators produce their influence?

It is well established that children from low socio-economic-status (SES) families generally do not achieve academically as well as middle-class children. While a number of researchers have related this finding to various aspects of the differing environments of lower- and middle-class children, there is considerably less evidence describing environmental factors associated with performance differences solely within an economically disadvantaged population. Data from third-grade children from the Longitudinal Study indeed confirm the existence of wide ranges in cognitive aptitude and academic achievement among children of relatively homogeneous SES. To further our understanding of development and contribute to the planning of environments to facilitate that development, it is obviously of critical importance to discover the unique characteristics of children and their environments that do not fit the generalization that low social class equals low achievement.

Analysis to date of the massive amount of data collected has been focused on examining relationships among various large sets of information from particular domains. In these investigations an attempt has been made to examine the consistency of findings across several status categories (i.e., child's sex and race, family socioeconomic status, and geographical location). But one of the frustrations experienced in doing large-scale research is the impersonal aspect of such group analysis and the consequent decreased awareness one has of individual study participants. Every so often one hears a tester's or teacher's salient comment about a particular child; in some instances a local agency or newspaper article reports a critical family event. But to a large extent the individual developmental histories of study children remain unknown to the researcher who, to operate efficiently and in accord with relevant statistical models, must constantly reduce the data collected into a limited set of variables.

Given the multiple and interacting nature of influences upon any behavior and the error contained in any measurement technique used, the magnitude of correlation obtained between psychosocial variables and the young child's functioning is understandably moderate at best, accounting for only a small amount of the behavior examined. Moreover, we do not know the extent to which various aspects of the child's development are appropriately assessed by statistical models that assume a linear growth model. The present study was an attempt to generate hypotheses concerning those combinations of factors which enhance or interfere with the child's early grade-school performance. Intensive case studies were prepared for those study children who, on a third-grade achievement test, were: 1. significantly above or below the average performance for children of similar ethnic and income status in basic school skills of reading and math or 2. significantly deviant from the level predicted by their performance on a test of pre-academic skills at age four.

It should be noted that such an approach is not seen as an alternative to or substitute for previous analyses, but rather as a supplement to them. We recognize that the problems indicated above are not eliminated by this approach. However, an intensive study of extreme cases should serve to highlight significant factors (and/or combinations and sequences of factors), i.e., those environmental events or personal dispositions that covary with school performance. Thus, close examination of the preschool and primary grade programmatic information gathered should help delineate critical factors in the child's early school experiences. Those factors/processes not identified previously in the larger sample can then serve as hypotheses to be tested in subsequent experimental studies.

The findings in this report should also be relevant to the current controversy regarding early identification and screening of preschool children. Intensive study of observer ratings and test performances obtained during the age period 3.5 - 5 years should indicate the extent to which assessment of cognitive, perceptual, affective, and social functioning in preschool low-income black children, a group which in general can be classified as "at risk" with regard to functioning successfully in school, can serve to: 1. identify early those areas of functioning needing remediation and 2. suggest individualized modes of treatment. Equally important, the findings may suggest early indices of gifted functioning. Thus, by multiple analytic strategies we hope to contribute to the further understanding of the complex interacting influences upon children's development so as to provide a basis for informed socio-educational intervention.

SAMPLE

The sample for the current report is a subsample from the ETS-Head Start Longitudinal Study. Sample selection procedures and initial sample characteristics for the Longitudinal Study are presented in Project Report 71-19 (Shipman, 1971). Briefly, in the fall of 1968 four regionally distinct communities were selected which 1. had sufficient numbers of children in grade school and in the Head Start program, 2. appeared feasible for longitudinal study given expressed community and school cooperation and expected mobility rates, and 3. offered variation in preschool and primary grade experiences. The study sites chosen were Lee County, Alabama; Portland, Oregon; St. Louis, Missouri; and Trenton, New Jersey. Within these communities, elementary school districts with a substantial proportion of the population eligible for Head Start were selected. In each school district an attempt was made to test all non-physically handicapped, English-speaking children who were expected to enroll in first grade in the fall of 1971 (i.e., children of approximately three-and-one-half to four-and-one-half years of age).

In 1969, mothers were interviewed and children tested prior to their enrollment in Head Start or any other preschool program. For this initial four-site sample at least partial data were obtained on a total of 1875 children, with Lee County and Portland constituting 60% of the sample. Sixty-two percent of the sample was black, with boys comprising 53% of the overall sample, 54.5% of the black sample, and 50.5% of the white sample. For the three sites in which children had the opportunity to attend Head Start in the second year of the study (1969-1970), 37.2% of the sample attended Head Start, 11% attended other preschool programs, and 51.8% had no known attendance in Head Start or other preschool programs. In Lee County, where Head Start was a kindergarten program, 41.7% of the initial sample attended Head Start, 19.1% attended other preschool programs, and 39.9% had no known attendance in Head Start or other preschool programs. While racial composition of the Head Start sample varied by site, substantially more blacks than whites attended Head Start; only 13.3% of the children enrolled were white. For a variety of reasons, the St. Louis site was dropped in the third year of the study and the 353 subjects there lost from further longitudinal study. In June of 1974, the six-year longitudinal sample contained 1017 children in <u>three</u> sites. Thus, except for the loss of St. Louis, attrition over six years was limited to about one-third of the original sample, with losses distributed equally across sexes and sites, but relatively greater for whites in each site. The six-year longitudinal sample went from 62% to 72% black across sites.

The current analysis focused on children from the longitudinal sample (i.e., those who were tested or their mother interviewed in Year 1[1]) who were below the 1969 Office of Economic Opportunity poverty guidelines as determined by the parent interview given during the year Head Start was available to study children. Since the number of white families in the study meeting these criteria was relatively small, only black children were included to eliminate the possibility of racial confounding. Scores on the Year 6 Cooperative Primary Tests were necessary to define the

[1]Throughout the report "Year" refers to year of the Longitudinal Study.

Year 1 = January to August 1969 (child age 3½-4½);
Year 2 = September 1969 to August 1970 (child age 4½-5½);
Year 3 = September 1970 to August 1971 (child age 5½-6½);
Year 4 = September 1971 to August 1972 (child age 6½-7½);
Year 5 = September 1972 to August 1973 (child age 7½-8½);
Year 6 = September 1973 to August 1974 (child age 8½-9½).

extreme groups, which markedly reduced the size of the sample available for this analysis since achievement tests were administered only in target classrooms (i.e., classes with 50% or more study children who had been previously tested). Thus, the sample for the current report (henceforth referred to as the "total sample") consisted of black children from Head Start-eligible families who were identified in Year 1 and had scores available on the Year 6 Cooperative Primary Tests. The total sample consisted of 100 boys and 86 girls. From this economically disadvantaged sample the highest and lowest achieving children were selected by three different methods which will be discussed below. Although most children were identified by all three methods, some children satisfied the selection criteria for only one method.

The third-grade Reading and Math subtests of the Cooperative Primary Tests (Cooperative Test Division, ETS, 1967) served as the index of Year 6 achievement. The Cooperative Primary Tests are a nationally standardized achievement test battery developed by ETS and designed for use in grades one through three. The tests are group administered, with the child responding by making an "X" on the one of the three response alternatives s/he believes is correct. There is no special instruction to the student about guessing, and there is no correction for guessing in the scoring. The teacher is instructed to allow a reasonable amount of time for all students to finish. In order to provide practice with this type of item, the pilot test included in the test package was administered first. Both forms of the Reading test consist of 50 items, some of which assess the comprehension of individual words, while others require the student to extract a key element from a sentence or paragraph, or provide some interpretation, evaluation, or inference based on the sentence or paragraph. The Math test consists of 60 items covering the following topics: number, symbolism, operation, function and relation, approximation, proof, measurement, estimation, and geometry. Straight computation is not emphasized, but rather an attempt is made "...to test major concepts of mathematics in their emergent state" (Cooperative Test Division, ETS, 1967). Form 23B of both Reading and Math was administered.

The first method selected children for the extreme groups on the basis of their raw scores in Reading and Math. The twenty-five highest and twenty-five lowest scoring black Head Start-eligible children, irrespective of sex, were identified separately for the two subtests. Each of the resultant groups thus contained approximately 14% of the total sample, and the means of the high and low groups were more than two standard deviations apart. Within this group the ten highest and lowest scoring boys and ten highest and lowest scoring girls were then identified. Table 20-1 presents the means and standard deviations on Reading and Math for the total black Head Start-eligible longitudinal sample and for groups identified by this method. These values can be compared to the national standardization sample for the Cooperative Primary Tests where the Reading mean was 36.1 with a standard deviation of 8.6 and the Math mean was 39.4 with a standard deviation of 9.0.

TABLE 20-1

Means and Standard Deviations on Reading and Math for the Total Sample and Extreme Raw Score Groups

Group	*n*	*M*	*SD*
Reading			
Total Sample	174	25.16	8.32
High-Combined Sexes	25	39.36	2.87
Low-Combined Sexes	25	13.80	1.83
High-Boys	10	39.10	2.77
Low-Boys	10	12.80	1.32
High-Girls	10	41.30	1.89
Low-Girls	10	14.00	2.11
Math			
Total Sample	181	28.50	8.43
High-Combined Sexes	25	42.80	3.21
Low-Combined Sexes	25	16.68	2.81
High-Boys	10	44.30	3.61
Low-Boys	10	15.70	2.71
High-Girls	10	42.90	2.38
Low-Girls	10	16.60	3.17

The second method selected black Head Start-eligible children whose performance was significantly better or worse than predicted from Year 1 scores on the Preschool Inventory (PSI) (ETS, 1970). The 64-item PSI was selected as the predictor because it is a highly reliable test of preschool achievement and had the highest loading on the general information-processing factor defined in Year 1 (Shipman, 1971). Since age at time of testing was known to affect PSI scores, the scores were age-adjusted by regressing total scores on age at the date of testing. The age-corrected PSI scores where then used in standard least-squares regression equations to obtain a predicted score for each child in Reading and Math. Separate regression equations were used for boys and girls. For boys the correlation between Year 1 PSI and Year 6 Reading scores was .36 (regression weight b = .29), while for girls the correlation was .45 (b = .39). The correlations between PSI and Math performance were .25 (b = .23) for boys and .35 (b = .29) for girls. Separately for Reading and Math, the difference between the actual and predicted scores for each child was computed, and for each subtest the ten boys and ten girls with the greatest positive difference scores were selected; similarly, the ten boys and ten girls with the greatest negative difference scores were identified. Due to regression to the mean, the highest (and lowest) predicted scores were substantially closer to the mean than the highest (and lowest) actual scores. Thus, most of the children selected by this deviation from prediction method also were selected by the first "absolute score" method.

To avoid apparent mislabeling for some children caused by the regression-to-the-mean effects of this second method, a third method was used which identified children whose initial PSI scores were one standard deviation above (or below) the average of the total sample and whose Year 6 Reading and Math scores were one standard deviation below (or above) the mean. Thus, these were the children showing the greatest change in achievement performance. Since the mean PSI score was 23.25 with a standard deviation of 9.89, any child with a score of 13 or less was considered low on the PSI and any child with a score of 33 or more was considered high. By this criterion 15 boys and 7 girls, or about 12% of the sample, were defined as low while 10 boys and 15 girls (about 15% of the sample) were classified as high. The mean of the Reading scores was 25.16 with a standard deviation of 8.32; thus scores of 33 and above were considered high, while scores of 17 and below were considered low. For the Math scores (mean of 28.5 and standard deviation of 8.43), high scores were those of 37 and above, while low scores were 20 and below. The deviation sample resulting from this method of selection comprised those children in the low-high and high-low categories for each of the subject areas. The 10 children in this group--4 in Reading, 5 in Math, and one who was included in both the Reading and Math areas--were chosen for particularly intensive case study.

DATA COLLECTION AND PROCESSING PROCEDURES

General Strategies

To achieve the broad goals of the study the measurement strategy required selection of a variety of measures that would help describe more adequately the complex interrelationships and structure of children's abilities and characteristics over time and permit determination of their interaction efforts with particular preschool and primary grade programs. Measures encompassing objectives claimed by preschool and primary grade programs were included along with measures of development that social science holds as important for human functioning. Measures also were included that would help delineate basic cognitive, affective, and social processes and their courses of development. Tasks were selected to allow continuity of measurement across age periods, through the use of vertically equivalent forms over time, and multiple measurement of the same variable (within a context) across several age periods so that possible developmental shifts in expression could be monitored. Process rather than static variables were emphasized, especially those process variables involving parent-child and teacher-child interactions, such as modes of information-processing and reinforcement strategies. To the extent possible, measures were included which tapped functional characteristics or perceptual and cognitive styles affecting learning, such as individual differences in ways in which children approach a task, kinds of cues selected, strategies of organization, speed of decision and response, and persistence. Implicit throughout was the belief that only for the intermediate purpose of structural analysis and derivation of measures within domains could one separate cognitive, perceptual, social, and affective domains or study the child without taking environment into account.

The six years of research with the longitudinal study sample have included a total of about twenty-five-and-a-half hours of testing for each child, four-and-a-half hours of interviews with each of their mothers, an hour-and-a-half of observing each mother-child pair working together on tasks, and a physical examination for each child. In addition, there have been eighteen days of observing each Head Start class, and three days of observing kindergarten, first, second, and third-grade classes, two half-hour periods of watching each child during "free play" in preschool, about four hours of each Head Start, kindergarten, first, second, and third-grade teacher's time to supply information about herself and the children in her classes, an hour from each Head Start aide, more than an hour of each Head Start Center Director's and principal's time to describe the preschool centers and elementary schools in general, and many consultations with community agencies to obtain information about the environments in which the children live.

The major variables toward which these information-gathering efforts have been directed include: 1. The Family, both status and process variables, that is, those variables describing what the family is (e.g., ethnic membership, occupational level) and what it does (e.g., the mother's teaching styles with her child and her attitudes toward the schools and the learning process); 2. The Teacher, including such things as background characteristics, attitudes, abilities, teaching goals; 3. The Classroom, both program components and teacher-child and peer relationships; 4. The School, physical characteristics and organization as well as relationships between teachers and administrative staff; and 5. The Community. The largest percentage of measures included, however, were those designed to tap several aspects of 6. The Child, e.g., health information and cognitive, perceptual-motor, affective, and social development.

Data Collection Procedures

Community support and participation were essential if meaningful, useful data were to be obtained. Community leaders and administrators were consulted, and written intents (not merely consents) to participate in the study were sent to ETS by both community agencies and local school boards. Field operations were organized around local staff who served as coordinators, interviewers, testers, and observers. For the first phase of data collection, household canvassing and parent interviews, ETS subcontracted with the New York City firm of Audits and Surveys (A&S) to locate eligible children and then complete a 90-minute ETS-prepared interview with each eligible child's mother or mother surrogate. The interviewers, all female and matched by race with respondents, were recruited from the local communities, with A&S staff responsible for both training and supervision. In subsequent years of the study, parent interviews were conducted in a similar manner except that ETS assumed the training and supervision responsibilities that had been subcontracted to A&S. During the child's Head Start year the mother was interviewed in the testing center; home interviews were again obtained when the child was nine years old.

During the first study year individual child tests and mother-child interaction tasks were administered by local women, most of whom were black housewives with limited work experience. While the usual educational credentials were not required, experience in working with young children was considered highly desirable, as was the ability to read well and speak with ease. After four to five weeks of training, final selection of testers was made by the project director and a senior member of the research team. Testing was monitored by the local coordinator and by ETS regional and Princeton office staffs. Training procedures were essentially identical in later years except that with increased experience the training period could be reduced to three weeks. In the early years of the study, test centers were located in churches or community recreation facilities, while in later years testing was done in rooms available in the individual schools or in mobile vans parked outside of the school. Each year, individual tests were grouped into two or more batteries, with each battery usually administered in a single session with a child. Each battery included measures representing the range of areas being assessed; the order of tests within batteries reflected consideration for the need to balance types of responses (active vs. passive, verbal vs. nonverbal), and to stimulate and sustain the child's interest.

In the second year of the study a variety of measures were used to assess the preschool experience of all children enrolled in Head Start or other preschool classes in the urban sites. Random time samples of individual children's behavior were collected throughout the year with PROSE, a structured observational procedure. Also, an attempt was made to obtain personal-social ratings of these children in the late fall and spring. Two trained local women observed the child's behavior during "free play," and later resolved any discrepancies in their independent ratings in order to form a single consensus rating on each scale. Global Classroom Ratings describing teacher-child and peer interactions were similarly obtained, except that observations for this instrument were not limited to "free play" periods. Global Classroom Ratings and Teacher Questionnaires were obtained in target classrooms for each subsequent year of the Longitudinal Study, with a target classroom defined as any class containing 50% or more study children. In grades 1-3 the observer who made the Global Classroom Ratings also provided information for the Assessment of Classroom Programs Inventory. Also, in grades 1-3, each teacher in a target classroom was asked to rate study children and their classmates with the Schaefer Classroom Behavior Inventory and the Enhancement of Learning Inventory. The local site coordinator explained the procedures and each teacher received a small honorarium for completing the tasks.

In the primary grades several group-administered measures were obtained. Group achievement tests were administered in the spring by the classroom teacher in target classrooms. The local coordinator explained the procedures for group testing and was available to assist the teacher as needed. Local ETS staff administered the Coopersmith Self-Esteem Inventory to all third-grade target classrooms to enhance the child's feeling of confidentiality in the information obtained. At the end of each school year attendance, standardized test, and report card information were obtained from each school for study children.

Data Processing

The data from all of the above measures were scored and coded at the item level by Princeton office staff, and all scoring and coding was double-checked. The coded data were keypunched and independently verified, after which the individual data tapes were edited for appropriate ID listing and for out-of-range and logical inconsistencies in coding. To facilitate analysis across different measures and time periods, merge tapes for each study year were prepared which comprised all derived family and child scores from the separate task tapes. For more detailed description of data collection and processing procedures see Project Reports 72-18 (Shipman, 1972b) and 75-28 (Shipman, McKee, and Bridgeman, 1976).

RESULTS AND CONCLUSIONS

As might be expected, the case studies revealed the multiple determinants of academic success or failure; on first reading, each child's record appeared to have a unique history of causal antecedents. Among the many child, family, and school variables examined, no one score or composite of scores was consistently associated with level of academic achievement. When examining the extent to which children were categorized as exceptional according to geographical region, family structure, sex, and preschool attendance, only consistent differences according to site were evidenced with more children from Lee County doing poorly and more children from Portland doing relatively well in reading and math. However, the extent to which site differences reflect differences in initial sample characteristics, or in geographical region, urbanness, preschool teacher certification, preschool program sponsor, and age of preschool entry (all of which are confounded with site in this sample) or other unmeasured relevant variables is unknown. Since most of these Head Start-eligible children had actually attended Head Start, preschool experience per se did not differentiate high- and low-scoring children; however, in checking those children who had been retained in first or second grade, a more severe index of poor school progress, a higher percentage of children who had not attended preschool was found. Moreover, for those Head Start children who later attended a follow-through program the data suggested the positive impact of continued broad comprehensive services to the children and their families. When examining teacher background characteristics, (i.e., age, years of schooling, and amount of teaching experience), it was found that at any one grade level most teachers had children in both the high and low categories; gross school variables such as school size, class size, and percentage of minority students also revealed no consistent differences although there was a trend for schools with more support staff to have more children in the high-achievement groups. Such findings point to the importance of investigating specific teacher-child interactions for understanding school effects.

Point-biserial correlations obtained between a selected group of family status, situational, and process variables and the child's designation in high or low reading and math groups indicated that even within this restricted SES sample of economically disadvantaged families, differences in parental educational level, physical resources in the home (i.e., amount of material possessions, extent of physical crowding), and encouragement of school-relevant skills and attitudes (e.g., frequency of reading to their four-year-old child, level of educational aspirations and expectations) were associated with the child's later school progress. Similar findings were obtained by Greenberg and Davidson (1972) and Stedman and McKenzie (1971) in their research with high- and low-achieving low-SES urban northern black and southwestern Mexican-American children, respectively. Low-income families are not a homogeneous group. The lack of association obtained between parental occupational status and children's academic achievement again highlighted previous reported study findings (Shipman et al., 1976) on the apparent different meaning of this variable for black and white families.

These data are consistent with the extensive research literature on the important relationship of early home influence to the young child's school performance (e.g., Bronfenbrenner, 1974; Hanson, 1975; Hess, Shipman, Brophy and Bear, 1969; White, Day, Freeman, Hantman and Messenger, 1973). Although status/situational and process variables may share considerable commonality in their prediction of the child's subsequent reading and math performance, the process variables help provide important explanatory information and programmatic clues that are not obvious from status characteristics alone. As was pointed out in a recent extensive discussion of relationships among family status, situational, and process variables and children's academic achievement (Shipman et al., 1976), status characteristics may be viewed as providing differential opportunities for various processes to emerge. Thus, a higher level of parental education is associated with greater academic knowledge, increased awareness of public affairs and popular culture, more informed perceptions of school, and continued seeking of new knowledge as in reading books and magazines (cf. Hyman, Wright and Reed, 1975), all of which may have impact on the child's knowledge and motivation for learning. In addition, by providing differential opportunities for the parent's participation in society, there may be indirect effects upon the child via parental attitudes and child-rearing behaviors acquired through such experiences. Another example of the interrelation among status, situational, and process variables is the commonly found association between low economic status, high household density, and parental use of physical punishment with their children. These negative effects of crowding have been shown to be exacerbated by additional stresses in the home (Booth and Edwards, 1976). Family process variables are thus considered as the underlying mechanisms by which child outcome differences associated with family status characteristics are created and maintained.

A variety of measures of the child's functioning at age four were found to be useful in identifying children likely to do well or poorly during the course of their acquisition of basic school skills of reading and math. Such measures were not limited to those in the cognitive-perceptual area, but included tasks assessing affective behaviors (i.e., self-esteem, cooperation) and cognitive styles (i.e., reflectivity). These findings suggest that a number of preschool measures of child's cognitive, affective, and social functioning may indicate early strengths and weaknesses relevant to the child's later school functioning, perhaps in part due to their reflecting children's differential responsivity to early intervention. Further analyses of data collected at ages five and six are likely to suggest other important areas of inquiry with some measures not found to be differentially predictive at age four becoming so at a later developmental stage. For example, preliminary analyses suggest this is the case for the reflectivity-impulsivity dimension assessed with the Matching Familiar Figures Test and for academic achievement motivation which newly emerges during the child's attendance in a preschool program. The positive use of such measures as initial screening instruments to provide guidance for tailoring programs to meet children's needs should be emphasized as contrasted with their use in making placement decisions which may act as self-fulfilling prophecies. Preschool assessment can facilitate the provision of programs geared to the individual needs of children rather than those planned on the basis of ascribed needs of children according to various status characteristics.

But a major conclusion from these data is that these family and child variables are not necessarily associated with exceptionally high or low academic achievement; for any one of these variables or a composite of home or child variables much of the variance in individual scores remains unaccounted for. Also, the correlations do not provide rationales for the degree of association obtained. Thus, to obtain clues to the nature of moderating variables it was decided to study intensively those children who showed the greatest absolute deviation in cognitive-perceptual performance, whether in a positive or negative direction, thereby taking into account potential interactions among family, child, and school variables and also differential sequences of school experiences.

The emerging causal hypotheses derived from this intensive case study approach may be grouped into three major categories of locus of change: the child, the home, and the school. Within each of these broad classifications, a number of subcategories can be derived. For example, change in the child's cognitive-perceptual performance can be viewed as a function of change in the child's physical well-being (e.g., a serious illness or accident leading to sensory impairment and/or absence from school, remediation of an interfering defect, gradual "catch up" with developmental lag arising from premature birth); emotional status (e.g., becoming more or less shy and inhibited in responding to an unfamiliar adult in a testing situation, being more or less willing to attempt a response when the questions become more difficult); motivation (e.g., changes in the child's valuing of school performance, in his or her expectancies for success in performing school tasks, and in his or her enjoyment in the school situation); and in general cognitive strategies (e.g., changes in ability to attend, reflect upon, differentiate). As the case studies clearly exemplified, however, rather than acting in any simplistic compartmentalization these changes in the child's functioning should be viewed as dynamic interdependencies among physical, affective, social, and cognitive behaviors. For example, for some children, preschool attendance appeared to affect most their self-confidence and ease in relating to others; these changes in personal and social variables later enabled them to better attend and assimilate academic instruction. For others, acquisition of new pre-academic skills in preschool appeared to be causally related to their increased social and affective competencies. Nevertheless, except for one child for whom a serious accident did seem to account for the striking decrement in performance, the above postulated changes which were evidenced in the case histories examined could not be viewed as sufficient causes. Examination of other case histories reflected similar events but without the same consequences.

In examining responses to the three parent interviews obtained when the child was four, five, and nine years of age, examples were provided for changes in family status, situational, and process variables. Changes in status and situational variables included those in family structure, employment status, welfare status, material well-being, home ownership, crowding, mobility, etc. Attitudinal and behavioral changes were noted also, reflecting changes in feelings of alienation, powerlessness, and optimism, in child-rearing practices, and in participation in school-related activities. Again, there was no one area of change that was unique for families of "exceptional" study children.

Similarly, examination of programmatic information gathered regarding the schools and classrooms children attended yielded no striking contrast at any one grade level. But, when examining the data sequentially, a pattern did emerge for children in the exceptional positive deviation category; a cognitively stimulating atmosphere where the teacher was rated at least moderately warm had been present for at least several years. For example, what may have started as small increases in the child's knowledge of school-relevant information, confidence, task orientation, and achievement motivation in a Head Start preschool program was apparently reinforced and enhanced by teachers in kindergarten and later primary grades. Most of these children (in contrast to many others in the study sample) never had teachers who were described as unenthusiastic, unprepared, using primarily negative reinforcement techniques, or providing little cognitive stimulation.

The most common picture that emerged for those children who showed the most gain in academic achievement was the previously mentioned continuing warm and stimulating classroom environment combined with a home environment that provided the child emotional support in general and support for school activities in particular. Examples of parental school-supportive activities included visiting the school, participating in classroom activities, knowledge of the child's functioning in school, higher expectations for the child's educational attainment, and, in some cases, the parents' involvement in their own continuing education.

It must be emphasized that for these "deviation" cases the above examples of supportive activities emerged following the initial parent interview. In some cases they reflected changes in parental behavior as a function of the preschool program the child attended. For example, in one family, the mother began by visiting her child's preschool program, later became a volunteer classroom aide, and by the time the child was in third grade had returned to school for a GED high-school equivalency certificate and was enrolled in a local community college. Both parent and child showed parallel educational growth. But it appeared obvious that the home did not impact on the child's progress in a sole or independent fashion. The child's preschool and grade school experiences were directly facilitating not only to him but to his mother, and thereby also acted indirectly on the child. The mother obtained information and emotional support in the school setting. In response to greater acceptance she participated more; and from such participation there appeared to develop an increased sense of efficacy and optimism with greater awareness and use of community resources to meet family needs.

Another example of parallel child and family growth is seen in the following case. During the first two years, Mary (fictitious name) was generally moody, restless, and uncooperative in the testing sessions, both with her mother and the testers. She appeared quite timid and shy with strangers. Her mother, estranged from her husband, and living on welfare, also appeared somewhat aloof and negative. She reported having no friends or relatives and rarely went out. Mary attended a summer Head Start program prior to kindergarten, subsequent to which she appeared less shy and socially immature. She also performed better on the Year 3 measures. Classroom observations indicated that she attended a highly motivating, stimulating first grade. Her teacher provided considerable feedback and intellectual stimulation, often using unplanned incidents that occurred. Students appeared happy and involved and the teacher individualized the curriculum to a great extent. Mary prospered in this environment and her teacher described her as a mature, responsible, and excellent student. Mary's attitudes toward herself and school improved considerably and she did well on the various measures we administered that year. She continued to have a warm, individualized, and stimulating classroom in second and third grades. Mary's school records got progressively better, both academically and emotionally; she was described as having matured socially, as being a responsible, well-liked classmate, and as exhibiting a very high level of persistence in her schoolwork. Meanwhile, her mother appeared considerably less alienated, held high aspirations for her child's educational attainment, and had enrolled in a community college. Mary, a shy, uncooperative four-year-old, was at age nine, a confident, happy child enjoying school and performing well.

Another child, the youngest of 15 children, was very nervous and shy during initial testing. Not used to being required to do things on his own, he refused several tasks and cried often. The next year he attended Head Start. According to his mother, Head Start "changed him in every way," but especially in helping him learn to play with other children and become more independent. When seen again at the testing center he was no longer reserved and shy. In addition to these increased social skills his test performance showed he had gained much from the cognitive stimulation of the preschool program and also from his daily viewing of Sesame Street. Moreover, his parents continued to provide a very warm, affectionate home environment. Both parents were highly supportive of school activities; they read to their son often and had high educational aspirations for him. Despite the many children in the family, the mother's interview responses reflected a very differentiated and realistic appraisal of her child's strengths and weaknesses. In kindergarten he was described as having made very good classroom social and emotional adjustment and was a happy, independent, and able learner. His first grade classroom appeared generally unstimulating, but the children were attentive and studious and the teacher tried to individualize the curriculum in a generally open, permissive environment. In contrast to Head Start he reported liking school "only a little bit." His performance in school and on our test batteries, however, remained above average. Fortunately, his classroom experiences were much more positive thereafter. His third-grade class, organized for team teaching, was a particularly happy, orderly, and stimulating environment. The teachers were affectionate and spent much of their teaching time with individual children. Again, home and school together provided a nurturing and supportive environment for the child's growth.

Just as the above cases exemplify the realization of the

child's potential for growth when home and school work together to provide an emotionally supportive and cognitively stimulating environment, the next example indicates the tragedy that evolves when home and school not only fail to interact, but when there is a lack of communication and coordination among those adults representing various social agencies purported to serve the child. When first seen at the testing center, John (fictitious name) was outgoing, friendly, and verbal, responding well to the variety of tasks in the four-day battery. He lived with his mother and two older sisters in a small crowded apartment with few conveniences or possessions of his own. During the mother-child interaction sessions, he showed considerable initiative in responding, and was highly task-oriented and attentive. His mother was affectionate and provided him with frequent positive feedback and praise. Although she was somewhat limited in her presenting of task-relevant information, the child learned the task quickly and well. When seen the following year at age four-and-a-half, John continued to perform well on the many diverse tasks administered, and testers consistently described him as an attentive, friendly, verbal boy with whom they enjoyed working. He attended a Head Start program and was described by his teacher as socially mature, creative, and quick to learn. His kindergarten teacher gave a similar appraisal, although she noted he seemed somewhat bored. His individual testing that year continued to indicate above-average cognitive and social competencies. When interviewed in first grade, he expressed strong liking for school, especially reading. The teacher rated him as very task-oriented, friendly, and non-aggressive. However, he changed from public to private school in first grade and when he transferred back to public school in second grade he began to show increasing absenteeism. His test performance, however, continued to be adequate. That year his teacher rated him as only somewhat attentive in school. In third grade he continued to perform well on individual tests, but when interviewed again about school he expressed considerable dislike, especially for reading. His teacher described him as not at all attentive in his school work and not friendly with his classmates. On the group achievement tests he scored significantly below the mean performance level for other black Head Start-eligible study children. During the home interview the mother repeatedly expressed concern about her son. She reported that within the past two years he complained increasingly of stomachaches necessitating increasing absence from school. He finally had to be hospitalized and was tentatively diagnosed as having a stomach ulcer. The mother felt her son's problems were due to emotional upset over not having a father. Although badly wanting to help her son, she did not know what to do. There was no indication of communication between home and school, no sharing of information, no provision of resources. Teachers at different grade levels apparently were not questioning the discrepancies in teacher ratings and attempting to understand and counteract their cause. Nor was the physician who treated this child consulting with his teachers or obtaining counseling help for him or his mother. Yet without such communication, such combining of knowledge and resources, how likely is this child, particularly one who is economically disadvantaged and of minority status, to reverse his downward achievement trend? Instead, a horrendous cycle of absenteeism, little if any academic progress, negative reinforcement, reduced academic motivation and interest, and increasing anxiety and negative self-evaluation has been set in motion.

In other cases, early gains gradually or abruptly disappeared in the absence of home and/or school support. One four-year-old study child lived with her parents and four siblings in a bare two-room apartment with no toys, books, or TV. A grandmother babysat when the mother went to work. At age five this child attended Head Start. The teacher was affectionate, enthusiastic, and stimulating and worked with the children in various-size groupings to match individual needs and preferences. Angela (fictitious name) was happy with newly discovered toys and materials and improved in her test performance. There was continuity of enthusiasm, affection, and stimulation in Angela's first-grade classroom, and she received special reading instruction to continue the progress she made in preschool. At the end of the year, it was recommended that she not continue with the special instruction. Her teacher noted that Angela was "definitely capable of reading but needed constant encouragement." Unfortunately, she did not receive the attention and encouragement she needed. Subsequent classroom observations in third grade revealed that the teacher offered no stimulation of thinking and displayed no affection or enthusiasm; efforts at individualization were rare. The home interview revealed no parental encouragement or stimulation of intellectual activities and little knowledge of their daughter or her progress. This case and the many others clearly indicate the need for working with the total ecology of the child if we truly care and wish to serve our nation's children well.

Before concluding this description of study findings it must be pointed out that there were cases where examination of the many accumulated bits of information provided no apparent clues as to causal factors for exceptional academic gain or loss. Some children appeared to have everything working against them, an exceedingly impoverished, continuing stressful, non-supportive home environment, and a sequence of unexceptional classroom settings, but they still evidenced strong academic skills in third grade. Of course, the consequences of these negative factors may appear later. One such child has begun to express increasingly negative statements about himself and his family, negative feelings which if continued may increasingly interfere with other areas of functioning. However, it is also clear that despite the extensive and in-depth assessment provided in the present study, we have only begun to tap the surface of the crucial dynamic factors in the child and his or her environment which affect performance in the school setting.

Generalizations

1. Any particular aspect of individual functioning must be evaluated in the context of other aspects of the developing organism and the environmental conditions in which the organism is behaving. For example, development of affective and intellective behaviors were found to be closely intertwined and knowledge of behaviors in one domain aided interpretation in the other whether for understanding responses to the tester or to teachers and peers in the classroom. Similarly, intellectual and motivational correlates of variation in the child's health and physical status were evidenced.

2. Furthermore, the implications of many variables become understandable only after examining that variable and its interactions developmentally. This suggests a theoretical approach which considers developmental changes in both the child and the environments in which that development is embedded, and more extensive use of longitudinal designs. It also implies that providing "exceptional" children such as those in the present sample with appropriate learning environments requires a historical perspective which a cut-off score does not suggest.

3. Not only do home and school variables, particularly parent-child and teacher-child interactions, influence the child's behavior, but most such effects are reciprocal and not unidirectional (e.g., the case history of "John").

4. Interactions of individuals and the environments in

which they function are dynamic; predictability of a child's achievement from early indices of the home environment should not be interpreted to mean that these predictors necessarily determine the child's achievement. Families, children, and schools can and do change, with corresponding changes in the nature of their interactions, and such change can be facilitative or harmful. In contrast to some interpretations of early childhood research findings, for example, White and Watts (1973), the age period 3-6 is not just a period of refining established relations.

5. In many cases, developmental progress was gradual across the time intervals in which measures were administered. In addition, growth in one domain often served as a precursor to growth in another; thus, development in one area may proceed in seemingly irregular spurts and be inappropriately assessed by traditional linear analytic methods. We need to develop greater sensitivity to measurement and interpretation of such changes and their cumulative effects so that we can enhance positive growth and counteract possible negative influences. These considerations also suggest the importance of long-term evaluation of intervention efforts. It may take several years of small cumulative gains before such gains are large enough to be statistically significant which may account in part for some of the "sleeper" effects recently reported for upper-elementary grade low-SES children who had experienced early intervention programs (Palmer, 1976; Seitz, Apfel, and Efron, 1976).

6. As a corollary, facilitating influences usually require continuing reinforcement to maintain their positive effects. For example, most youngsters in Head Start evidenced increases in pre-academic skills, task orientation, achievement motivation, and social skills in relating to their peers and to other adults. The academic gains generally were not maintained, however, when the grade-school program apparently did not capitalize on children's acquired skills and motivation. The finding by Coleman and his colleagues (1966) that disadvantaged children are more affected by the quality of teaching may be more crucial as children's sensitivity to their school experience is heightened by programs such as Head Start. For those children who showed the greatest gain in academic skills between age four and nine, following Head Start attendance there was a continuity of facilitating school experiences; at each primary-grade level these children had enthusiastic, warm, positively motivating, cognitively stimulating teachers who taught in a one-to-one or

small-group setting. Such continuity in facilitating school experiences is particularly non-existent for a sizable minority of low-income children who move frequently between schools, a situation common to many urban areas. Moreover, this continuing warm and stimulating school environment was combined with a home environment that provided the child emotional support in general and support for school activities in particular.

7. Finally, in reviewing the information gathered one becomes acutely aware of the multiplicity of positive and negative factors for those children in these extreme achievement categories. Thus, it is not a particular parent, teacher, or child attitude, attribute, or behavior, or a particular social setting, but the cumulative effects of their multiple interactions. Moreover, for different children, different clusters of variables appear to be differentially effective, suggesting the need for multidimensional assessment of individuals and their environments.

The present case study approach has generated a number of hypotheses that should be investigated further in the larger study sample. In future analyses, particular attention will be paid to investigating the complementarity of home and school influences, differential effects for congruent and non-congruent instructional sequences in relation to child characteristics, and the nature of the complex interactions among affective, social, cognitive, and perceptual development. Subsequent analyses might examine whether home and school influences operate in an additive or interactive fashion in their impact upon the child's educational progress. Also, there is need for more precise delineation of the meaning of continuity of experiences. To continue to meet the child's developmental needs continuity may necessitate change, not continuation of experience. Again, a "building block" notion of dynamic transactions (cf. Sameroff, 1975) appears to provide a more adequate conceptualization of what occurs in these environmental interactions. Also, further efforts to delineate the most predictive composite at each age within SES, sex, and race subgroups for those measures administered during the first four study years should provide guidance to current efforts at early screening and identification of children with potential learning disabilities. There is also considerable need for more research aimed at understanding those children who show outstanding resilience amidst considerable environmental stress. When examining these case histories one cannot help but be impressed by the strengths one perceives in the children and in their families. Most studies in the literature, however, have focused on pathology; our understanding of such strengths is meagre at best.

As case histories in this study indicate, low socioeconomic status and minority group membership do not necessarily imply low school achievement. The children showed a wide range of aptitudes and abilities. Moreover, parents and teachers do make a difference. Thus, findings of this study are supportive of the importance of early parent-child interactions as well as the child's early acquisition of school-relevant skills and motivation and those programs such as Head Start which emphasize the parents' involvement in the child's educational experience. In describing the interrelatedness of family status, situational, and process variables, the data also suggest the potential positive impact of economic aid to impoverished families in raising competence levels in the children (i.e., even small differences in material possessions and household density were associated with children's higher achievement) and the necessity for coordination of services to support the child and his/her family. These findings and the several case histories described are consistent with those projects recently reviewed by Meier (1976) in suggesting that cognitive gains are likely to be largest and to be sustained when there is support in the total ecology of the child, not just in the quality of parent-child interactions alone, but also in adequate health care, nutrition, housing, and general family support. They also support his proposal for Neighborhood Family Development Centers to coordinate comprehensive service, training and research functions as a basis for modifying the total ecology of the developing child.

The data also indicated the potency of classroom interactions on the child's progress. Similarly, in his recent book, Bloom (1976) challenges the schools to provide all children with appropriate learning opportunities and describes a mastery approach that had promising results with older students. The importance of the complementarity among socializing influences, however, was evident in the present sample. Parent-to-child or teacher-to-child models appear too simplistic for characterization of minority children's achievement behaviors. Sustained intellectual growth depends on the quality of relationships established between parent, teacher, and child. More research and development activities are needed which focus on elaborating the mechanisms by which home and school can work more effectively together to enhance the child's development.

The children in the present sample would be considered by most as "children at risk," but in following six years in their lives we see no inevitable sequence of events which could not have been otherwise determined. Those case studies which exemplified the nurturance and acceleration of competencies during the six-year span of the study speak out against those who accept the inevitability of increasing despair and failure for low-income minority children in school. Our responsibility is to create situations where such children are typical, not exceptional. These children had a family able to provide love, concern, and support for their school activities, teachers who provided them with the necessary encouragement, stimulation and reinforcement for learning in a manner responsive to their particular learning styles, and they were not beset by physical or other problems interfering with their ability to respond adequately and progress. We must coordinate our nation's resources to assure no child receives less. It is hoped that this study provides some clues to the theoretical considerations and applied strategies that will contribute to that undertaking.

This is an abridged version of Project Report 76-21, Notable Early Characteristics of High and Low Achieving Black Low-SES Children, authored by Virginia C. Shipman, which was prepared for the Office of Child Development, Department of Health, Education, and Welfare under Grant H-8256.

REFERENCES

Bloom, B. S. Human Characteristics and School Learning. NY: McGraw-Hill Book Company, 1976.

Booth, A., and Edwards, J. N. Crowding and family relations. American Sociological Review. 1976, 41, 308-321.

Bronfenbrenner, U. A report on longitudinal evaluations of preschool programs. Volume II: Is early intervention effective? (DHEW Publication No. [OHD] 75-25). U. S. Department of Health, Education, and Welfare, Office of Child Development, 1974.

Coleman, J. S., Campbell, E. R., Hobson, C. J., McPartland, J., Mood, A. M., Weinfeld, F. D., and York, R. L. Equality of Educational Opportunity. Washington, D.C.: U.S. Government Printing Office, 1966.

Cooperative Test Division. Handbook: Cooperative Primary Tests. Princeton, N. J.: Educational Testing Service, 1967.

Cooperative Tests and Service. Preschool Inventory Revised edition - 1970: Handbook. Princeton, N.J.: Educational Testing Service, 1970.

Greenberg, J. W., and Davidson, H. H. Home background and school achievement of black urban ghetto children. American Journal of Orthopsychiatry. 1972, 42, 803-810.

Hanson, R. A. Consistency and stability of home environmental measures related to IQ. Child Development. 1975, 46, 470-480.

Hess, R. D., Shipman, V. C., Brophy, J. E., and Bear, R. M. The cognitive environments of urban preschool children: Follow-up phase. Chicago: University of Chicago Press, 1969.

Hyman, H.H., Wright, C.R., and Reed, J.S. The enduring effect of education. Chicago, IL: University of Chicago Press, 1975.

Meier, J. H. Current status and future prospects for the nation's children and their families. Paper presented at the meeting of the National Association for the Education of Young Children, Anaheim, California, November 1976.

Palmer, F. H. The evidence for early childhood intervention and subsequent elementary school performance. Paper presented at the meeting of the American Psychological Association, Washington, D.C., September 1976.

Sameroff, A. J. Early influences on development: Fact or fancy? Merill-Palmer Quarterly. 1975, 21, 267-294.

Seitz, V., Apfel, N. H., and Efron, C. Long-term effects of Intervention: A longitudinal investigation. Paper presented at meeting of the American Psychological Association, Washington, D.C., September, 1976.

Shipman, V. C. Disadvantaged children and their first school experiences: Structure and development of cognitive competencies and styles prior to school entry (PR 71-19). Prepared under Grant H-8256, Department of Health, Education, and Welfare. Princeton, N.J.: Educational Testing Service, 1971. (ERIC Document Reproduction Service No. ED 068 496)

Shipman, V. C. Disadvantaged children and their first school experiences: Structural stability and change in the test performance of urban preschool children (PR 72-18). Prepared under Grant H-8256, Department of Health, Education, and Welfare. Princeton, N.J.: Educational Testing Service, 1972 (b). (ERIC Document Reproduction Service No. ED 078 011)

Shipman, V. C., McKee, D., and Bridgeman, B. Disadvantaged children and their first school experiences: Stability and change in family status, situational, and process variables and their relationship to children's cognitive performance (PR 75-28). Prepared under Grant H-8256, Department of Health, Education, and Welfare. Princeton, N.J.: Educational Testing Service, 1976.

Stedman, J. M., and McKenzie, R. E. Family factors related to competence in young disadvantaged Mexican-American children. Child Development. 1971, 42, 1602-1607.

White, B. L., and Watts, J. C. Experience and environment: Major influences on the development of the young child. Englewood Cliffs, N.J.: Prentice-Hall, Inc., 1973.

White, S. H., Day, M. C., Freeman, P. K., Hantman, S. A., and Messenger, K. P. Federal programs for young children: Review and recommendations. Vol. III: Recommendations for federal program planning. Department of Health, Education, and Welfare Publication No. OS 74-103. Washington, D.C.: U. S. Government Printing Office, 1973.

NORMAN P. ERBER, Ph.D.

Associate Professor of Audiology
Washington University
Central Institute for the Deaf
St. Louis, Missouri

21

Optimizing Speech Communication in the Classroom

The perception of speech by a hearing-impaired child is a very complicated and delicate process which depends on the successful interaction of numerous variables. The purpose of this chapter is to describe the important role of the classroom teacher in optimizing oral communication. I shall present a simple model of the communication chain that will help us understand some of the factors that affect how hearing-impaired children comprehend spoken language. It is important to establish a model, in this case a pictorial outline, in order to examine the nature of communication systematically.

COMMUNICATION MODEL

Figure 21-1 diagrams eight major steps in oral communication: 1. The speaker formulates the intended message in his brain. 2. This is converted to nerve impulses which cause his articulators to produce the acoustic and optical signals of speech. The speaker monitors his own output through several feedback channels simultaneously (e.g., auditory, proprioceptive). 3. The coded acoustic and optical signals from the speaker are transmitted through acoustic and optical environments, respectively. 4. These signals may pass through speech-reception aids, which make some dimensions of the signal more prominent to the child. 5. The child's sensory systems receive the communication signals and convert them to nerve impulses which are conveyed to his brain. 6. These neural signals are integrated and interpreted by the child on the basis of previously acquired linguistic rules. 7. Aspects of the child's behavior indicate to the speaker whether the child has received and interpreted the intended message correctly. 8. If the child indicates that he has interpreted the message correctly, then the speaker may attempt to transmit a subsequent message. If, however, the child indicates that he did not understand, then the speaker may attempt to transmit the message again, perhaps in a slightly different way.

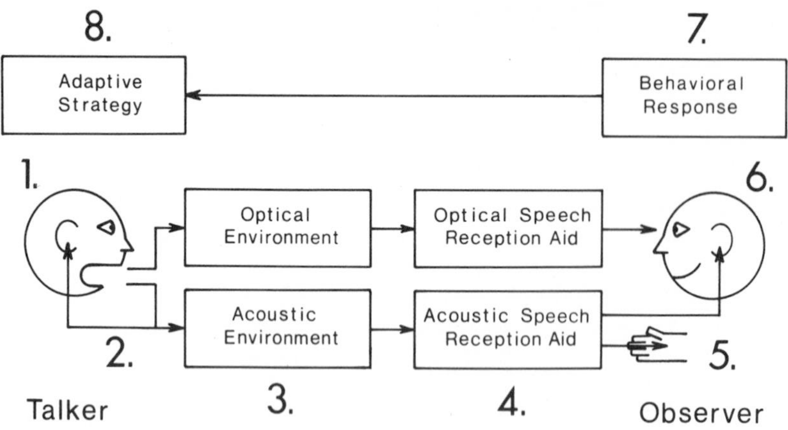

FIG. 21-1
A simple model depicting eight major steps involved in oral communication with a hearing-impaired child.

Of all the factors depicted here, probably the one that contributes most to a child's ultimate speech-perception abilities is his hearing capacity. This term, "hearing capacity," does not mean the same thing as "pure-tone audiogram" but instead refers to the child's potential for perceiving amplified speech through his ears, which is a function of the condition of his sensory and neural structures. Unfortunately, this seemingly most important factor, the child's inherent hearing capacity, cannot be modified by the classroom teacher; she may only work to maximize its use. The child also brings with him several other personal characteristics which the teacher cannot control, for example, his age, academic history, previous oral/aural experience, intelligence, personality, and parental interest.

It is important to note, however, that the child (with his personal characteristics) forms only one or two segments of the entire communication chain. Most of the other vital links are primarily the responsibility of the classroom teacher. These include the effective use of available sensory aids (e.g., an amplification system), careful control of potential distractors in the teaching environment, and creative application of instructional materials, methods, and strategies.

THE TEACHER'S RESPONSIBILITIES

I have briefly listed some of the factors in the speech-communication chain that tend to be the responsibility of the classroom teacher. Let us now consider how much each variable seems to contribute to successful speech perception, and how the teacher may improve communication in each case.

Sensory Aids

With regard to the amplification system, it is the teacher's responsibility to insure that her speech signal is amplified to an appropriate listening level and is delivered clearly with reliability to the child. This requires frequent and careful monitoring of batteries, settings, earmolds, cords, etc. Obviously, a dead battery or clogged earmold can make a hearing aid non-functional. The teacher also should routinely check the condition of the child's outer- and middle-ear, as the additional threshold shift caused by a conductive loss can seriously interfere with aural communication (Osberger and Danaher, 1974).

For moderately and severely hearing-impaired children, the selection of a hearing aid, choice of gain setting, and earmold fit are extremely important factors in successful reception of speech. For such children, speech perception scores on word-identification tests can be improved by more than 30% when amplified acoustic cues from a hearing aid are added to visual cues from lipreading (see Erber, 1971a). Conversely, auditory word-recognition scores can fall 30% or more if the speech intensity is allowed to decrease as little as 10-55 dB below the optimal level (Erber and Witt, 1977). Maximum use of acoustic cues by hearing-impaired children tends to occur only within a narrow range of sound levels. This will restrict how far a teacher can move from the hearing-aid microphone and still maintain acoustic contact with the child.

The value of a hearing aid is much more difficult to determine for a profoundly deaf child, especially with conventional word-identification test materials. For example, lipreading performance with amplified cues from a hearing aid is likely to differ only about 1-15% from lipreading alone (Erber, 1972). And a profoundly deaf child's auditory speech-perception scores are likely to be low regardless of whether his hearing aid is amplifying sound properly or not (Erber and Witt, 1977). There is evidence, however, that a profoundly deaf child can identify the stress patterns of words much better when he uses his hearing aid at an appropriately high level than when he listens near threshold (Erber and Witt, 1977). Thus, a malfunctioning aid or a low signal level can deprive him of potentially useful speech-pattern information (a 40-60% decrement). Research will indicate whether teachers can help profoundly deaf children to increase their use of these pattern cues during auditory- (or vibratory-) visual perception of speech.

The greater the child's hearing loss, the more he will rely on his vision for perception of speech. Visual impairment among hearing-impaired children is relatively common (see Levin and Erber, 1976), ranging between 20-40% of the sample tested. Certain visual abnormalities can diminish speech perception to a considerable degree, ranging from an estimated 30% decrement in lipreading performance for a child with 20/50 visual acuity to a 70% decrement for a child with 20/200 vision (Romano and Berlow, 1974). A teacher should be alert for common behavioral symptoms of visual disorder, such as crossed eyes, squinting, or complaints of headache, all of which may denote the need for ophthalmologic care. For children who already use eyeglasses for correction of vision, the teacher must continually check for dirty or cracked lenses or loose frames, which can reduce visual perception. In cases where a child is known to have a vision disorder which is not correctable (e.g., reduced visual fields, color blindness), the teacher can accomodate to that child's special needs by providing optimal seating, or by using large type, special illumination, or unusual color contrast.

Classroom Environment

Regarding the acoustic environment of the classroom, noise and reverberation in the vicinity of the teacher and child (that is, in close proximity to the hearing-aid microphone) can have serious detrimental effects on speech communication by moderately and severely hearing-impaired children. These negative changes in auditory or auditory-visual perception can be moderately large (30-50%) under very poor S/N ratio conditions (Erber, 1971a) or when reverberation is high (see review by Olsen, 1977). If the teacher decreases the distance between herself and the hearing-aid microphone, she can easily minimize the disruptive effects of poor acoustic surroundings. The teacher should be particularly attentive to unnecessary noise generated by the children themselves and suppress it, as this is the source most likely to interfere with classroom communication.

A few studies have examined how the optical environment, such as light and talker angle, distance, and level of illumination can affect visual perception of speech through lipreading (Erber, 1971b, 1974a). Increasing angle and distance both have been shown to produce decrements of from 10-20% in word-recognition through lipreading under extreme conditions (e.g., angles greater than 45° or distances between 20-50 feet). Large reductions in light level, on the other hand, do not seem to decrease visual perception of speech to a great extent (5-10%), at least over short time periods. That is, fatigue that may occur during the day under low levels of illumination has not been a major topic of investigation.

The arrangement of materials beside and behind the teacher can be important. Teachers have reported that the visual attention of young children may shift from the teacher's face, as she speaks, to colorful pictures or toys in the vicinity. Classroom visitors also are a common distraction. Although the disruptive effect in these cases cannot easily be quantified, the teacher can plan the arrangement of furniture and displays to minimize optical competition in the teaching environment. The teacher often has considerable control over the optical environment of the classroom. To optimize conditions for visual perception of speech, she should face the primary source of light, keep viewing distances short and desk arrangements compact, and eliminate potentially distracting objects and surfaces from the teaching area.

Clarity of Speech

The clarity of a teacher's speech is a function of the

positions and movements of her articulators as she attempts to communicate a message. A child's ability to perceive this message accurately will depend on the degree to which the acoustic and optical components of the teacher's speech signal match the child's internalized standards of oral language. In general, clarity is enhanced by slightly slowed, careful articulation with an effort to provide moderate emphasis to each syllable. A teacher may obscure her speech acoustically, by high vocal pitch or low intensity, or optically, by large teeth or a small immobile mouth. Her rapid or imprecise articulation can cause misperception through both auditory and visual modalities. Comparisons between naive talkers and those experienced in communication with deaf children have shown that differences in vowel, consonant, and word intelligibility through lipreading as great as 20-30% can occur (Pintner, et al, 1941; Pesonen, 1968). Small differences in acoustic word intelligibility of males and females also have been shown to exist (Pascoe, 1975). One study has described differences in the syllabic patterns of different talkers (Knudsen, 1928).

Moderately large differences in speech clarity (and thus intelligibility) probably exist between experienced and inexperienced teachers, but considerable differences in speech clarity even may exist between teachers with similar amounts of experience. Several studies have demonstrated that it is possible for one to achieve small improvements in acoustic speech intelligibility through specific training and feedback (Black, 1956), but general principles to generate uniformly high speech clarity, or intelligibility, among teachers of deaf children have not yet been developed.

Message Structure and Content

Research and classroom experience both have shown that the teacher's choice of message can strongly affect speech perception by a hearing-impaired child. This is most likely to occur when the child has limited vocabulary, knowledge of language, or experience with typical conversational sequences. But it also is true that certain speech stimuli are inherently easy or difficult - even for people with acquired hearing losses who possess large vocabularies and sophisticated language. For example, it is well known that the stress pattern of a word can influence its intelligibility. Spondees tend to be more intelligible than trochees, which in turn are easier to identify than are monosyllabic words. This occurs both for auditory and visual perception (Erber, 1971b). Short, simple sentences of familiar form tend to be more intelligible through lipreading than are long, complex sentences (Hannah, 1974; Clouser, 1976). Less is known about the effects of sentence length and structure on auditory perception through the impaired ears of a young child.

Clinical observation suggests that the teacher can enhance both auditory and visual perception of speech by inclusion of speech elements, words, or phrases that are known to be distinctive. That is, careful construction of a sentence can enhance its intelligibility to a hearing-impaired child (can at least insure that the child is aware of the intended meaning). Messages that are appropriate to the situational context also are more likely to be understood. Careless or unplanned sentence construction may result in only partial transmission of the message acoustically or visually. Thus the structure and content of the message can make the difference between comprehension and perceptual confusion (a difference of up to 100%), especially for a child with minimal knowledge of language.

Methods and Strategies

The methods and strategies that a teacher uses may appear both in her initial attempts to communicate and also in remedial attempts if earlier trials have failed. Many special teaching techniques seem to be useful, for example, contriving daily experiences to stimulate classroom discussion (Golf, 1974), motivating children by creating a need to communicate orally (Moog, 1975), emphasizing individual or small-group instruction (Pollack, 1974), applying special reinforcement methods to inform the child of correct perception and to reward it (Doehring, 1968), and using formal non-speech complements to oral communication such as cued speech (Cornett, 1967) or phonetic signs (Schulte, 1978). Common clarification strategies that teachers frequently employ include repetition, emphasis, syntactic change, and use of informational prompts (Erber and Greer, 1973).

Some teachers use a form of "adaptive communication" (Erber, 1977), in which each exchange of speech with a hearing-impaired child is considered an informal test at particular levels of stimulus and response (summarized by the matrix in Figure 21-2). The teacher uses the child's responses to indicate whether the child is functioning adequately at the communication level that she has chosen. At any given time, the teacher decides to increase or decrease complexity depending upon whether recent perceptual tasks have resulted in success or failure. In addition, these choices will be influenced by the emphasis the teacher chooses: 1. to transmit information accurately through messages constructed for high intelligibility; or 2. to expand the child's knowledge of language by using vocabulary and syntax which may be only marginally familiar.

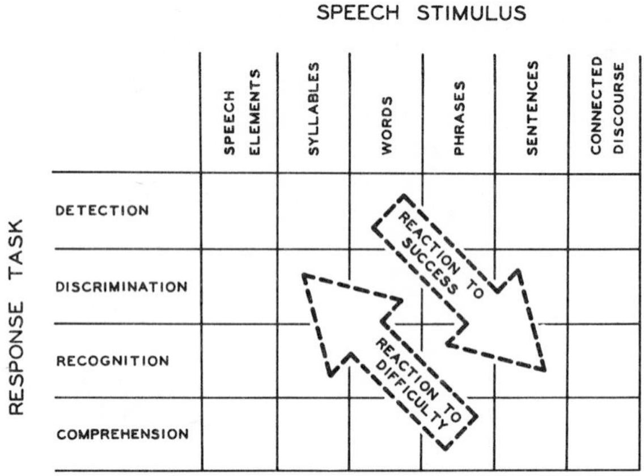

SPEECH STIMULUS

RESPONSE TASK

	SPEECH ELEMENTS	SYLLABLES	WORDS	PHRASES	SENTENCES	CONNECTED DISCOURSE
DETECTION						
DISCRIMINATION						
RECOGNITION						
COMPREHENSION						

REACTION TO SUCCESS

REACTION TO DIFFICULTY

FIG. 21-2
A communication skills matrix. The child's speech perception abilities are evaluated at each level of stimulus-response complexity. These measures are used to specify directions for instruction and practice in communication. Two adaptive strategies are shown. (From Erber, 1977).

Research has not clearly specified the role of particular teaching strategies in the aural habilitation of hearing-impaired children. Certainly, it is important for teachers to choose instructional strategies that maintain the child's interest and motivation and that provide continuity between units. But our experience suggests that exclusive use of conscious communication strategies is much less necessary for moderately and severely hearing-impaired children than it is for children who are profoundly deaf. Those with moderate and severe impairments often perceive speech accurately through combined auditory and visual modes, respond correctly, and consequently receive frequent reinforcement from their teachers.

Profoundly deaf children, on the other hand, often may misperceive spoken messages on the first try, respond incorrectly or not at all, and get discouraged during difficult oral communication tasks. They may resort to acquisition of information through situational cues and gestures, in addition to minimal acoustic and optical cues. Many teachers feel that systematic strategies are necessary to prevent, or at least minimize, the consequences of communication difficulty during critical points in a child's development. The communicative progress of a profoundly deaf child strongly depends on repeated opportunities to experience success in speech perception. It takes a skillfull teacher to accomplish this goal orally - through manipulation of messages, situational context, speech clarification, and verbal prompts - without resorting to excessive gesture or other forms of manual communication.

To summarize, experience suggests that teachers usually do not need to depend on extraordinary methods and strategies for enhancing the perceptual development of a moderately or severely hearing-impaired child, provided that he listens through a functioning hearing aid, that he attends to his teacher in a relatively quiet environment, and that the teacher uses moderate care in speech production. On the other hand, minimal conditions of careful articulation, hearing aid function, and classroom environment do not seem sufficient to insure the rapid development of speech (and language) perception in a profoundly deaf child. Instead, in such cases, a teacher must be able to construct messages, apply oral instruction methods creatively, and be able to select confidently from a repertoire of remedial strategies if communication difficulty should occur. Failure to apply appropriate strategies when needed can mean the difference between communicating orally with the child or not doing so (i.e., an 80-100% effect).

CLASSROOM MANAGEMENT QUOTIENT (CMQ)

Several years ago, Downs (1973; Northern and Downs, 1974) proposed the "Deafness Management Quotient (DMQ)" to help a clinician decide whether a particular hearing-impaired child should attend a school that emphasizes oral/aural communication methods or one that follows a Total Communication philosophy. Rating scales for hearing-threshold level, IQ, family support, etc., provided the "objective" data for this important decision. Although the validity of the Downs' proposal continues to be debated, it has caused educators to carefully examine the criteria that they use to make their placement and planning decisions.

In the preceding discussion, I have specified numerous factors -- controlled by the classroom teacher -- which can influence a hearing-impaired child's learning of receptive oral communication skills. These variables also can be organized into a format similar to that of the DMQ, but in this case into what might be called a Classroom Management Quotient (CMQ). This would consist of a set of personal rating scales to help a teacher decide whether she is providing particular hearing-impaired children with the optimum conditions for oral/aural communication learning (e.g., instructional behavior, classroom environment, use of sensory aids)

(Table 21-1).

Because the conditions required for successful speech perception tend to vary as a function of the child's hearing capacity, it seems reasonable to weight these factors somewhat differently for teachers of children with different hearing impairments. Although it is premature to assign specific weightings to the various factors, it may be possible to describe their relative importance in the development of speech-perception skills. For example, for a child with a moderate or severe hearing impairment, the teacher's proper use of functioning amplification equipment, and the quality of the acoustic environment, seem to be most important, because without quiet and without the talker close to the microphone, meaningful acoustic cues cannot reach the child and his valuable hearing capacity will be wasted. For the profoundly deaf child, the teacher's ability to structure the intended message, and the optical clarity of her speech, probably are the most important factors, as a visually-oriented child is unlikely to comprehend unplanned or imprecise speech patterns, especially early in his communicative development. Remedial strategies would rank high in importance also, as a teacher must know how to skillfully manipulate the oral stimulus and its situational context to help the child understand speech. The reason for this sort of relative ordering is not to point out any lack of importance of a factor (each is important in its own way), but to emphasize the critical nature (extreme importance) of certain variables for successful communication by certain children.

CONCLUSION

Numerous variables influence oral communication between a teacher and a hearing-impaired child (see Figure 21-1). The child's hearing capacity, intellect, and personality are not easily modified; these form the raw material for development. But many other factors are primarily the responsibility of the classroom teacher, including use of sensory aids, control of the environment, and application of materials, methods, and strategies. Depending on the child's auditory abilities (primarily), some of these factors seem to be much more important than others. If the teacher is careful to optimize the conditions under which she teaches, the child will learn to perceive speech with maximum ease. We must develop a systematic approach to insure that this happens in every case.

TABLE 21-1

A set of rating scales to be used for self-evaluation by a teacher of hearing-impaired children. The teacher can use these personal ratings to help determine whether (s)he is providing optimal conditions for oral/aural communication.

	very poor ... very good
USE OF AMPLIFICATION SYSTEM	/....../....../....../....../....../....../....../
ACOUSTIC ENVIRONMENT	/....../....../....../....../....../....../....../
OPTICAL ENVIRONMENT	/....../....../....../....../....../....../....../
CLARITY OF SPEECH CUES	/....../....../....../....../....../....../....../
MESSAGE CONTENT AND STRUCTURE	/....../....../....../....../....../....../....../
REMEDIAL COMMUNICATION STRATEGIES	/....../....../....../....../....../....../....../
INSTRUCTIONAL METHODS AND MATERIALS	/....../....../....../....../....../....../....../

ACKNOWLEDGEMENT

Preparation of this manuscript was supported by Program Project Grant NS 03856 from NINCDS to Central Institute for the Deaf.

REFERENCES

Black, J. Voice communication: A bibliographic and annotated summary of ten years of research. Office of Naval Research, Contract N6onr-22525, NR 145-993, Ohio State University (1956).

Clouser, R. A. The effect of vowel consonant ratio and sentence length on lipreading ability. Amer. Ann. Deaf. 1976, 121, 513-518.

Cornett, R.O. Cued speech. Amer. Ann. Deaf. 1967, 112, 3-13.

Doehring, D. G. Picture-sound association in deaf children. J. Speech Hearing Res. 1968, 11, 49-62.

Downs, M.P. Hearing screening for children revisited. Scand. Audiology Suppl. 1973, 3, 71-93.

Erber, N. P. Auditory and audiovisual reception of words in low-frequency noise by children with normal hearing and by children with impaired hearing. J. Speech Hearing Res. 1971a 14, 496-512.

Erber, N. P. Effects of distance on the visual reception of speech. J. Speech Hearing Res. 1971b 14, 848-857.

Erber, N. P. Speech-envelope cues as an acoustic aid to lipreading for profoundly deaf children. J. Acoust. Soc. Amer. 1972, 51, 1224-1227.

Erber, N. P., and Greer, C. W. Communication strategies used by teachers at an oral school for the deaf. Volta Rev. 1973, 75, 480-485.

Erber, N. P. Effects of angle, distance, and illumination on visual reception of speech by profoundly deaf children. J. Speech Hearing Res. 1974a, 17, 99-112.

Erber, N. P. Pure-tone thresholds and word-recognition abilities of hearing-impaired children. J. Speech Hearing Res. 1974b 17, 194-202.

Erber, N. P. Developing materials for lipreading evaluation and instruction. Volta Rev. 1977, 79, 35-43.

Erber, N. P., and Witt, L. H. Effects of stimulus intensity on speech perception by deaf children. J. Speech Hearing Dis. 1977, 42, 271-278.

Golf, H. R. Strategies for teaching 4- to 8-year olds. Proc. 46th Meeting Conv. Amer. Instructors Deaf. Washington, D.C.: U.S. GPO, 1974, 267-270.

Hannah, E. P. Speechreading: Some linguistic factors. Acta Symbolica. 1974, 5, 57-66.

Knudsen, V. O. "Hearing" with the sense of touch. J. Gen. Psychol. 1978, 1, 320-352.

Levin, S., and Erber, N. P. A vision screening program for deaf children. Volta Rev. 1976, 78, 90-99.

Moog, J. S. Language instruction determined by diagnostic observation. Volta Rev. 1975, 77, 561-570.

Northern, J. L., and Downs, M. P. Hearing in Children. Baltimore, Md.: Williams & Wilkins, 1974, 268-270.

Olsen, W.O. Acoustics and amplification in classrooms for the hearing-impaired. In F.H. Bess (ed.), Childhood Deafness - Causation, Assessment, and Management. New York: Grune and Stratton, 1977, 251-266.

Osberger, M. J., and Danaher, E. M. Temporary conductive loss in students with severe sensorineural deafness. Volta Rev. 1974, 76, 52-56.

Pascoe, D. P. Frequency responses of hearing aids and their effects on the speech perception of hearing-impaired subjects. Ann. Otol. Rhinol. Laryngol. 1975 supp. 23, Vol. 84, no. 5, 1-40.

Pesonen, J. Phoneme communication of the deaf. Ann. Finnish Acad. Sci. 1968, 151, Series B.

Pintner, R., Eisenson, J., and Stanton, M. The Psychology of the Physically Handicapped. New York: F.S. Crofts & Co. 1941, 144-148.

Pollack, D. An acoupedic program. In C. Griffiths (ed.), Proceedings of the International Conference on Auditory Techniques. Springfield, Ill.: Thomas, 1974, 139-146.

Romano, P. E., and Berlow, S. Vision requirements for lip-reading. Amer. Ann. Deaf. 1974, 119, 383-386.

Schulte, K. The use of supplementary speech information in verbal communication. Volta Rev. 1978, 80, 12-20.

Summary Impressions

BARRY A. KAUFMAN, Ed.D.

Assistant Professor of Education
Washington University
Graduate Institute of Education
St. Louis, Missouri

22

What We Have Learned— Prospects for the Future

I want to take the opportunity to thank Dr. Simmons-Martin and her staff for perhaps the finest and most intellectually stimulating professional conference I have ever attended. University professors are usually in the position of giving out information; rarely do I have the opportunity to take in information and honestly say I have learned something. It is indeed a pleasure to summarize the proceedings of this International Conference on Parents and their Young Children. As the title of my summary statement suggests, I will focus on what I have learned and what future directions can be charted. When I use the term "learning" I do not take it to mean the often stated psychological definition of a change in behavior. For me learning is a new level of insight, a new consciousness, a new vision of reality, a new awareness. I come to see and act on the world in a way that continues to contribute to my understanding of human behavior and myself. During this conference I have come to understand the world of hearing-impaired children and their parents in a totally new perspective. For this I am grateful.

My formal professional training and present activities focus on the issues and problems related to early childhood education and child development. Prior to this conference I only had a superficial and somewhat stereotyped understanding of the concerns related to the education of the young hearing-impaired child. My own research and teaching is concerned with the social, educational, and intellectual needs of the so-called normal child. Therefore, my remarks will be cast in the context of what I know about the developmental and educational needs of children in general. I have organized this summary into three specific components. Just as the traditional approach in American education has emphasized the 3 R's of Reading, wRiting, and aRithmetic, I often analyze educational issues into the three P's of Philosophy, Psychology, and Pedagogy. Philosophy provides an analysis of the various societal issues, psychology permits an analysis of the principles of knowledge acquisition, and pedagogy allows for an analysis of the teaching-learning process. Although each of the three analytic lenses will be discussed separately, it should be understood that they represent an integrated and articulated whole. One cannot simply isolate philosophical concerns from the more pragmatic activities generally discussed in the area of psychology and pedagogy. I take as a given statement that the whole is greater than the sum of the parts. Therefore, I hope my summary will provide the reader with a somewhat more unified conceptualization of the various papers that were presented at the conference. No attempt will be made to summarize individual presentations.

My analytic perspective on future directions will essentially focus on what I saw missing from the conference. I do this not so much as a criticism of omission, but rather as a means of charting a future course related to the issues and problems on intervention with parents and their young children with communication disorders. As a professional concerned with the mainstream of early childhood education and child development, I believe I can provide some insight into some of the current trends in psychology, and educational research that are not yet widely used by your community of investigators. I see this as a unique opportunity to increase communication between the world of "regular" education and "special" education.

PHILOSOPHY

An important philosophical point I wish to raise was originally stated by Ira Gordon (Chapter 2). I am referring to the ecological or systems analysis aspects of parent-child interaction. Gordon identified four ecosystems of human interaction that reflect the interface between the needs of the individual child and the needs of the society. I am most concerned with the articulation between the microsystem, identified by Gordon as the smallest unit of analysis, i.e. the mother-child dyad, and the macrosystem composed of the institutional organizations of our society, i.e. schools, communities, and government. I found most of the papers presented at the Conference focused on the microsystem with little reference to societal implications. Because of the methodological characteristics of contemporary psychological and educational research, subjects under investigation are often isolated from socio-political realities. Empirical research, either under laboratory conditions, or tightly designed experimental field conditions, tends to generate data and interpretations of the data that represent contradictions to prevailing sociological concerns. If on one hand, as Burton White suggests, nothing can substitute for the continuous and nurturing relationship of a mother and infant; such data needs to be examined against the backdrop of a macrosystem analysis that indicates that either out of economic necessity or personal career motivation, more and more women are going to work. Scientific data related to human behavior needs to be examined within the context of social change. Microsystem analysis divorced from the realities of the macrosystem will only serve to engender feelings of guilt and personal blame around the parenting process. I hope that at future conferences of this nature, investigators will begin to apply an ecological analysis to the problems of mother-child interaction. Mothers and children do not exist in isolation from the complexities of a changing social system.

A theme that underlay much of the Conference was the issue of the oral _vs_. the manual approach to the education of the hearing-impaired. What concerns me is that some participants addressed the question in terms of _isms_. An ism implies an ideology and very often a doctrine. By definition, ideological differences are not open to empirical verification but are primarily a function of an individual's beliefs, values, and attitudes. One cannot say that capital_ism_ is better than commun_ism_ or vice versa unless one is willing to acknowledge the particular philosophical value differences inherent in each of the particular political systems. Isms generally impede communication, are rallying cries with little recognition of the other side of the picture, and often imply a rigid and unyielding position. The issue of the oral or manual approach to the education of the hearing-impaired child suggests an either/or approach. As an outsider looking into the field of deaf education, I find it somewhat disconcerting to see the field split on ideological grounds rather than on philosophical grounds as reflected in a basic set of beliefs, assumptions, and values. My own philosophical position suggests that polar opposites provide a motivating force for growth and understanding. Nothing exists within the human condition that is 100% wrong. New levels of understanding come about as a result of recognizing the internal contradictions that exist in any doctrine.

The process of the growth of knowledge within a given discipline parallels the development of knowledge acquisition within the individual. I will elaborate upon the constructivist nature of learning in the section on psychology. However, it should be noted that knowledge acquisition, whether within the individual or society, results from a resolution of cognitive conflict. Philosophical differences cannot be reduced to simple slogans or combative "camps". Perhaps the crucial differences in the oral and manual approach are so fundamental and broad that syncretism is impossible, and only rapprochement is possible. If indeed this is the case, as in the language of early childhood education, perhaps the possibility exists for "parallel play" often found in preschoolers in that the protagonists are separate, but equal and mutually tolerant.

PSYCHOLOGY

A single psychological theme that dominated many of the presentations can be summarized by one word, "interaction". The chapters by White, Gordon, Levenstein, Shipman, and Anderson all suggest an interactivist approach to the developmental process. Implied in each of these presentations is the notion that it is through the active rather than reactive behavior of the infant that cognition develops. It was not very long ago that the baby was viewed as a helpless and passive organism subject to either a predetermined maturational plan, or completely influenced by environmental controls. Through the pioneering work of Jean Piaget, Burton White, and others too numerous to mention, the baby is now conceptualized as an active and to a large extent purposeful organism. The infant constructs knowledge and seeks out information from the environment. The child is in a constant reciprocal and dynamic interactive system with his/her environment. Contemporary child development research suggests that the unit of analysis be the interaction as a whole rather than simply behavioral responses or environmental contingencies.

As a student of Piaget, I am pleased to see the interactivist perspective becoming widely accepted in research and teaching with hearing-impaired children. The work of Piaget, I believe, can provide a unique perspective to the problems facing researchers, teachers, and parents in the education of these children. I would also suggest that the work of John Dewey be re-examined in the light of our new understanding of child development. As a philosopher-psychologist-pedagogist, Dewey's work can provide a rationale and conceptualization for the educational process of the hearing-impaired child. No one was more concerned with the psychological needs of the child on a microsystem level and the needs of a democratic society on a macrosystem level. American education has a tendency to forget its heros. I believe that the work of Dewey speaks directly to the interactive nature of the developing child and how to translate such a process into a meaningful educational program.

What I found missing from a psychological perspective relates to the interpersonal needs of the young child. Most of the papers focused on general cognitive organization and the more specific issues of language, speech, and communication. From a traditional child development orientation, the total needs of the child must include the area of social-emotional development. I can appreciate the immediate concerns of the research and teaching community of children with hearing or communication disorders; however we are dealing with a whole child and therefore must address the questions of interpersonal and social development.

Within the past few years there has been a rethinking through of the traditional Freudian system of a child's personality development. Since 1960, humanistically-oriented theories related to the emotional development of the child have suggested interesting approaches in the education of young children. It is not enough for parent-infant programs for the hearing-impaired to focus only on the language and communication aspects of development. Too often, so much emphasis is placed on language and communication that the emotional aspects of the child's life are generally ignored. In terms of future directions, I would hope that parent-infant programs for the hearing-impaired would begin to examine the rich literature related to the interpersonal development of the child. A basic assumption of contemporary child development is the emphasis on the whole child. Described in the literature as the human potential movement, humanistic psychology, or personal growth movement can provide exciting new dimensions to the parenting process.

PEDAGOGY

Another theme that seemed to dominate a number of the papers relates to the professional relationship of the researcher, teacher and parent. Issues of pedagogy should be addressed within the framework of meaningful questions that relate to the needs of researchers, parents, and teachers. In the final analysis, pedagogy becomes the instrument of our philosophical and psychological perspectives. Perhaps the most exciting aspect of this conference was evidenced by the continuing reference to the need for all individuals concerned with the problems of hearing-impaired youngsters to listen to each other. Teacher-effectiveness research has for many years attempted to isolate the variables that go into a good teaching-learning environment. Literally volumes of research reports, dissertations, and government sponsored projects have tried to identify those aspects of the teaching-learning process that seem to best meet the educational needs of the child. Project Follow-Through of Head Start was a massive attempt to find out which approach to early childhood was most effective. After some ten years of research, the data is still unclear and for all practical purposes has contributed little to the day-by-day needs of the classroom teacher.

A growing number of educational researchers now feel that a more qualitative approach to classroom research is necessary. They argue that quantitative methods with behaviorally specified outcomes does not capture the ongoing teacher-child relationship. Psychometrically oriented classroom research is now giving way to a more phenomologically based mode of inquiry. Termed ethnographic research, investigators of this school conceptualize the classroom a social system or unique culture. Ethnographic research draws on the traditional field methodology found in anthropology and sociology. Rather than attempting to isolate and statistically operationalize classroom behaviors, ethnographic researchers search for meaning and understanding within a human interactive environment. All participants within a social system are considered primary. The classroom is viewed as a complex social system that must be understood within the context of all the participants. Phenomological inquiry is more consistent with the underlying assumptions of the interactive conceptualization of child development. Therefore, if we assert that the process of development is essentially interactive in nature, then we will need to rely on more qualitative methods of research.

It has been my experience that the major communication gap that exists between researchers and teachers is that researchers generally try to reduce human interactions into quantitative terms while teachers and parents tend to describe their world in qualitative terms. More often than not the teacher is forced to translate qualitative events into quantitative behaviors. Perhaps in future conferences we will begin to see more naturalistic and ethnographic research reports. If indeed teachers should talk to researchers, researchers must respond with appropriate methodologies that reflect the problem being investigated. In my opinion, classroom research for the hearing-impaired would do well to look at the emerging modes of inquiry generally termed ethnographic or participant observation. Nowhere was this need more evident than the data reported by Dr. Virginia Shipman. Teachers and parents do make a difference. However it is often difficult or impossible to come up with quantitative measures to isolate exactly what it is that makes a difference. Dr. Shipman's longitudinal study clearly points out that characteristics such as warmth, supportive environment, individual attention, and enthusiasm make a difference in a child's learning experience. Intensive designs or case studies as represented by the work of Dr. Barbara Anderson are essential to the improvement of the instructional process. Pedagogy can best be served by a pluralism of research methodology. Questions should guide the appropriate inquiry strategy; not the other way around.

Conclusions

The complexity of issues makes it difficult to provide a concise and comprehensive summary. I believe the entire movement of early childhood education is at an important crossroad. The underlying assumptions of early childhood education can provide a unique perspective to the current issues and problems being faced by researchers, teachers, and parents concerned with the hearing-impaired child. The work of Froebel, Montessori, Dewey, Piaget, and Simmons-Martin can greatly contribute to the deeper understanding of the child and his/her family. I am convinced that the whole-child approach inherent in early childhood education could provide a meaningful structure for the future growth and development of the parent-infant education movement regardless of handicapping condition.

Conclusions

The International Conference on Parents and Young Children was conceived as a series of presentations requiring synthesis from a group of theorists, researchers, early education programmers and policy developers from varying parts of the world. In this setting they considered basic issues, current trends and major developments across areas which relate to children with hearing impairment and other communication disorders. A summary of these issues, trends and developments is presented below.

Basic Issues

The basic issues grow out of very complex sociological, political, and economic changes in the relations among institutions such as the family, the school and the government, and seem to have been exacerbated by the current Public Law 94-142. Among the basic issues were the following:

a. The roles of parents and teachers -- mutually exclusive or supportive?

b. The support for education -- private or public?

c. The nature of research -- field related, ethnographic or traditional?

d. The pedagogical procedures -- traditional, behavioral, or developmental?

e. The nature of learning -- thinking or behaving?

f. The early habilitation of the deaf -- classroom or parent oriented?

g. The input system -- unisensory, bisensory or multisensory?

h. Measurements -- family factors, parent-child interaction, language.

Current Trends

The heuristic objective of stimulation through identifying the knowledge base seems self evident. When knowledge and practice are in harmony, success can be anticipated. Therefore, by looking at both the research and the processes, a synthesis can take place which may result in a positive influence on the child's development. Among the trends identified by the participants were the following:

a. Early intervention focusing upon language development concomitant with cognitive development.

b. Visual as well as auditory perception entering into classroom strategies.

c. A movement from a deficit emphasis on a child's ability and potentiality to an emphasis on differences.

d. Interest in discerning the nature of the "knowing" process as different from learning and thought.

e. A transactional view of the family whereby intellectual, cultural, and emotional considerations enter into intervention.

f. Concern with psycho-dynamic theory as it applies to children as well as parents.

g. Parent-child dyad, a setting offering opportunities for research and training.

h. Research becoming broader and more humanistic in definition of educational objectives, and correspondingly more flexible in program assessment.

i. Increasing importance of language formation as a specific behavioral target for study.

j. Inclusion of the immediate postnatal period in the study of the infant.

Major Developments

Of all the major developments, the most important seemed to be a change in emphasis which has led to a more inclusive, a global view of education. There are far-reaching major developments in the areas of language, cognition, perception, and learning, with a saltation of important research available in caregiving, parent roles, teaching and intervention. Among the significant developments reported at the conference were these:

a. Broadened concern with human behavior to include the first three years of the child.

b. Parent-child interaction and the child's language development demonstrated as measurable.

c. Parents importantly involved in early childhood education programs learning to be better caretakers and teachers of their young children.

d. Movement from traditionally structured programs to an eclectic examination of a variety of dimensions and approaches.

e. Consideration and identification of the precursors of language and cognition in early infancy.

f. Application of psycho-dynamic theory to humanistic education.

g. Directed attention to the whole child which includes linguistic, cognitive, affective, perceptual, social, and psycho-motor development.

h. Broadened concept of cognition to include such variables as language judgement, creativity, motivation, and responsivity.

We fervently hope that the above presentation will engender positive developments for children with communication disorders. A conference and publication of this type does not pretend to offer established routes for future travel. Rather, it presents, as a cartographer's rough sketch, the roads and rivers that have been traveled, sometimes easily, sometimes not. To the readers is left the projection of this experience in choosing the trail ahead.

Subject Index

a b c d e f 9 g 0 h 1 i 8 2 j